FIRST AMERICAN EDITION

OF THE WORKS OF THE

REV. D. W. CAHILL, D.D.

THE HIGHLY DISTINGUISHED

IRISH PRIEST, PATRIOT AND SCHOLAR:

CONTAINING

A BRIEF SKETCH OF HIS LIFE,

THE MOST IMPORTANT ADDRESSES, SPEECHES, CONTROVERSIAL SERMONS &c. DELIVERED IN IRELAND, ENGLAND AND SCOTLAND,

TOGETHER WITH HIS

CELEBRATED LETTERS TO LORD JOHN RUSSELL, LORD PALMERSTON, THE DUKE OF WELLINGTON, THE EARL OF DERBY, THE EARL OF CARLISLE, &c. &c. &c.

BEING THE MOST INTERESTING WORK

EVER PRESENTED

TO THE CATHOLIC PUBLIC.

BOSTON:

PATRICK DONAHOE,

23 FRANKLIN STREET.

1855.

INDEX.

TO THE READER.

We present to public attention, in book form, the Letters, Discourses, Responses and Controversial Sermons of that eminent Divine and Scholar, the Rev. D. W. CAHILL, whose eloquent and manly voice and pen, have, like the bursting thunderbolt, cast dismay and confusion among the ranks of his country's oppressors and persecutors—when pestilence, plagues and famine, and an unfeeling and tyrannical Government and its subservient agents, had swept Ireland of millions of its bravest sons and daughters, and levelled their humble habitations to the earth—when annihilation would seem inevitable—then in Ireland's supposed weakness, degradation and humility, her heartless despoilers would feign re-enact and legalize a new edition of the desecrated "Penal Laws," which have crimsoned Ireland's verdant soil with blood, and consigned many a Holy Divine and Scholar to the scaffold or banishment for life from an ancestorial inheritance. To meet, and counteract in embryo, these contemplated evil designs of the Government, and an intriguing Cabinet, we find this invincible and uncompromising champion of the Church—the philanthropic, patriotic and eloquent orator, pen in hand in the field, confronting the degenerate "Iron Duke," or upsetting the wily schemes of a Palmerston or a Russell, and awakening from her lethargic slumbers the Courts of Europe, which would have soon fallen victims to English intriguing, and deceitful and designing emissaries, with bland faces and craven and hollow hearts, who with a smile of deception and a tongue of suavity, were plotting destruction wherever they went.

Whether we view the Rev. D. W. Cahill, amidst impending threats and frowns, undismayed, bearding the insatiable and growling lion, or in his astronomical researches, with mind absorbed among the heavenly bodies, scanning the starry firmament, and defining each luminary orbit and revolution, with the ease and familiarity we would define or depict objects momentarily exposed to observation—or, his philanthropic and patriotic heart overpowered as he reflects over some death-scene of starvation, where his last shilling administered to the corporeal wants, whilst his eloquent voice conveyed the last consoling words, ere his holy hand extended the Unction, or the anxious soul started from its earthly tenement on its celestial journey of eternal bliss—no matter in what capacity we regard the Rev. D. W. Cahill, we must pronounce him the greatest living man in Europe at the present period.

PREFACE.

To wrest from oblivion, and collect in a neat volume the Letters and Discourses of this distinguished and learned Divine has been our object— knowing how unwieldy, and how liable to destruction newspapers are, the only manner in which anything of his productions has appeared in this country as yet. But did we say to *wrest from oblivion?* No, while there remains an honest descendant of "the Island of Learning and of Saints;" an uncontaminated descendant of the line of Kings and chiefs—of patriots and warriors—of Statesmen, poets and wits—of honest, industrious and manly fathers, or beautiful, virtuous, religious and affectionate mothers—so long as there remains a living remnant of the Celtic race, that has not abandoned their God, their country or their faith; so long will a Cahill live in the hearts of his country people, and all discerning admirers, of genuine worth—and to such we humbly present this volume.

A BRIEF BIOGRAPHY OF THE REV. DR. CAHILL.

THE distinguished divine and scholar is now in the full vigor of his age and intellect—he is approaching his fifty-third year. He is the son of a gentleman well known in the midland southern portions of Ireland, as an eminent engineer and surveyor, and was thus almost necessarily, from his earliest years, practised in those exact sciences upon which in a larger degree, eminence in those professions are dependent. Thus,—and in those early years it is when instruction is imparted to command success, and when skill is acquired with a readiness almost intuitive—was laid the foundation of that scientific eminence for which, in after life, Dr. Cahill has been remarkable.

By the female side, the subject of our sketch is of Spanish descent; his patronymic is thoroughly Celtic, and the whole temperament and habitudes of the man, so far as the discipline of the priest permits them to be manifested, develops, in an extraordinary degree, the characteristics of both these ancient races. The Rev. Gentleman's *physique*, too, is indicative of this descent. His complexion is brown, his hair dark, his eyes black, and deeply thoughtful; his person tall, and of massive yet graceful proportions; he presents, in these respects, a personification of the attributes of both peoples, most striking and demonstrative. In stature, Dr. Cahill far transcends the ordinary, standing not less than six feet five inches.

The Rev. gentleman is a native of the Queen's County.

in Ireland, and a subject of the diocese of Kildare and Leighlin, over which presided, when he was a young man, the celebrated Dr. Doyle, the 'I. K. L.' of the pre-emancipation period. The tendency of studies which he inevitably entered upon, the combined Spanish and Celtic temperament, the physical development with which nature had endowed him, tended naturally, one would almost say, to direct his views toward the army, which, in those days, presented a noble field to the aspirant after military fame, and a theatre upon which engineering skill and scientific knowledge were sure to rise in fame and station. Accordingly young D. W. Cahill was originally intended for the army. A more glorious field of operation, however, awaited him,— a warfare more noble and more suited to the powers he has since displayed—a contention in which he has won a fame, which no facilities in another career could have ever equalled, and from which Christianity, it is hoped, has reaped some harvest, and mankind been the gainer. The young intended soldier rejected, like St. Ignatius, the colors, the war-steed, and the cannon, to enlist under the banner of the cross; and while yet a youth, entered upon those studies which qualify the man to become the minister of God, and the servant of the altar.

The Rev. Dr. Cahill was, at an early age a student of the lay side of Carlow College, after which he studied, for some time, under those masters of education who have outstriped all other professors of the sciences, the Jesuits Here, having entered somewhat upon those studies more appropriate to the profession he had chosen, he was distinguished as a scholar. In due time he entered Maynooth, and commenced that course of severe study and rigid discipline, which have rendered that ground so eminent, and made its *alumni* so eminent as scholars, so self-denying as priests. At Maynooth, Dr. Cahill read a full course of theology and natural philosophy, under the distinguished professors of that time, Dr. Delahogue, and Dr. McHale, now the illustrious Archbishop of Tuam. In Hebrew and the cognate studies, he became a great proficient under Dr. Browne, for many years past the exemplary Bishop of Dromore. Under Dr. Boylan, who was himself an ornament of the Irish Prelacy, he studied German, French and Italian, in all which languages our Reverend Friend obtained such proficiency, as placed him amongst the most proficient not only of his age, but of his college.

Having completed the usual but severe routine of the minor ordinary studies, the Rev. Gentleman then received orders, and was selected to the Dunboyne establishment, of Maynooth, where he spent an additional period of years in reading a more advanced course of theology and ecclesiastical history. In due time he was taken into full orders in the Church, of which he is now so happily an ornament.

We have not spoken of the *éclat* with which the subject of our notice went through his college studies; we may say one for all, that the capacities then manifested were such, and so prominent, as to prefigure the maturity of their present development. The estimation in which he was held *at home*, where his qualities were best known, was shown by his being selected for the professorship of natural philosophy in Carlow, then under the Rectorship of the Right Rev. Dr. Doyle, himself a *literateur* of the most distinguished character; and, as a proof his talents were recognised beyond the sphere in which they were exercised with so much efficacy, we may mention that the degree of Doctor in Divinity was conferred upon him by the Pope.

In Carlow college, he continued for some years to teach not only natural philosophy, but mathematics and astronomy; in which latter science, we believe, he possesses an eminence not exceeded by any man of our day.

As a scholar in practical science, we should mention that the Rev. Doctor studied chemistry, as a laboratory student, under the late Dr. Barker, of Trinity College, Dublin; a gentleman who produced such celebrated pupils as Sir Robert Kane and others.

So far of Dr. Cahill as a student and a professor, the rest is known to all his countrymen; it may briefly be communicated to others. After a residence of some years in the Colleges of Carlow, the Rev. Gentleman, at the earnest desire of many distinguished personages, who being Catholics, were desirous of having their children educated in the faith, as well as in the higher sciences, transferred the sphere of his operations to Dublin. For many years subsequently the Doctor had a seminary at Seapoint, near Blackrock, which, for eminence and respectability, was not exceeded by any in the country.

During all this time Dr. Cahill was known as a preacher of singular force and clearness, and of great, yet simple, eloquence — characteristics, which his scientific acquirements, and knowledge of ancient and modern classics, qualified him largely to put forth. He was invited, consequently, to preach in many and distant portions of the kingdom of Ireland and in this country also, upon important occasions. At whatever inconvenience to himself, he never negatived these applications, which are so frequent; the result was, that he gave up the seminary to proclaim more and more the great truths of the gospel to the world.

CONVERSIONS IN ENGLAND.

LETTER OF THE REV. J. COLLINS TO THE REV. D. W. CAHILL:—REPLY OF THE REV. DR. CAHILL.

The following correspondence has taken place between our distinguished countryman, the REV. DR. CAHILL, and the REV. J. COLLINS, recently a clergyman of the Church of England, and who has become a convert to the Catholic faith within the last few days:—

Crooked Billet Hotel, Liverpool, May 31, 1851.

REV. AND DEAR SIR.—Permit an anxious clergyman; sixteen years an active minister of the Church of England, and has labored the most of that period in this nation, to address you on, to him, an all-important subject.

For years I have been dubious of the position which the Church of England—the undefined and extravagant vagaries of private judgment; the numerous and conflicting sects; the levelling divine mysteries with human reason; the discarding the sacrament of baptism through the caprice of a state official, and the want of a spiritual head to the scholar and conscientious, are mournful and alarming reflections.

Following up the legal motto, "*Audi alteram partem*," I attended your lecture lately, in Liverpool, on the Sacrifice of the Mass. Many points about which I hesitated, were *lucidly unfolded* and *convincingly impressed*; on a subsequent conversation on the Real Presence and Transubstantiation, many doubts were dissipated, and, though some doctrines are mysterious still, which appear "as through a glass darkly," yet, "I am determined to trust, where I am unable to trace."

I am a Master of Arts of my University, and hold testimonials from dignitaries, clergymen and congregations, perfectly satisfactory.

I leave my church with anguish, and feelings similar to those experienced in parting from a beloved parent, yet I cannot be wrong in following the example of so many learned and good. I henceforth profess myself a Catholic, if permitted to enter the fane from which my forefathers strayed.

I have the honor to be, Rev. and Dear Sir, your very faithful servant,

JOHN COLLINS.

REPLY.

St. Mary's Church, Liverpool, May 31, 1851.

My Dear Rev. Friend.—I feel urged thus to address you in the language of warm affection, in order to give you a hearty welcome, as you set your foot for the first time within the wide-spread and time-honored walls of the universal church.

I have never read in so few words a more comprehensive statement of the incongruities of the Protestant Church, than you have put forward in the second paragraph of your valued communication. Alas! reformed England has no Church, since she separated from the communion of Tertullian—she is in the "position" of a body without a head, the members deprived of spiritual life, having no source of spiritual vitality—she is in the "position" of a withered branch broken off from the trunk, and producing no meritorious fruit; and hence, I am not surprised at your doubts of the spiritual position. Her "numerous sects," as you appropriately call them, are the sure indication of the storm that rages over her spiritual domain. They are the clear result of an ecclesiastical disturbance—they are the palpable demonstration that the national faith is shattered into fragments. Like the swelling surges of an agitated sea, these acts multiply, and rise, and foam as the tempest rages; and they contrast strongly with the solemn repose and universal calm which reigns over the boundless empire of the Catholic Church.

Private judgment, in "its vagaries," has thrown down all the ramparts of Christianity, and has actually blotted out the Gospel; it has taken away the Seven Sacraments, and destroyed Purgatory and the Holy Sacrifice of the altar; it has denied the Divinity of Christ, and has disputed the personality and the existence of the Holy Ghost: it has corrupted the Bible, and has robbed mankind of their title-deeds to their future inheritance—in a word—it has pulled down the whole fabric of the New Covenant, and has left nothing behind except the soul, standing alone in the wide waste of doubt and Atheism, with no mark to direct reason and faith, save the canopy of the skies and the boundless horizon.

I do believe, that Lord John Russell, in "his official caprice," is the greatest enemy the Church and State of England ever had; he has insulted the Catholic world; he has paganised the Protestant creed; he has degraded the British constitution; and, if not stopped in his capricious career, he will lower the dignity of the crown. Hence, I do not wonder that the scholar and the Christian should leave an establishment where trick, and stratagem, and caprice, and despotism, and mere human laws are substituted for confidingness, honor, order, charity and the ordinances of God.

I feel very happy, indeed, by your remarks, in reference to our interview. I have ever felt intensely the strong conviction, that no Protestant could long remain detached from the true Church, if he permitted his mind and heart to yield to a calm and unprejudiced investigation of the truths of our holy religion. You, my dear friend, are now the best judge of the truth of this assertion; and I pray God, that many may be induced to read your letter, and to follow your example. There can be no doubt of the necessity of a sacrifice in the New Law, as the established, essential worship of God; and surely, the cross were the fulfilment of the bloody sacrifices of Old Law; the Last Supper was the fulfilment of the priesthood, and the offering of Melchisedech. If bread and wine, then, were the *type*, surely bread and wine cannot be the *fulfilment;* if so, the typical thing and the thing typified, would be the same thing. The type was the *shadow* of some future perfect *reality;* and surely the *shadow* and the *reality* cannot be the *same thing*. Hence as the offering at the Last Supper was the reality of Melchisedech's type, it follows, necessarily, that it must be as *exalted above the type*, as the priesthood of Christ was above that of Aaron, and the atonement of the cross, above the blood of oxen. This reasoning furnishes a demonstration to prove that the new priesthood and the essential sacrifice, will be continued through all-coming time, "to show forth His death till He come." And hence the Catholic Church has now a sacrifice which is a perfect propitiation for sin, an offering suited to all the conditions of divine worship, and a gift to present to the throne of mercy worthy the acceptance of God.

My dear friend, it is a melancholy and most deplorable fact, that there is no worship worthy of God in the Protestant Church, as they neither have a priest to offer, or any offering to make, which is the essence of worship. That church has actually gone back to Judaism by celebrating the type and the memorial of bread and wine—that is to say, they preserve the slender taper of the Old Law to direct and to light their steps, although the sun itself has risen in the skies, and pours a burning flood of light over the spiritual creation. How wretched and foolish to see men (who read the Scripture,) *kneel down* in their plain senses before bread and wine in the New Law—that is, they adopt a type, or a memorial, or a shadow, in the face of a *perfect fulfilled* covenant. May God enlighten them. They deserve pity, to see them like fools, hold up the light of a farthing candle to direct the world, while the sun stands blazing in the meridian. It is Judaism to adopt this ceremonial, and it is blasphemy to kneel before avowed bread and wine.

The man who searches is not certain of truth; the man who changes his belief to a newer creed, cannot dare to say, that the all-wise unchangeable God dictates these novelties and contradictions. Now, if a witness, who doubts, and hesitates, and changes his evidence, would not, or could not be believed by an honest jury at a petty court, surely a doubting, changing testimony to FAITH cannot be received at the tribunal of God. Clearly then, there never was, or never can be *Divine Faith* in the Protestant Church—that which is *unworthy* to be human, cannot *deserve* to be divine.

I fully appreciate, and I entirely enter into your feelings of anguish on leaving the Protestant Church; but, being guided by the inspiration of the Holy Ghost, your sorrow will soon change into joy; and as many of your brethren (who rank amongst the best and most learned men of the present age) have set you an example, you form an additional member of the glorious band, who within the last few years have broken family ties—have given up station and emolument, and, at the sacrifice of every worldly advantage, have yielded to their convictions in joining the faith of Augustine and Jerome, of Irenæus and Chrysostom; ranging themselves under the victorious colors that are seen flouting the skies, above the old infallible rock on which Peter has planted the eternal standard.

I beg to say, in conclusion, that while I advocate the principles of my church, and while I am prepared to die, if necessary, in its defence, I have never uttered one word from the pulpit in disrespect to the conscientious creed of Protestants; and moreover, I say, no matter what provocation I may receive in England, I shall never deviate from this charitable and inoffensive course, which I have observed since I entered on public life, and which I hope to practice to my death.

I am about to proceed to Manchester, where I shall remain for a month; and in the meantime, I beg to recommend you to the care of my dear friend, Rev. Mr. Sheridan, of St. Mary's, Liverpool; who, I take leave to say, is one of the most zealous, and disinterested, and perfect Catholic clergymen in England.

Believe me, my dear Rev. Friend, faithfully and attached brother in Christ.

D. W. CAHILL, D.D.

To the Rev. JOHN COLLINS, M.A.

ADDRESS TO THE CATHOLIC INHABITANTS OF GREENOCK,

DELIVERED ON THE 26TH OCTOBER 1851.

ON Sunday the 26th ult., DR. CAHILL preached in the Rev. MR. DANAHER'S church in Greenock, the church was crowded to excess, and many persons were compelled to go away for want of room. On the following day, a deputation of the Catholic inhabitants of Greenock, waited on the Rev. Gentleman with an address, expressing their admiration of his high attainments, and his exertions in the cause of religion and of his suffering country. DR. CAHILL replied as follows :—

GENTLEMEN :—I cannot find any form of language capable of expressing my feelings of grateful acknowledgment for the address you have just read. I have never received a more distinguished compliment; and I can no more hope to imitate the style, or your composition than I can repay your affectionate kindness. When I heard that address, I felt that you had been unconsciously drawing my picture from an image of me which your own ardent fancy had painted; and it is to your warm Irish hearts, rather than your deliberate judgments

I am indebted for the flattering copy. I can read, however, from your eloquent words, an inspiring lesson to stimulate me to an ambitious attempt of approaching the exalted reality which your patriotism has sketched.

In my strictures on the English minister, I only claim the merit of a feeling heart, and the advantage of a *Continental* observation. The history of Europe has unfolded, within the last five years, many a fierce revolutionary struggle excited by English diplomacy; and it points out many a concomitant attempt to uproot the creed of Jerome, and to tear the triple crown from the brow of the successor of the fisherman. My merit merely consists, in sounding the alarm through the world against this unexpected, this unexampled, this secret, and this perilous perfidy; and, like the shepherd's whistle during the night, I am only a mere voice amidst the darkness of my country; but I have aided by that voice in collecting together the scattered flock, and arresting the treacherous wolf in his stealthy, ravening career. And if I have succeeded in publishing the woes of Ireland in foreign countries, I have only transcribed the history which is carved on the deserted villages, and on the red graves of my unhappy country. Who could fail to write the eloquence of the heart, while beholding the faithful Irish banished from the homes of their forefathers—seeing the tottering, naked grandfather, carrying in the trembling arms his starving grandchild—and hurrying in thousands towards the emigrant ship, as to a place of refuge from persecution, famine, the poorhouse, and the coffinless grave? And who could stand on the oozing pit, where the naked remains of thousands of half-starved victims lie in rotting masses below, and not write in words of fire on the cruelties and the woes, which, like a torrent, has swept without control over unfortunate Ireland, and carrying away in the devouring flood, abandoned thousands of my poor faithful countrymen? Cold must the heart be, which speak *icicles* while looking into the furnace of persecution; and unfeeling and *coward* must be the bosom which could talk in bated breath and whispering humbleness, while the flesh of the murdered Irish poor *protrude through the clay, on the top of the putrid masses that rot below.* I am, therefore, only a faithful copyist of Whig cruelty—of what my heart has read and committed to its eternal memory.

I feel extremely happy that my exertions at Greenock, have been so successful, as you state, but you give me the merit which most appropriately belongs to yourselves. All education is imperfect without the knowledge of God's law; and the man who, in the deserted cabin, teaches the orphan child the faith of Christ, and the Lord's Prayer, fills a higher office than the accomplished scholar, who, beneath the gilded ceiling of the imperial palace, instructs the son of a king in philosophical science, the history of thrones, and the conquest of nations.

Gentlemen, again accept the ardent expression of my sincerest gratitude, and believe me to be, with lasting and distinguished regard, ever faithfully your devoted humble servant,

D. W. CAHILL.

CONTROVERSIAL SERMONS,

BY REV. D, W. CAHILL.

This eloquent Divine delivered two controversial sermons on Sunday, 21st. of December, 1851 at St. Peter's Catholic Church, Seel street, Liverpool.

The subject of the first one was " *The Bible, as interpreted by private judgment, false as a rule of Faith.* "

" Long before eleven o'clock, says the *Dublin Tablet,* the hour announced for the discourse, the sacred edifice was crowded to excess, and several well known clergymen belonging to the Protestant Church, and a large number of their flocks, were present. A considerable number of persons, who came at the time appointed, had to return, as they could not procure places, and many others were content to stand outside the doors, and hear as well as they could under the circumstances. The Rev. Gentleman came before the altar habited in his surplice and stole; he was accommodated with a seat. The most profound attention was observable throughout his brilliant discourse, which lasted nearly an hour and a half. It was indeed a master-piece of eloquence. "

We are able to give to our readers a complete analysis of this sermon, as it was published by the above named journal.

The second sermon was preached on the evening

of the same day in the same church, which, as the *Tablet* says, was thronged as full as in the morning. The subject was "*The Real Presence in the Blessed Sacrament,*" which he proved in the most convincing manner to all who heard him. The very Rev. Divine, that journal adds, has won golden opinions from all parties in that city, by his moderation and the inoffensive manner in which he put forth the powerful truths on both subjects."

ANALYSIS OF DR. CAHILL'S SERMON.

"The Bible as interpreted by private judgment, false as a rule of Faith."

The distinguished orator commenced by stating, that he hoped to prove by the clearest evidence, that the Bible, as interpreted by private judgment, was false as a rule of Faith; and he then proceeded to show that from the creation of the world up to the time of Moses there was no written work in existence whereby true believers could have been directed or governed; and yet, after all, Faith had been handed down pure from generation to generation, from father to son, and so on. There was no law written as regarded Faith; so that at least for a period of twenty-six hundred years after the creation of Adam, man had no written book to guide him as a rule of Faith, and yet God was worshipped by man, and the true Faith preserved all that time without a written book, and God's law was obeyed.

The law was imparted by God to the Patriarchs, and by them it was handed down from one generation to another; so that, according to the doctrine that the Bible was a rule of Faith, how could man have been saved in the Old World until the coming of Christ? When Christ came on earth, and died for the redemption of the world, he descended into Hell—Limbo—to preach the glad tidings of redemption to the souls that were there—not by a book, but by the authority of his word. He had there to tell them that the Faith which they had held from the creation of the world—which had been handed down from father to son—had been accomplished in his death.

The Patriarchs were not guided or governed by any written law, but by the authority which they had received from the beginning, and which they imparted from one to the other—from generation to generation.—There was therefore, no written book from the commencement, but the faith was communicated by word of mouth, and living authority, and he (the Rev. Preacher) would submit that, that was a very strong point.—For twenty-six hundred years the Church of God was governed, not by written words, but by true living authority communicated to her by God himself. He would now come to the New Law, as established by Christ—for up to the time when he made his appearance upon earth, salvation was obtained, not from books, but from the living authority which existed without any book. Coming, therefore, to the New Law, he wanted to know where it was written, or ordered to be written, as an authority to be guided by? It was not written, but it was spoken law. If it had been necessary for Christ to have written a book on the subject, He would have done so, or He would have commanded one to have been written; but the fact was, that Christ never during His life on this earth, wrote a book, nor did He speak about having a book written. He said to His Apostles that he would send the Holy Ghost, who would teach them all things, and bring to their minds whatever He had told them—and whatever he had told them He commanded them to do. He did not say to them, "write a book," but He commanded them to go and preach the gospel all over the world—not by writing, but by teaching by word of mouth.

When, then, did the sanction of the first book appear on the subject after the death of Christ? Not for three hundred and seventy-five years after the death of Christ. It was that time, before the stamp of the Church was put upon any book—not but that the Scriptures were written and in possession of the Church before it, but they had not been stamped with the seal of authority up to that period. The Old Testament had been written by Moses—the New Testament had been written, and was in the possession of the Church; but, as he before observed, they were not stamped with the authority of the Church for nearly four centuries after the Gospel was preached (not written) by Christ and his Apostles. No book was used during that time; but the Gospel existed, and salvation was obtained through the Church, speaking by the living authority alone.

There were twelve Apostles, and out of those, only five wrote books. He would ask if it were necessary, why did not the remainder write? The four Evangelists wrote three works, not as general to the Church, but at the special request of individuals. Mathew wrote at the solicitation of the people of Palestine; St. Mark at that of the people of Rome; St. Luke to an individual; and St. John wrote, to put down a heresy that had arisen amongst some early Christians. The writings were not general, but written locally, and for local purposes, not as the guidance or rule of Faith. Suppose that Queen Victoria had occasion to write to an individual in Liverpool relative to some local act of parliament, did any one think, she would sit down and write the whole code of laws by which England is governed to that individual? So it was with the Scriptures. If they were written for the government and law of the whole Church it would be clearly so stated and set forth; but they were not; they were written for local and special purposes, without reference to the general government of the Church, which was preserved in the Church itself from the beginning.

The Rev. preacher then stated in detail to whom and for what purposes the Gospels, the Acts, the Epistles, and the Apocalypse were written, and stated that the Church, as the depository of all truth, had by her authority set her seal on the Scriptures, but that it was not until nearly four hundred years after Christ that she thus collected and set apart the sacred volume we now possess. Yet, the Christian Faith existed before that. Christ did not say to His Apostles, "Go and write to all nations in my name," but, he said, "Go and teach, and preach to all nations:" and St. Paul expressly states, that Faith comes by hearing alone. Now, hearing must come from one living man to another living man, who, by speaking, communicates the Faith to him—that Faith having come down from the earliest times to its possessor, through the authority of the Church. A man cannot hear with his mouth or his eyes, but with his ears he can hear what the mouth utters to him. Christ was a living man, and he spoke to living authorities, who, in their turn, spoke also to living authorities in the Catholic Church, and thus the Faith was preserved pure and spotless down to the present time, and would ever continue so to the end of time. It was clear, therefore, that Faith came by hearing, that Faith being spoken by the authority of the Church, and that was the Faith and the belief given by Christ to His Church on this earth.

His first point, was therefore proved; and his second fact, was equally strong. It was avowedly admitted that for nearly four hundred years after Christ, that there was no book stamped with the authority of the Church. If the rule of Faith of the Catholic Church was confined to books of Scripture, many of those were lost; but, notwithstanding that, the Faith was fully and entirely preserved in the Church, for he had received his Faith from his spiritual Fathers in the Church as pure and spotless as the stole he wore. He was the legitimate descendant of that Faith, and would not part with it but with his life, nor would any other Catholic in the world. Suppose the Scriptures were the rule of Faith, why they ought to have the whole Scriptures; but they had not the whole, as it was well known, that nearly the half of the books were lost; but yet, the Catholic Church preserved the Faith whole and entire. If a man kill another, he violates the Fifth Commandment, and although he did not violate any of the other ten, yet he could not be reconciled to God, until he returned to grace and repentance; and, in the same manner, if a man violated any one of the dogmas of Faith, he could not preserve a part thereof: so that if the Scriptures were a rule of Faith, man should have the whole, and not a part, of what he founded his Faith upon. Catholic Priests were reviled, and charged with not reading the Scriptures; and they were further charged with preventing the people from reading them.

Now, he would tell such parties, that every Priest at his ordination was obliged before the Bishop, with his body prostrate on the ground, and his hands stretched out, to take one of the most solemn oaths that man could take, that for the remainder of his life, he would devote at least one hour and a quarter every day reading the Scriptures. So that any one who asserted that Priests did not read the Scriptures, told a falsehood. They say also, that Priests prevent the people from reading the Scriptures—that is another falsehood. Also, let any man go into any shop in England where books are sold, and he would get the Scriptures to purchase, if he had money to pay for them. In fact, that was a matter of mercantile speculation; but see how easy it was to choke two such bold lies as were constantly uttered against Catholic Priests and Catholics. But, he would ask, how could the whole Scriptures be read? Where were the lost books to be found? He would now come to that point, and show how many books were lost: and this he would prove from the books that remained of the Scriptures.

In the Book of Numbers, xxi. 14, there is the following passage—"Wherefore, it is said in the Book of Wars of the Lord." Now, where was that book? It was not to be found—it was lost. In the Third Book of Kings it is stated, that Solomon wrote 3,000 proverbs; there was not more than 1,500 to be found—the rest are lost: and in the same book it is stated, that he wrote 105 canticles; there is not the half of that number to be found in the present Bible; they are lost. Then, there it is stated, that there was the Book of Nathan the Prophet—there is no such book now; it is lost. In the Book of Chronicles, it is stated, that the acts of David are written in the Book of Samuel the Seer, and Nathan the Prophet—no such books are to be found; they are lost. There was an Epistle of St. Paul to the Colossians lost. St. Paul wrote five Epistles to the Corinthians, but we have only two of these. There were altogether twenty-three books belonging to the Bible lost—twenty from the Old Testament, and three from the New; so that if the Bible was to be a rule of Faith, how could it be proved that the whole Bible existed?

If a man made his will, and left his son his property, and that in the course of time, twelve men on their oaths, came to decide on that will, and found only the half of it in existence, would they, or could they as honest men, say that it was the man's will? It was manifest, therefore, that there was a time when there was no Bible; yet Faith existed; and it was equally manifest that the Bible as interpreted by private judgment, was false as a rule of Faith. Catholics respected the Bible, but they did not make it the rule of their Faith; but they respected it and believed it, because the Church had sanctioned it—that Church which was unchanged and unchangeable. How was that portion of the Bible preserved? Why, from the fall of the Roman Empire in 475, for nearly nine centuries, every country in Europe, was in a constant state of revolution, confusion, and civil war: and where was religion, piety, literature, Faith, and morals preserved all that time? In the faithful repository and bosom of the Catholic Church—that was known all over the world,—history records it. And how was such preserved? By teaching the doctrine which was confided to the Church by Christ and his Apostles—the living authority being in the Church.

It followed, that those who made the Bible the sole rule of Faith, ought to have the whole Bible, which they had not, and if they had not, why they must be in doubt every moment about their Faith. They could not be certain of the truth or of the Faith, and therefore they must be in the dark, and to be in doubt on such a matter, was to be always in a state of unhappiness. Moses wrote a portion of the Old Testament, but it was admitted on all hands that for twenty-six hundred years before he wrote, that no book of the law existed, yet the Faith was preserved all that time by the Patriarchs, who handed it down, one from another. Christ said to his Apostles, when speaking of the Scribes and Pharisees, not to do as they did, but to observe what they said, for they spoke the law with their lips, but their hearts were unsound—do not as they do, but do what they say. They taught the law of Moses, who was dead fourteen hundred years before that time. The command of Christ was in the imperative mood—do not what they do, but what they say: so that here again Faith came by hearing.

He would ask those who followed their private judgment, and made the Bible the rule of Faith, if they understood Hebrew, for the Old Testament was written in the Hebrew, and then translated into Syro-Chaldaic; and the New Testament was written in Greek—he would ask a man depending on private judgment, then, do you know Hebrew? He would answer, no. Then how could such a man say that he founded his Faith on the Bible, when he did not know whether it was truly translated or not?

The same thing must be said in reference to the New Testament; and in both cases, such a man after all his boasting, was depending not on his own judgment, but on the judgment of others, of whom he could know nothing, not even their names. Now, would it not be better for such parties as he alluded to, to depend on the Pope and the Bishops whom they did know, than to depend on parties whose names he was ignorant of? He would ask such persons—"Is there any person in your Church who cannot read?" He would be answered—yes. Then, how do you teach persons to form their Faith by private judgment? By teaching them the Catechism. Yes, but where do you get that Catechism? From other authority. Then, where is your private judgment? You don't get it from your private judgment, but from authority, as you call it, of which you are totally ignorant. The Protestant Clergy were obliged to swear to the truth of the Thirty-nine Articles, and where did these Articles come from? They came to them on the authority of an Act of Parliament; and yet, such clergymen were obliged to swear before God to the truth of such Articles. Acts of Parliament were made by the House of Commons and the House of Lords, which comprised about 1,000 persons, including old Bishops, all differing in religion, and many having no religion at all; and yet, these were the persons upon whom Protestant Clergymen, and Protestants were to rely for their rule of Faith—whose judgment they were obliged to obey, in swearing to the Thirty-nine Articles.

He would ask—if the Pope and the Bishops of the Catholic Church, who had preserved the Faith for so many hundred years, pure and spotless, were not better authority than such men as he alluded to? He then alluded to the Acts of Parliament made by Cranmer in the reign of Edward VI., and contrasted such Acts with the conduct of the Popes and Bishops who governed the Catho-Church, and who preserved the Faith of Christ as it had been given to them by Him and the Apostles. Up to the time of Luther in 1517, the authority of the Popes and Bishops was acknowledged all over the world—Purgatory, prayers for the dead, invocation of the Saints, and satisfaction for sins—all were acknowledged; but when Luther threw off the authority of the Church, he flung aside those dogmas, because if he retained them, he must obey the authority of the Pope; and from that time to the present, his followers had been gradually getting rid of everything they thought proper—all on private judgment, of course.

He alluded to the Gorham case, and the decision thereon. In the same manner the Protestant Church got rid of the Sacraments; and he would ask, what belief had they now? There were the Unitarians; many of whom he knew to be learned men, and by the same process of private judgment they denied the Divinity of Christ; in same manner the Greeks denied the personality of the Holy Ghost. The Protestants first began to take the slates off the house, then they took away the roof, next the pillars; and lastly, they carried away the walls, and left nothing behind; all from private judgment, of which, they confessed themselves to be totally ignorant, for they depended not on their own, but on the opinion and judgment of others, of whom they knew nothing whatever. Such was their Faith.

He then referred to the Acts of Parliament made on the subject of the Church of England government, and Lord John Russell's opinions, which governed such Acts, and concluded by stating, that persons who were depending on the Bible as a rule of Faith, as interpreted by private judgment, were the most inconsistent in the world, and that they stood alone in the world, in the midst of the most frightful doubts and perplexity, which nothing could remove from their minds. They should, therefore, have recourse to the only true and infallible test of Faith, which lay alone in the bosom of the Catholic Church from the earliest time, and would continue so to the end of the world. After resuming his argument, he concluded by passing a well-merited compliment on the Christian Brothers who had charge of the schools, whose cause he advocated, and showed all the good they had done.

REV. DR. CAHILL'S ADDRESS

TO THE

CATHOLICS OF LIVERPOOL AND BIRKENHEAD.

This letter was intended to prevent the Catholics from walking in public procession on St. Patrick's Day. He gave the five following reasons for so doing. 1st. That it never had been in any part of Ireland a public procession solely ni commemoration of St. Patrick, but in honor of the holy cause of temperance. 2nd. The meeting of the Catholics might be deemed as a menacing show of physical force, and as a challenging attitude. 3rd. The degrading scenes of intemperance of some few, may be ascribed to the whole Irish race and creed. 4th. By a supposed or real insult, personal conflicts, or general riots with all their bad consequences, have been the results of these processions. 5th. If anything tending to arouse social animosity is criminal at all times, on a Sunday or Holiday, must be of deplorable affliction to the Church. The eloquent Divine exhorts the Irishmen to save virtuously a few pounds, and give relief to the many suffering poor Irish exiles who have been banished from their country by a cruel, persecuting Cabinet, making the English towns crowded with the "wretched victims of English misrule, who fly from Ireland to seek shelter in England, from injustice and famine, and to earn their bread in honest industry and hard labor."

An exhortation to make England their home, concludes this letter : he advises his countrymen " to identify their minds with her interests, and to form a real *bona fide* integral part of her community." By an observance of his recommendation, and their obedience to the voice of the Catholic Church, they will convince Lord John Russell and his perfidious colleagues, that they have not succeeded in gagging the mouths, and tying up the hands of the Irish priesthood.

SAINT WERBURGH'S BIRKENHEAD, *Feb.* 13*th*, 1852.

BELOVED BRETHREN AND FELLOW-COUNTRYMEN : This is the first time I have had the pleasure and the privilege of addressing you by a public letter; and, as I am about to speak to you in the name of religion, and under the sanction of the Catholic clergy, I feel assured that I shall command your willing and prompt obedience to any request I may find it necessary to make. Therefore, with perfect respect, and with warm affection, I beg of you, or rather command you, to abstain on next Patrick's Day, from your annual custom of walking in public procession. I am induced to make this request from a variety of cogent reasons, the force of which, under the existing circumstances, and from a clear view of the case, you will yourselves, readily admit.

Firstly—Then, we have never had, *in any part of Ire-*

land, within my remembrance, a public procession through the streets, solely in commemoration of St. Patrick. We have had public processions of the Temperance Societies during several years past in Ireland, and St. Patrick's Day has been appropriately selected for that purpose, in order to celebrate, on the patron day of the Apostle of Ireland, the triumph of Irish virtue over the most degrading vice, and the most brutal debasing habit that could pollute the human heart, weaken our reason, and stain the soul. But on those occasions, the procession was not intended in commemoration of Saint Patrick, but in honor of the holy cause of temperance. I have seen these assemblages at different times, formed solely of the pledged members of the Society, headed by the Catholic clergy, accompanied by several respectable members of the Society of Friends, and composed of Protestant and Catholic tradesmen, all united in one charitable brotherhood of virtue, and vying with each other in advancing the cause of reason, sobriety, order, and religion. Surely, therefore, you cannot feel an objection at my earnest request, to give up a procession which has no precedent in the history of Ireland, or in the commemorative festivals of your country.

Secondly—However laudable may have been heretofore the intentions of our countrymen in these public demonstrations, our meeting at the present moment, might be deemed as a menacing show of physical force, and as a challenging attitude of illegal and public intimidation. From the recent insults inflicted on our country and our creed by the lies and the perfidy of the present Government, your Protestant neighbors and fellow-townsmen might feel uneasy, lest in your accumulated numbers, and your just indignation, you might be betrayed into any expressions of recrimination, or into any breach of the peace; you must judge of their feelings by your own, and as their political processions justly give you offence, you must not yourselves sanction the practices which you condemn in them. True, you have no arms in your hands, nor do you walk in commemoration of a political and national triumph, but numbers even without arms (at the present time,) has the appearance of a challenge, and cannot be viewed without apprehension by any dispassionate observer; it is in itself calculated to engender bad feeling, to awaken embittering recollections, to lead to a breach of the peace, and must therefore be discountenanced by every sound thinking man, as mischievous and subversive of the public social order.

Thirdly—It has often happened, that the *friendly* meeting of the morning, has ended in the *riot* of the evening; that the *sober* multitude of the mid-day have been disgraced by the degrading scenes of intemperance at night: and the bad conduct of some few (as is always the case,) has been ascribed to our race and our creed, as a national reproach, and as an essential vice of our name. Surely, you will not contribute by any act of yours to perpetuate this unjust accusation, but rather to wipe away by a superior character of peace and order, any stigma which have been cast upon us by the recklessness, or the misguided patriotism of a small section of our countrymen.

Fourthly—In some instances, a supposed or a real insult, coming from a suspected quarter along your line of procession, has led to personal conflict or general riot; and the subsequent dismissal from employment, the loss of situation, the punishment inflicted by Courts of Justice, imprisonment, and all the consequent misfortunes of idleness, poverty, and beggary, have been more than once the afflicting and melancholy results of the insane celebration of a day, which, in place of being the memorial of national piety, has been often incongruously converted into the signal of mutual revenge. You will, therefore, agree with me, that every true lover of Ireland, and of her invincible name, will aid in putting a stop to the revival of any act which would tarnish our national virtue, imperil our mutual strength, or defeat our essential future combination.

Fifthly—Anything that tends to rouse social animosity, to awaken religious hostility, is criminal and wicked of course, at all times and in all places; but scenes such as I have described, become on a Sunday or on a Holiday, subjects of deplorable affliction to the Church, which commands that so solemn a festival as the 17th of March, shall be kept holy by all the faithful, in proportion to the benefits conferred by our Patron National Saint, and to the imperishable deposit of Christian faith, of which this day is the joyful sacred commemoration. Your compliance, therefore, with these views of mine, will give satisfaction to the clergy who love you, will honor the religion you profess, and will be a lasting testimony of your obedience to the letter and spirit of your faith.

I have been informed, on an authority which I cannot

doubt, that, on one occasion, the loss of employment, aris ing from circumstances such as I have described, deprived the working classes, within one month of no less a sum than twelve hundred pounds, or thereabouts: and hence, if you will now kindly follow my affectionate counsel, and thus avoid a similar loss, you can subscribe a few pounds of the virtuous saving, and give relief to the many suffering poor Irish exiles, who, being banished from their country by a cruel, persecuting Cabinet, stand at your doors every morning, begging a morsel of food to save them even for one day from the ravages of hunger, inflicted by unjust laws. This is an appeal to your hearts, which you cannot reject; and the man who, on next Patrick's Day, would be seen wasting money, and drunk and riotous, would appear before me as wanting in common feeling to our poor countrymen, and I should consider his conduct on this occasion as a palpable departure from the obedience due to ecclesiastical authority, and a violation of the personal respect which I humbly claim as due to myself.

It is very easy for those who are ignorant of the persecutions of Ireland, to find fault with the conduct of Irishmen in England; but the residence of one year in our unhappy country, would convince the most incredulous, that no nation in the whole civilised world has ever endured so much persecution, and borne their heavy misfortunes with such national fortitude and national honor. If common justice were done to the Irishmen at home, the English towns would not now be crowded with the wretched victims of English misrule, who fly from Ireland as from a furnace, to seek shelter in England from injustice and famine, and to earn their bread in honest industry, or hard labor.

* * * * * * * * * *

And if I could add one word more of advice, that word would be an advice to make England your home; to identify your minds with her interests, and to form a real *bona fide* integral part of her community. This idea gives a fixed aim to all your exertions, and cannot fail, in the end, to have a decided salutary influence on your temporal interests and social position. Irishmen live in England and Scotland as in a place of transit. They mean to stay in these countries only till they will have acquired the means of returning home or going to America. This feeling is highly patriotic, but it is romantic and imprudent. They live in Great Britain like travellers in a ship; they care little about the safety of the vessel except during the passage; and as a matter of course, the captain and the crew always look on them with suspicion—treat them as strangers, and only entitled to a temporary civility, perfectly careless of their after fate; and hence the intention of not making England your home produces a habit of recklessness; engenders an unsteadiness of conduct injurious to fixed interests, and subversive of the sincere English friendship which a sober permanent residence never fails to secure.

Under all these circumstances, then I call on you, (as one who loves you, and who could die for you if necessary) to fulfil my earnest command on next Patrick's Day. Keep that remarkable and eventful holiday with becoming sobriety; remain at home during the evening, with your little families in peace and quietness, set an example of order and edification to your children, and God will pour a rich blessing on your obedience and your conduct.

But, above all, convince Lord John Russell and his perfidious colleagues, that they have not succeeded in gagging the mouths, and tying up the hands of Catholic clergy; tell him in words that cannot be mistaken, that the priests are your magistrates, and that their words are more powerful than an armed police; proclaim by your good order, that the Popish bishops, whom he attempted to disrobe, consume, annihilate, and after that to deport to the colonies, are not dead yet; but on the contrary (as we say in Ireland) "*are alive and kicking*;" and let him know, that when I choose to address you under the sanction of the church, I can command you to do what I please, and that you will neither walk, nor drink, nor sing, nor dance, but according to my pleasure, I hope soon to meet you in a public assembly, where, from the bottom of my heart, I can return you thanks for a conduct which obeys the church, pays respect to the civil authorities, advances your own interests, and offers a lasting, and a distinguised compliment to me.

Believe me, beloved brethren and fellow-countrymen, to be for ever your ardent friend, and your devoted Irish priest,

D. W. CAHILL, D.D.

ADDRESS AND PRESENTATION TO THE REV. DR. CAHILL,

FROM THE

UNITED SONS OF ERIN SOCIETY, LIVERPOOL.

The result of the address to the Catholic inhabitants of Liverpool and Birkenhead, were, that a deputation from the United Sons of Erin Society waited on Dr. Cahill, and assured him, in the name of those whom he exhorted not to walk in public procession on next St. Patrick's Day, that his advice would be followed to the letter. Afterwards, they presented him with a beautiful gold snuff-box and the following address. The box bore this inscription: "*From the Members of the United Sons of Erin Society to the Rev. D. W. Cahill, in token of their admiration of his virtues, talents, and patriotism.*" The box was manufactured in Dublin, and bears, as the motto of the Society, four hands united, to signify the union that ought to exist among the children of the four provinces of Ireland (Leinster, Munster, Ulster and Connaught;) and under them are the words: "*United we stand—divided we fall.*" The Irish harp, surmounted with a wreath of Shamrocks, crowns the devices, and gives a rich appearance to the whole.

ADDRESS TO THE REV. DR. CAHILL.

Rev. and dear Sir:—We, the members of the United Sons of Erin Society, have long desired this opportunity of expressing to you our admiration and respect for you. As Irishmen, we cannot but feel pride in you, as a distinguished advocate of civil and religious liberty, and, as Catholics, we are honored by your virtues, talents, and scientific attainments. While therefore, we deplore the ruin and desolation which was fallen upon our common country, we rejoice to think that your life is an illustration of the fidelity and devotion with which your Reverend predecessors in the ministry of the Gospel, clung to their invincible faith, when all things else were wrested from them ; and you will pardon us, for adding that your missionary labors forciby remind us of those bright and glorious days in Ireland's history, when her priests and her philosophers went forth, from her hospitable shores, and distinguished seats of learning, as venerable and illustrious apostles of Christianity and civilization to the various nations of Europe.

Approving as we do, the sentiments contained in your admirable letter to the Catholics of Liverpool, we have resolved to abstain from celebrating the approaching anniversary of our patron saint by a public procession. In adopting this resolution, from a conviction of its propriety, and in obedience to your desire, we do not wish to be regarded as surrendering any right which is recognised by law and usage. We believe, however, that the interests of Irishmen in this town will be best promoted by avoiding all such public displays as would irritate the feelings of our British neighbors, whose bad passions have been too much excited for sectarian and party purposes, and we are prepared and determined to prove by our conduct on the anniversary of our National Saint, that we can make sacrifices to further the ends of peace and charity.

We would here beg to remark, that our purpose, as a society, is morally and socially to elevate our fellow-countrymen in Liverpool, and by word and example, to disarm, as far as possible, those English (perhaps unconscious) antipathies and prejudices, of which a poor and down-stricken people are invariably made the certain victims. We are therefore, anxious to produce among the Irishmen in Liverpool a perfect unity of feeling and action ; to abolish, as far as we can, all provincial distinctions between natives of the same country, and to excite among them a just appreciation of that harmony and unanimity, the absence of which has hitherto considerably impaired their effieciency in public affairs, and detracted from that social and political influence, which, constituting as they do, nearly one-third of the entire population of this great mart of commerce, they might otherwise possess.

In this work you have given us, by precept and example, most valuable aid. We beg, therefore, on this account, and for the reasons we have already assigned, that you will accept this gold snuff-box, as a small but sincere token of our gratitude, admiration, and respect which we entertain for your person and character. Signed on behalf of the Members

DENIS ARKWRIGHT, *Chairman.*

LIVERPOOL, *February* 20*th.*

DR. CAHILL'S REPLY.

ST. WERBURGH'S BIRKENHEAD, *February* 20*th*, 1852.

BELOVED FELLOW-COUNTRYMEN: —As I had read, through each succeeding paragraph of your most valued, and most complimentary address, I found my mind insensibly and agreeably carried back to the days of Ireland's past history, and I felt my heart excited by feelings of far higher interest and pleasure, than of mere personal gratification. I am not at all surprised, that you exaggerate into the largest proportions any slender pretensions of mine, while you have your eyes fixed on my Irish predecessors in the Catholic Church; and I am quite sure that in your fond and glowing panegyric on me, you have mistaken me for one of those glorious ecclesiastical ancestors of mine, whom you had in view, when your hearts composed the flattering document now before me. But the picture you have drawn shall be carefully studied by me, and I shall make an effort to approach the original, and many a glorious masterpiece of Irish sanctity, and Irish learning, and Irish patriotism, is planted in every page of our distinguished and checquered history, to publish to the coming and unborn generation of Irish priests, their ecclesiastical lineage, their unsullied name, their eminent services, and their unconquered faith.

The historical monuments of ecclesiastical Europe, at this moment, bear venerable and imperishable testimony to the ancient celebrity of Ireland, in letters and faith; the churches dedicated to St. Patrick, to St. Martin, and to St. Bridget, proclaim from their tottering foundations throughout the neighboring Continent, that they received the Gospel from the famed missionaries of Ireland ; and following the idea suggested by your historical observations, the surrounding nations must acknowledge, that whatever perfection they now possess in religion and learning, they lighted their first torches of Christianity and civilization at the sacred fires which burned on the ancient altars of Ireland. But, alas, and alas! this was a long time ago; when the Irish owned Ireland—when there was no poor in our land—when our shores were the mart of national abundance—when our hearts were free, our limbs unfettered, our race unproscribed, our names respected, and our doors the hospitable retreat of the stranger. Alas! beloved countrymen, this was a long, long time ago! but though, still far away in the darkness of ages, it is a holy and an inspiring practice to direct our piercing and searching thoughts through the long silent night of our sad history; and as we gaze on the sparkling firmament of our ancient glories, sigh for the coming auspicious morning, when the sun of Ireland shall rise again over a *united people*, a free nation, and an emancipated faith. This holy thought, should be the subject of our universal morning prayer, and our vesper songs, in order that the voice of liberty and of patriotism, shall never be silenced through the struggling vicissitudes and the dark mysterious history of our country.

> "Let Erin remember the days of old,
> Ere her faithless sons betray'd her,
> When Malachi wore the collar of gold,
> Which he won from the proud invader;
> When her kings with standard of green unfurled,
> Led the Red Branch Knights to danger,
> Ere the emerald gem of the Western world
> Was set on the crown of a stranger.
>
> On Lough Neagh's bank, as the fisherman strays,
> In the clear cold eve's declining,
> He sees the round towers of other days
> In the waves beneath him shining;
> Thus shall memory often, in dreams sublime,
> Catch a glimpse of the days that are over,
> And, sighing, look through the waves of time,
> For the long-faded glories they cover."

I had written to you in the name of the Catholic clergy, and I asked permission to add my own sincere request, and my affectionate counsel; and now, on their parts and on my own, I return to you my most grateful thanks, and very deeply felt acknowledgments for the very prompt respect, and the willing obedience with which you have adopted my views. I can add nothing to the paragraph which you have written on this point; your own words are your highest eulogium; and they prove to the clergy of Liverpool, that your obedience to their authority and to my request, is the motto, which, in imitation of your fathers, you have written on the front of your banners; and they demonstrate, that love of country, pure patriotism, and ardent nationality, are imperishable words carved on your hearts as well as on your flags, but that the love of your Church and of your Faith is the unfading device, which shall ever move in the van, in lofty preeminence, and shall for ever take undisputed precedence of every other historical memorial in all your national demonstrations.

I should be the last man in Ireland, who could think of crushing the public expression of your cherished nationality during your residence in England; and the fondness with which you cling to every sacred feeling that swells your rising bosom for Ireland, is an additional argument to prove how much you have sacrificed in the first instance to obey the church, to respect the laws, and to honor me. Neither the clergy of Liverpool nor I, ever can, or shall forget the debt we owe you for this act of your obedience, which is at once the public guarantee of social harmony in your city, and of universal advantage to yourselves. I wish you to understand me on this point. I do not mean that you should never have any public demonstration on certain state occasions that may be named by your committee.

This assumption would be demanding too much, might condense your feelings under too perilous a pressure, and might end in a disastrous and fatal explosion. I mean no such thing. I know too much of the world, and vastly too much of Irish ardor, to think of enclosing the feelings of one hundred and thirty thousand men, women, and children in a nutshell. What I mean and advise—and (I may as well say it) *command*—is that you shall have no *procession*, no offence to your fellow townsmen, no endangering of the public peace, no violation of the law, no embittering demonstration of physical force, no profanation of a holiday, no immoral results of your assemblages, and no national reproach affixed to your name. This is my clear meaning; but the request is not intended to prevent you forming an evening party, holding a soiree, calling a public meeting, appointing a chairman, adopting useful resolutions, and having these joyful, social, and peaceful proceedings enlivened by a brilliant orchestra, and terminated by one loud cheer for Ireland.

Can there be any idea more glorious than an evening spent in the manner I have described, without offence to God or man, and in the harmonious commemoration of our love of Ireland? On the following auspicious day the sun will rise on a happy community, respected by the civil authorities, beloved by the clergy, happy with your little children and families, and in peace with yourselves and with all the world.

The cordial co-operation which your society has given me this day, by following the advice which I have offered to the Catholics of Liverpool, places your corporate character in an eminent position of prominent public order, which must be long recollected to your advantage, by every advocate of the public peace, and by every lover of Christian morality. From the affectionate respect which I entertain for the United Sons of Erin's Society,

I feel pride and pleasure, that you have been the first public body which stamps with your approval and united support the address to which I have referred; and I feel confident that the character which you have earned and won from the public concurring testimony, shall never be forfeited on your part, by any act at variance with the expectations now so anxiously felt towards you. There can be no doubt of the fact, that a united, well organized, and properly directed society of Irishmen, can effect much good towards the relief, advancement, and social stability of our countrymen in Liverpool; and as the stream runs muddy or clear, according to the character of the source where it rises, it is undeniably true, that your personal example and official character, will give a corresponding tinge to your public transactions, and will be felt by the remotest object of your corporate care. But, alas! as I conclude your third paragraph, you remind me of the chief, inherent misfortune of Ireland—our own internal divisions. Alas! these suicidal conventions have ever, through all our past history, weakened our national strength, defeated our combined efforts, given power to our enemies, and ultimately enabled the despoiler and the tyrant, to forge chains for our enslavement, and to bind our hands, enfeebled and exhausted by mutual conflicts, in permanent bondage and degradation.

If there be any one precipice of Irish woe which has no bottom, it is the awful depth of the disasters inflicted on our name, and on our ill-fated race by our mutual jealousies; and if there be any one warning more than another, which I could give to my beloved countrymen, it would be to avoid the fate which has enabled England to enslave our country, to rob us of our inalienable rights of civil and religious liberty, and to make a barren waste, a howling wilderness, and a universal putrid churchyard in our ancient country. And how happy shall I be, if, by any advice of mine, I shall be instrumental in uniting these scattered children of the four Irish provinces into one Irish family, one fond national brotherhood, and bound together by the lasting principles of order, patriotism, and religion. This would be a confederacy of virtue, possessing resistless power in all the private and public walks of civil and social life.

I have never on any former occasion, felt greater pleasure than I now experience, from the public compliment which you have this day paid to me; and the valued and valuable gift which you have kindly presented to me, shall ever remind me of your distinguished regard for me, and of my deep debt of grateful acknowledgments to you. I therefore thank you with the warmest sincerity, and I hope very soon to have the extreme pleasure of meeting you all in public assembly, when, at the top of my Popish Irish voice, and in the sweet tones of our own accomplished Irish brogue, I shall imprint the inspired cutting remarks of our national bard on your attentive Irish hearts:—

" 'Twas fate they say, a wayward fate,
Your web of discord wove,
And while your TYRANTS JOINED IN HATE
You never joined in love.

And hearts fall off that ought to twine;
And men profane what God has given;
And some are heard to curse the shrine
Where others kneel to heaven."

Believe me, beloved fellow-countrymen, your attached and devoted Irish priest,

D. W. CAHILL, D.D.

ANNIVERSARY DINNER IN HONOR OF SAINT PATRICK'S DAY.

The anniversary of the natal day of the Patron Saint of Ireland, for 1852, was celebrated by the Catholics of Glasgow at a public banquet in the large hall of the Tontine Hotel, the walls of which were tastefully festooned with evergreens for the auspicious occasion. The *Glagow Free Press* speaks in the followings terms of this feast :

The presence of the illustrious Dr. Cahill—aptly termed by the Chairman—" the flower of the Irish priesthood "—imparted unwonted *éclat* to the proceedings, and never, indeed, were we called on to record festivities on such a scale of magnitude as those which this year were held in honor of St Patrick. The Rev. Patrick Hanley discharged the duties of the chair with an ability and tact which were the theme of general commendation. Upwards of 200 sat down to dinner.

After proposing and speaking to several toasts, the chairman said—" The health of our respected friend, Dr. Cahill." (Drunk with all the honors, and one cheer more).

Dr. Cahill on rising to reply, was accorded a reception, which for the warmth of its enthusiasm, we have never seen equalled in any public assembly, the audience getting on their feet *en masse*, and cheering for several minutes.

After a few words on Lords Russell and Palmerston, he commenced by modestly declining the high eulogium conferred by the Chairman on his services, which only consisted in his knowledge of the sad history of Ireland; if in his sympathies he seemed to weep, it was because he followed tens of thousands of his persecuted fellow-countrymen to the tomb, and because he dipped his pen in their graves. Every Irish heart, would have done what he did.

The patriotic Divine cast a glance of anguish over the present state of Ireland, as compared with the time in which St. Patrick first set his Apostolic foot on its soil; then, it was the seminary of Europe; now, it is stormed by the emissaries of Satan. Catholicity is almost natural to an Irishman: it cannot be effaced from his heart. An interesting anecdote on the Irish character, a vivid image on the celebration of the day of St. Patrick in several countries, and a splendid eulogium on the friendly crowded shores of young and vigorous America, and the blessings of liberty, prepare us for a pathetic apostrophe, and a prayer, followed by a picture of emigrants. On finishing his interesting discourse, the learned gentleman sat down amidst an enthusiasm of applause, and demonstrations of respect by the waving of handkerchiefs and continued cheering, " such, (*says the Glasgow Free Press*,) as we have never before witnessed in this city."

DR. CAHILL'S SPEECH

Mr. Chairman and beloved fellow-countrymen, I do believe there is no nation in the world able to shout with the Irish. Our countryman, Dean Swift, counseled the Irish people in his day, not to make speeches at public meetings for fear of the Attorney General. " Do not speak, " said he, " when you meet, as the law may punish you; but there is no law against shouting—hence, groan and shout. " And from that day to this, we can groan and shout better than any people in the whole world. Till I came here on this evening, I thought I could never forgive either Lord J. Russell or Lord Palmerston; but the speakers who have preceded me have inflicted such a castigation on them, that, with your kind permission, I will forgive them—not in this world—but in the next (laughter.) For this purpose, I must have the key of the Kingdom of Heaven, and also the key of the other place, in order that, when I first let them out, I can next let them in. (Roars of laughter, which continued for several minutes.)

Mr. Chairman, you have exaggerated my small services in reference to the public letters which I have written. Whatever merit I may have, consisted in my knowing well the history of Ireland. The history of other countries is learned from the cool pen of the historian, but that of Ireland is learned from the crimsoned tombs of the dead. The history of other nations is collected from the growing population and successful commerce, but the sad story of Ireland is gathered from the deserted village, the crowded poor-house, and the mournful swelling canvass of the emigrant ship. (Loud cheers.) You gave me too much credit for those slender productions of mine, and perhaps you are not aware that it was on the graves of the starved and shroudless victims of English misrule I stood when I indited the epistles. I dated them from the grave pits of Sligo, and the fever sheds of Skibbereen. If I seemed to weep, it was, because I followed to coffinless tombs tens of thousands of my poor, persecuted fellow-contrymen; and if my descriptions appeared tinged with red, it was, because I dipped my pen in their fresh bleeding graves, in order to give suitable coloring to the terrific page on which a cruel fate has traced the destinies of Ireland. (Enthusiastic applause.) It was not my mind but my bosom that dictated; it was not my pen but my heart that wrote the record.

And where is the Irishman who would not feel an involuntary impulse of national pride, in asserting, the invincible genius of our own creed, while he gazes on the crumbling walls of our ancient churches, which even, in their old age, lift their hoary heads as faithful witnesses of the past struggles of our Faith, and still, stand in their massive frame work, resisting to the last the power of the despoiler, and scarcely yielding to the inevitable stroke of time? (Long and loud cheering.) And where is the heart so cold, that would not pour forth a boiling torrent of national anger at seeing the children of forty generations consigned to a premature grave, or banished by cruel laws to seek amongst the strangers the protection they are refused at home?

Nature does not deny a home to the untutered savage that wanders naked over her boundless domain; even the maternal genius of the inhospitable forest gives a welcome asylum to her young; she brings them forth from her bare womb, suckles them on her stormy bosom, and feeds them at her desert streams. She teaches them to kneel beneath the dark canopy with which she shrouds the majesty of her inaccessible rocks : she warns them to flee from danger, in the moaning voice of the unchained tempests, and she clothes her kingdom in verdure and sunlight to cheer them in their trackless home. Well has the divine heart of Campbell given a preference to the savage beast over the ill-fated lot of the exiled Irishman, in these immortal lines which express the history of our nation—

> Where is my cabin door fast by the wild wood,
>   Where is my sire that wept for its fall?
> Where is the mother that watched o'er my childhood?
>   Where is my bosom friend, dearer than all?
> "Sad is my fate," said the heart-broken stranger,
>   "The wild deer and wolf to a covert can flee;
> But I have no refuge from famine and danger,
>   A home and a country remain not for me."

(At the conclusion of these lines, many of the assembly melted into tears, amidst the deepest sensation.) Oh! if St. Patrick were now to visit Ireland, what changes could not the historian recount to him since he first set his Apostolic foot on the soil? For many centuries after he died, Ireland enjoyed a profound peace, and a national prosperity. While, on the fall of the Roman Empire, most of the kingdoms of Europe rose up in vindication of their national rights, and all the neighboring nations were filled with the disastrous accompaniments and results of war; Ireland cultivated the arts and sciences, and practised the sublime precepts of the Gospel to perfection. She was the seminary where Europe was then educated, and whatever progress has been made by them in letters and religion, they must own that they lighted the torch of science and Faith at the sacred fires which burned on the altars of Ireland. No doubt, a storm has in later days been evoked from the abyss by the emissaries of Satan against this ancient creed. It has burst over Ireland with an awful violence, and in its devastating passage over our fine country, it has blown down the venerable institutions of past ages; it has rent the monarch oak, which crowned the forest with its lofty majesty—but the trunk and the roots were too strong to be torn by the rage of the hurricane; and here we are, the new growth of the flourishing branches sprung from the old stock, and likely to rise higher, and to spread farther than the parent tree, which, three centuries ago, reached to the skies over Ireland.

In fact, Catholicity, if I may so speak, is almost natural to an Irishman. He is, as it were, a Christian before he is baptized; he inherits Faith, by a kind of freehold grace, which St. Patrick has bequeathed to the most remote posterity of Ireland. You can efface every feeling from his heart but Catholicity; you can crush out every sentiment from his mind but the love of his altars; you may break him into pieces, and crush him into dust, but like the diamond in fragments, Faith shines in him to the last. (Loud, and long continued cheering.) The smallest particle of the Irish nature—the poorest, the most abandoned of Ireland's sons, reveals the sparkling inheritance as well as the most noble and lordly possessor: in fact, the darkness of the night is more favorable for seeing the native light of the fragment, than the golden hours of noonday sunshine; and thus the midnight of national trial, is the best time to behold the effulgence of Ireland's creed, and to test the essential splendor of her national Faith.—(Loud cheers.) Or, as our own bard has it:—

The gem may be broke by many a stroke,
  " But nothing can cloud its native ray,
Each fragment will cast a light to the last;
  And thus Erin, my country, though broken thou art,
There's a lustre within thee, that ne'er can decay,
  A spirit that breathes through each suffering part,
And smiles at thy pain on Saint Patrick's Day."

(At the conclusion of this sentence, the whole assembly burst into the loudest applause.) No doubt, you have heard the amusing fact of the Irish in a certain town in England, when, in 1850, they proceeded there to burn the Blessed Virgin in effigy. When all was ready for the idolitrous conflagration, the Irish were seen collecting in patches of tens and twenties, in the square where the faggots were prepared. The police observed, that each Irishman had a short, thick stick thrust up the sleeve of his jacket; and on asking what use they intended to make of these dangerous weapons in the present instance, one of the Irish said—"why then, your honor, we were afraid you might not have wood enough to burn the Virgin out and out, and we brought these few *kippeens, asthore*, to keep up the blaze." (Roars of laughter, which continued several minutes.) It is unnecessary to say, that the Virgin was not burned on that day; and the Irish on returning home, were heard saying to each other—*na bocklish, avick.* (Repeated roars of laughter.) Fellow-countrymen, this is certainly a great day for Ireland.

As your chairman has given me credit for having some knowledge of astronomy, I must take the liberty of informing the people of Scotland, that the length of the day and night in Ireland is twenty-four hours—(loud laughter)—and that it was twelve o'clock noon, in our colonies in the east, at about four o'clock this morning in Ireland; and again, that about this present hour, while we are filling our sparkling glasses, the Irish are just going to Mass, with the shamrocks in their hats, at twelve o'clock in America. The Irish soldier, therefore, on this morning, at four o'clock, saluted the glorious memory of St. Patrick, at the mouth of the Ganges; he began the shout in the east as the sun culminated over Pekin; and as the day advanced, and that shout rolled along the foot of Himalaya, it swept across the Indus, passed over the track of Alexander the Great, was heard in ancient Byzantium, disturbed the slumber of the sleeping brave in the gray field of Marathon, reverberated along the Seven Hills of Rome, and almost awoke, about ten o'clock this morning old Romulus on the banks of the Tiber.

Owing to the mysterious destinies of Ireland, and of our scattered race, there is not a spot, from the Yellow Sea to the Pillars of Hercules, from Garryowen to Melbourne, in which some merry Irishman does not on this day fix the green shamrock in his cap, and, with overflowing soul and wild transports of native joy sing the inspiring airs of his country, and chant aloud the magical tune of "Saint Patrick's Day in the Morning." (Loud cheers for several minutes.) But the commemorating voice of this day through primæval Asia and old Europe, is weak in comparison to the power it attains when it has crossed the Atlantic, and reached the friendly crowded shores of young and vigorous America. There, many a fond Irish heart welcomes the well-known cheers, as they burst in the patriot skies of Bunker's Hill: there the shout assumes the majesty of thunder as it rolls in peals, again and again repeated over the boundless prairies that skirt the Mississippi, and is echoed and re-echoed along the chiselled Alleghanies, until it dies away into silence about two o'clock to-night, as it re-echoes the placid, boundless bosom of the Pacific. (Great cheering.)

Thus round and round the globe, is the voice of Ireland this day heard by all mankind—thus her scattered and fated children sing the wild song of their native land to the stranger—thus they pour forth the patriot strains of their beloved country to the idolatrous Tartar; to the polished European, and the savage Indian; thus they stretch their united hands to each other on this day, and round the entire world they form a girdle of national love and patriotism, which reaches from the east to the west, and we couple the north and the south poles within the wide circle of our exiled but glorious affections. (No one except those who heard the conclusion of the sentence can form any idea of the wild enthusiasm which followed. After silence was again restored, and every ear again on the strain to drink in eagerly the burning language of the gifted orator.) He proceeded—Listen for a moment, about twelve o'clock to-night, and you will hear our own harp pour forth its Irish, plaintive voice from New York, acròss the broad enraptured waters of the Atlantic. Even now, if you will be quiet, you can audibly distinguish the shout of joy raised by seven millions of our blood, our race, and our Faith along the free shores of glorious, hospitable America.

Oh! America, how I love your green fields, because they are now the resting place of the wandering children of our country! I worship your lofty mountains and your rich valleys, because they afford an asylum and a barrier against the storms of adversity, which have swept away and withered the ancient homesteads of Ireland. I bless your majestic rivers, your magnificent lakes, because I behold the friendly canvass of your marine spread on their joyous waters, conveying my forlorn countrymen to a peaceful and plentiful home. Oh! America, I could die for your generous people, because they have opened their arms to welcome the ejected sons of St. Patrick!—I long to stand in the presence of the patriot, the accomplished Mrs. Tyler, and the incomparable ladies of America, that I may offer to them the deep homage of my grateful heart—that I may present to them the respect and the enthusiasm of the people of Ireland, for the withering chastisement they have inflicted on the sainted cruelty of the Duchess of Sutherland, and for the grateful dignity with which they have exposed the well-meaning hypocrisy of her noble committee. And I long to behold the country where the broken heart of Ireland is bound for, her daughters protected, her sons adopted: where conscience is free, where religion is not hypocrisy, where liberty is a reality, and where the Gospel is a holy profession of Divine love, and not a profligate trade of national vengeance. (Applause.)

How long, O Lord, wilt Thou hold Thy omnipotent scourge over Ireland, the most faithful nation of all the kingdoms that possess the Divine revelations from Heaven? But till Providence is pleased to staunch the flowing blood of Ireland, and to heal the wound; we, her persecuted sons, are bound to raise the cry of horror against our relentless oppressors; to keep up through each coming year and each century, the watchword of our sires for freedom, till the happy day of our deliverance. It is glorious to struggle for the redemption of one's country; it is base tamely to submit to the tyrant's frown—liberty, and then death, is preferable to slavery and life. Oh! eternal liberty—inheritance of the soul!

"Better to bleed for an age at thy shrine,
Than to sleep for one moment in chains."

(Wild and rapturous cheering.) Beloved fellow-countrymen, of late years I have had more opportunities of seeing the sufferings of the Irish than many others. I meet them at the seaport towns; I hear their complaints; I am familiar with their hard trials, and feel intensely their dire fate; and, in the midst of all their misfortunes, they never lose the native affections of their warm Irish hearts.

About the year 1849, I went on board an emigrant ship at the Custom-House in Dublin, in order to see the accommodation of the poor emigrants. While walking on the deck, I saw a decent poor man from the county Meath, with the ugliest dog I ever beheld, in his arms. He seemed to be keeping up a kind of private conversation with this dog, and occasionally he kissed him so affectionately, that I was led to speak to him, and made some inquiry about him. He told me that the dog's name was Brandy; that he and his mother were in his family for several years, and that he was the same age as his youngest child. (Loud laughter.) He continued to say, that on the day he was ejected, and his house thrown down, Brandy's house was thrown down, too; in fact, that the poor dog was exterminated as well as himself. That he took pity on him, brought him to Dublin, paid fifteen shillings for his passage to America, and that he would support him with his children as long as he lived. While we were speaking, the dog began to bark; on which I inquired what he was barking at. "Oh! Sir," said he, "he knows we are talking about the landlord. He knows his name as well as I do, and the creature always cries and roars when he hears his name mentioned." (Roars of laughter, which lasted several minutes.)

Oh, many a trial the poor Irish have endured during the last six years! Many a volume could be filled with the cruel persecution of the faithful Irish. From Galway to America, the track of the ship is marked by the whitened bones of the murdered Irish that lie along the bottom of the abysses of the moaning ocean. And yet those that have reached the friendly shore, still drag a heavy chain which binds them to their native land; still, they long to see their own beloved hills, and lay their bones with the ancient dead of their Faith and their kindred. And if death summons them beyond the Mississippi, or amidst the snows of Canada, or the pestilence of Mexico, they turn their fading eyes towards the day-star that rises over Ireland, and their last prayer is offered to Heaven for the liberty of their country—the last sigh to God, is made for the freedom of her altars.

DR. CAHILL AND THE HIBERNIAN FRIENDLY SOCIETIES.

Dr. Cahill's letter to the Catholics of Liverpool, produced an Address of the members of the Hibernian Friendly Societies, giving him the most sincere thanks for that letter, and assuring him of their esteem, regard, and unbounded confidence. They proved by various quotations from the English Code the legality of their Society, and showed its object to be that of law, order, and unity of sentiment.

Dr. Cahill in his affectionate response says: "he is made very happy by the practical evidence they gave to him of their voluntary obedience; he is proud of being the recognised peacemaker of that community; and entreats them to persevere in the observance of law, prudence, and union, as all illegal societies must fall. He hopes to see all the Irishmen in England living in mutual love; and to have very soon the pleasure of meeting them in Liverpool, to receive their pledge to abandon party strife, to love each other like brothers, and to stand together in one united confederacy."

TO THE VERY REV. DR. CAHILL.

VERY REV. AND DEAR SIR:—We, the officers and members of the First, Second, and Third Hibernian Friendly Societies, beg to tender to you the warmest expression of our best thanks for your admirable letter to the Catholics of Liverpool. We need hardly say, that you command not only the esteem and affectionate regard of your fellow-countrymen, but their unbounded confidence. We, therefore, take no credit to ourselves for at once complying with your advice and council.

We may here be permitted to remark, that our Society is founded on a perfectly legal basis. By its Thirteenth Rule, which is in strict accordance with the provisions of 10th George IV., chapter 56, as amended by 4th and 5th William IV., chapter 40, we are empowered to walk in procession with flags, banners and music. We may further add, that the object of the Societies in question, are purely of a benevolent and charitable nature. First, to support the sick: Second, to bury the dead: and, Third, to alleviate the miseries of the widow and the orphan. As a proof of this fact, the Second Hibernian Society has paid from the 1st of May 1847, to the 1st November, 1851, the sum of £861 for funeral expenses alone and the support of females.

Law and order, unity of sentiment among Catholics, and a total oblivion of all provincial distinctions, rank among the chief objects of our associations, and distinguish all our proceedings.

With these few remarks, and with profound respect for yourself personally, we have the distinguished honor, and the supreme happiness to be, Very Reverend and Dear Sir, your ever faithful and loving countrymen.

(Signed on behalf of myself and fellow-members.)

JAMES M'CORMICK, *Chief President.*

DR. CAHILL'S REPLY.

ST. MICHAN'S, DUBLIN, *Monday, March 1st,* 1852.

BELOVED FELLOW-COUNTRYMEN:—You make me very happy by the unqualified obedience which you show towards my late affectionate advice to my countrymen in Liverpool; you give strength to my words, and you add public respect to my name, by placing yourselves implicitly under my command; you raise my request to a level with the authority of your magistrates, and follow my will as you would submit to the law. There can be no compliment paid to me higher than this practical evidence of your voluntary submission; and there could be no public station in your city to which I would aspire with more ambition than to hold the distinguished rank of being the recognised peacemaker of a community of nearly half a million of inhabitants, healing old wounds, inspiring social union, effacing the memory of past contention, laying the foundation of public harmony, and cementing at the same time, into one confederacy of loyalty, order, patriotism, and love, every Irishman in Liverpool, without distinction of parish, or province, or name. This is avowedly a lofty station for any man to fill; I am grateful to you for this place; I value it exceedingly, and the more so, because it is a free public gift.

And now may I hope that you will never deprive me of the eminence to which you have raised me; that you will continue me in office; and that by your observance of law, and by prudence, and by union of national sentiment, you will enable me successfully to fulfil the duties of the responsible post which you have called on me to take. I promise to you on my part the most faithful services; and, I undertake to earn and to merit your kind and entire confidence. When next Patrick's Day will have terminated in public peace and social happiness, I shall consider myself *unregistered member* for the Borough of Liverpool; having, and holding my place, not from a majority of votes out of old rotten ten pound tenements, but from the devoted warm young hearts of my countrymen, from the sincere estimation of every lover of peace and morality, whether Protestant or Catholic, in the entire community. Let my brother members in the Borough, therefore appropriately attend to your politics and to your property, my parliamentary business is solely confined to your character and your lives; and with the blessing of God (as I hope to have a clear case,) I shall explain before *the first of next July* to the Home Secretary, the extent of my official services, and the support I expect at his hands.

The basis of your societies, appears from your statement, to be laid with prudence and judgment; as any society not invested with strictly legal conditions must fall, as surely as the leaves will fall in October. Illegal societies have within themselves an inherent internal cancer, which must of itself consume and dissolve the entire frame. They are like bastard seed planted in a bad soil, it never can come to perfection, it must ultimately perish; and I have never known an illegal society in Ireland which has not been *secretly founded by our deadly enemies*, encouraged by our relentless foes, carried on in blood, and ending in the transport ship or the reeking scaffold. With what pleasure, therefore, do I behold your societies, established on such clear legal foundations, and effecting such incalculable good amongst our poor but unparalleled Irish females—in feeding them, in clothing them, protecting them, sustaining them. Oh! such a Godlike work, to protect these innocent, ill-fated children, far from home, and to gladden their breaking hearts with kindness and charity.

I fondly hope to see the auspicious day, when I shall see all the Irishmen in Liverpool, and in all the other English towns, living in mutual national love. It makes the heart sick to see Irish against Irish, heart against heart, kindred and blood against kindred and blood. It is a national disgrace, and a national reproach; if we are faithless to ourselves, how can strangers rely on our fidelity? If we are enemies to each other, how can we complain of the persecution of strangers? Wolves do not devour each other—and there is no shame which causes such a crimson blush in the face of every real friend of Ireland, as to hear of Irishmen eating Irishmen's flesh; or, as Cromwell would say it, roasting each other on a spit for interest or revenge.

I hope very soon to have the pleasure of meeting you all in Liverpool; and one of the proudest moments of my life would be to find myself surrounded by the different heads of all your societies, from the four provinces, and to place your hands joined together within my hands, when I would make you all give a pledge to me, and before God, to abandon party strife, to love each other like brothers, and to stand together in one united confederacy of virtue, and order, for the remainder of your lives. I shall feel highly honored to become the Vice President of such an united body of men as I have here sketched, and you may command my services to any extent, and rely on me with most implicit obedience.

I thank you most sincerely for the remarkable expression of your respect towards me, and believe me, beloved fellow-countrymen, your devoted Irish Priest,

D. W. CAHILL, D.D.

REV. DR. CAHILL AND THE CATHOLICS OF GLASGOW.

The Catholics of Glasgow, numbering between two and three thousand persons, entertained the Rev. Dr. Cahill at a public Soiree in that city. The Rev. J. Danaher occupied the chair, and delivered the following introductory address:

LADIES AND GENTLEMEN. It now becomes my pleasing duty to call upon you for a demonstration of respect towards the distinguished individual whom we have the honor of entertaining this evening. (Great demonstrations of applause, which continued for several minutes.) — After the cheering had subsided, the Rev. Gent. in the course of his eloquent observations said—As a priest, a patriot, and a scholar, Dr. Cahill is entitled to our respect, esteem and admiration. (Loud cheers.) In this threefold capacity, he has now for years occupied a high position in the affections of the people. He has made his vast scientific acquirements subserve the cause of religion, and by his golden eloquence, has caused the learned, and the wealthy, and the great, to respect a creed which they were in the habit of regarding as a folly. (Cheers) During his stay amongst us, you have all become acquainted with his aptitude to illustrate Faith by the mysteries of nature. But, ladies and gentlemen, Dr. Cahill has established other claims on our admiration, which it is impossible not to advert on the present occasion. When on a recent occasion a tremendous deluge of woe swept over our country, prostrating the energies of a nation; when our countrymen become the victims of famine, and pestilence, and law; when men and women and children were sheltering in the damp ditches, and rotting off the earth one by one; when the workhouse doors were crowded with gaunt, naked, and hunger-stricken human beings; old women with the bones protruding through their skin, and children with the hideous fur of famine thick over their fleshless limbs; when the loud but unavailing wailing of famine rang from shore to shore, a surer index of a more indiscriminating slaughter than was ever effected by the hand of the destroying Angel; when desolation thus hung over the country, like a pestilential pall, eager to embrace within its deadly folds the wasted remnants of a devoted nation — this was the time above all others selected by a British ministry to proclaim war against our church, and this was the time above all others, that the champions of a free constitution showed their zeal for civil toleration by branding bishops, insulting priests mobbing nuns, pulling down churches, and preaching up infidelity; then it was that Dr. Cahill, in those powerful letters with which you are all acquainted, published to the world his indignation of the criminals and the crime, and inspired an universal hatred; or rather gave expression to an universal hatred, already inspired against enormities detested by God and execrated by man.

At the conclusion of his brilliant speech, the Rev. Chairman read the following address from the Catholics of Glasgow to the Rev. Dr. Cahill. It was printed on white satin with golden letters.

ADDRESS TO REV. DR. CAHILL.

Rev. Doctor.—The Catholic inhabitants of Glasgow, beg leave to offer you, on this festive evening their united expression of profound respect and affectionate regard. They unanimously hailed your visit to this city with feelings of joy and exultation, and they now bid you farewell with sentiments of increased admiration. We are proud of you as an Irishman —we value you as a patriot—and we venerate you as a priest.

When a hostile government planned and abetted the overthrow of Catholic monarchy on the continent of Europe, the cause of truth and justice was indebted to you for those letters which have unmasked the hidden treachery of our deadly enemies—which, in their wide circulation throughout the nations of the earth, have awakened a universal feeling of execration against this infidel conspiracy ; and which, have ultimately resulted in the final overthrow of this infamous scheme against civil and religious liberty.

There is no Catholic mind or Catholic heart in this empire, which does not feel an involuntary impulse of gratitude towards the name of Dr. Cahill, when we recollect the burning invectives which burst from your pen against England's cruelties during the famine and pestilence that afflicted your country. These noble appeals in favor of your poor countrymen, are written in all hearts, and are pronounced by every Irish tongue.

Whilst they consoled the poor victim in the wasting poor-house, and cheered the broken-hearted emigrant on his melancholy banishment from the home of his fathers, they will remain for ever in Ireland, an imperishable monument of the melting generosity of your heart, and the unquenchable love you bore your ill-fated country.

We confess here, publicly, that we thank a kind Providence for having raised up such a man in Ireland to defend our name and our faith. We are proud to feel that the man who at this moment possesses the affections of the whole heart of Ireland, by his patriotism—who takes his place next to the Liberator, in the public confidence, has wrung, at the same time, from our bitterest foes the expression of their admiration for the extent of those literary and scientific attainments which the public voice now willingly concedes to you, almost without a rival in this age of letters.

At one time, the public listen with ecstacy to your lectures on Astronomy—at another, we hear of your brilliant dissertations on Chemistry; again, the Press refers to the crowded audiences of the learned who attend you on Geology, Mineralogy, and the whole round of the varied branches of Natural Philosophy. But the most astonishing fact yet remains to be told—that is, while you are thus lecturing on different subjects, the churches are, immediately after, everywhere filled with thousands, hanging on words of almost inspired eloquence, and the Press is filled with these splendid letters, which start into existence almost in an hour.

Any of your avocations would be more than sufficient work for the most learned amongst us, and hence the aggregate of these labors can only be executed by the man, whose surprising attainments we are endeavoring to describe.

When we heard, through the public prints, that in Liverpool, Manchester, London, and elsewhere, you attracted whole cities after you wherever you went, we could never understand the circumstance, till we have been honored by your present visit to Glasgow. We now understand it, and we behold a tide of human beings—in fact, the whole Catholic population, following you wherever you go.

The result is, that an amount of moral good has been effected in this city through your discourses, which cannot be sufficiently appreciated. Reformations and conversions have been made in several instances, and in the short space of five weeks, since you commenced your lectures in our churches, we have collected several thousands of pounds for the various charities of the town.

We therefore beg leave to thank you—we are all desirous from our hearts to honor you—and with the united voice and prayer of the thousands who are assembled here this evening to bid you farewell. We join in a heurtfelt, universal prayer, that God may long preserve you, the ornament of the priesthood, and the fearless, invincible champion of your creed and your country.

The chairman was frequently cheered during the reading of the address, and on Dr. Cahill presenting himself was received with unbounded enthusiasm.

The *Glasgow Free Press* in alluding to the effect of this powerful speech, says:

"On bowing and taking his seat, an assembly of between two and three thousand ladies and gentlemen standing, the Rev. Gentleman was greeted with a demonstration of enthusiasm which was never,—which could not be surpassed—the gentlemen cheering and the ladies waving their pocket handkerchiefs."

REV. DR. CAHILL'S ADDRESS.

MR. CHAIRMAN LADIES AND GENTLEMEN: I am laboring on the present occasion under a deficiency, for which I am convinced you will pardon me, namely, I am afraid you will not understand me, in consequence of my Irish accent. (The conclusion of the sentence, like the wand of a magician, set the whole house in a roar.) I now beg to tell you with the deepest feelings of a lasting gratitude, that, although I have received many marks of public favor heretofore in Ireland and in England, I have never found myself placed in a position of such exalted distinction as on the present occasion. Surrounded as I am, not by hundreds but by thousands of gentlemen and ladies, by priests and people, I return my homage for your advocacy on this evening, of a great principle in thus honoring the individual who now addresses you. (Loud cheers.)

Your eloquent and valued address written on satin in golden letters, shall be preserved by me as long as I live ; it is a model of exquisite taste, and conveys impressions of affection which I shall carefully bind up with the most cherished feelings of my life; but there is an eloquence of soul which the golden ink could not express; and that silent thrilling language must be read in the merry faces, the sparkling looks, and ardent bosoms which reveal to my inmost heart the sincerity and the intensity of your feeling towards me. (Enthusiastic cheers.)

In associating me in the most remote connexion with the great O'Connell—(at the name of O'Connell the whole assembly rose and cheered)—you do me an honor which would raise even a great man to imperishable fame: as you illume me with a ray from that immortal name which sheds unfading lustre on the records of Ireland's saddest and brightest history, and which will live in the burning affections of the remotest posterity of a grateful country. (Loud and long cheering.) I am like a jolly-boat following a line of battle-ships, as I move in the foaming track of this leviathan guardship of Ireland. Large as I am, I am lost in the spray of the rudder; and no one who has ever witnessed the discharge of his broadside against the enemy, heard the thunder of his command, or saw the fatal precision of his aim, will ever think of comparing any living man to the great departed Irish champion. (Loud cheers.) And it was not the fault of our old commander if his invincible bark did not convey the liberties of his country to a successful issue—he sailed in shallow water, he was stranded by necessity; but no one has ever dared to say, that either he or his gallant crew ever quailed before danger, or struck their colors to the enemy. And when the returning tide rises and the breeze freshens, the old noble ship shall again set her sails before the wind; and, changing her name from Repeal to National Equality, her fearless crew shall again shout for freedom, and, with some future O'Connell at the helm, she will, and shall again face the storm, and ride the swollen flood in pride and triumph. (Enthusiastic cheers, which continued for several minutes.)

Whenever I go to Dublin, I pay a sorrowing visit to the tomb of our old commander, where I shed a tear over his ashes, and plant a flower on his grave. (Here the whole assembly audibly wept and sobbed.) I mourn for the lip of fire which was wont to kindle into resistless flame our universal patriotism; I grieve for the melting tongue that could dissolve the whole national will into a flood of resistless combination: and as I gaze on the dark vault that spans the horizon of Ireland, and see pretty stars shining in the Irish skies, I weep as I think on the brilliant sun that once careered in these skies in peerless splendor; the luminary which guided our destinies for upwards of half a century, but which now, alas! has set forever below the saddening west of time, leaving the crimsoned clouds, like funeral drapery, to shroud the fading twilight that hangs over his departed memory. (A loud burst of the most enthusiastic emotion rose from every bosom at the conclusion of this sentence.)

Oh, if he had lived to stand on the heights of Ireland, as the churchyards during the last seven years, sent their united wail of woe across our stricken land: oh! if he had lived to gaze on the red waves of the Atlantic, and heard the wild sinking shriek of Irish despair, wafted from the moaning abysses of the deep, as our kindred perished on their exiled voyage—he, and he alone, could raise a cry of horror, which would be heard in the ends of the earth—could shake the foundation of the nations, and wrench justice from even the iron bosoms of our cruel oppressors. None but he, could pronounce the funeral oration of the Irish, for he had a voice that could fill the world, and enchain the attention of mankind; and he alone had a heart to express the greatness, the perfection, the fidelity, the sufferings, and the death-struggles of his unfortunate country. He was Ireland's own son, the impersonation of her own heart—and he alone could sit at her bedside and speak words of consolation for the extermination and the massacre of her defenceless children. (No one can describe the rapturous cheers which greeted the orator at this part of his speech.)

Your allusion to my public letters, makes me very happy. There can be no doubt that England has endeavored, since the year 1815, to bring to a successful issue the largest conspiracy, ever perhaps, known in the whole world. When she placed Louis the Eighteenth on the throne of France, after the Battle of Waterloo, she found herself for the first time, for the last 700 years, virtually directing the politics, and practically planning the counsels of France. This was a bright opening to her intrigues and ambition; and from this period may be dated the commencement of a scheme, which for hypocrisy, anarchy, deceit, and infidelity, has no parallel in the history of the civilized world.

Secure in organizing an English party in France, she next proceeded to enslave to her views poor Spain, already demoralised, plundered, weakened, and exhausted by the presence of two contending armies. England, therefore, first planned the separation of her South American dependencies and allies, and hence she revolutionized all that territory into petty republics, and located a powerful, designing party in the Republics of Guatemala, Chili, Peru, Columbia, La Plata, and Monte Video. Spain herself, thus become an easy prey to her perfidious diplomacy; and hence, in the year 1832, she changed the succession to the throne, divided the nation into two hostile factions, and raised up at the Court an English party, which governs there at the present moment. She even made a bargain, which I am able to prove from undisputed documents, to lend money to the Queen's party, on condition of guaranteeing to her the repayment of the funds so given from the confiscation of all the Church property of the nation.

In the year 1833, she carried out the same design precisely, in Portugal; placed the daughter of a rebel son on the throne, advanced money for the execution of this palpable rebellion, on the condition of being repaid in the same way—namely, the confiscation of all the Church property in Portugal. Here again she planted her English party, who rule to this day the kingdom of Portugal. And with such desperate fidelity did England carry out her plans, that, within two years, she sold the churches in both countries, and converted them into theatres: she took possession of all the convents in Spain, both male and female; she seized all the large convents in Portugal: she banished from their cloisters, one hundred and fifteen thousand monks, friars, and nuns, who perished of hunger, affliction, and a broken heart. The debt due to England by Spain, has been already paid; but I am in a position to prove that the wretched Portuguese have not as yet, cleared off their unholy national mortgage to the English bankers, who, twenty years ago, advanced the money on English Government security. (Enthusiastic cheering.)

The Duke of Wellington has received many Protestant laurels from his campaign in Spain, and the partial historian pronounces glowing panegyrics on his honor and character in the Peninsular War. True, he paid, in gold principally, for the food of the English army there; but, he inflicted a thousand times more injury on that country than the plundering army of the French. Under pretence of depriving the French of any point of attack on the English, he threw down the Spanish factories, burned their machinery, beggared their merchants, ruined their commerce from that day to this, and has thus been a greater enemy to Spain, than the most savage Hun that ever spread death and desolation over that fine country.

I must tell you an anecdote of Wellington. About the year 1816, there was a tavern in old Barrack Street, having over the door 'the sign of the old goat.' The tavern keeper made a fortune by the call of the County Meath graziers, who frequented his house. He gave his daughter in marriage to a young man on the opposite side of the street, who, seeing the good luck of his father-in-law, set up a public house in opposition to the old man, and he, too, placed 'the sign of the goat' over his door, to deceive the customers. The old man then, in retaliation wrote, in large printed letters, under his sign, 'the real old goat.' (Loud laughter.) But soon changing his mind, as the Battle of Waterloo had taken place the year before, he ordered a painter to draw out the Duke of Wellington in full military costume, in place of the old goat. The painter did execute the work, but he forgot to efface the words of the old sign; and there the Duke of Wellington appeared with the General's truncheon in his hand, and having the words, 'the real old goat,' written under him.

(Roars of laughter, which lasted several minutes.) I tell you, now, that the real old goat was the most persecuting foe, the most deadly enemy, that Spain ever saw.

The English conspirators being now secure in the principal thrones of Europe, proceeded to Austria, where they encouraged the civil war which has reddened the soil in human gore, and has eventuated in the most disastrous results to that great Catholic country. Not a city, town, village, in Austria or Hungary, in which an English agent was not found working like the devil in his vocation of civil strife and national revolution: and it is an admitted fact, that the English party had become very powerful through every part of the empire. But Switzerland was the great focus, where the English party openly avowed their sentiments, and publicly threatened the Catholic powers of Europe with immediate civil revolution.

The world will be surprised to hear, that the English party and their confederates, amounted in that country alone to the astounding number of 73,000 sworn enemies of Catholic monarchy. I here pledge myself before this assembly, to prove the perfect accuracy of this statement. They next spread themselves into Naples, where the king, unaware of this English conspiracy, admitted them into his confidence, and gave them official places in his public schools. They ultimately succeed in forming a perfect network over the whole surface of Europe; and while they were laboring to lay the materials of a universal explosion beneath all the Catholic thrones, they were confederating all the Protestant powers to act with one simultaneous effort when the day of their matured plans should have arrived. (The entire assembly, who, up to this moment, listened with the most breathless attention to this statement, now gave vent to their feelings in one universal burst of applause.)

During all this time, England appeared kind to Ireland: spoke largely of Catholic monarchy in the Queen's speeches, and talked of honor and international law. But under this exterior of good feelings, she preserved feelings of the bitterest private rancor towards universal Catholic policy.

This conduct reminds me of an old Tory grand juror, from the hanging town of Trim, in Ireland, during the judicial reign of Lord Norbury. It was in the year 1818, when O'Connell was working for Emancipation. This old gentleman had dined with Norbury, heard him speak against Catholic Emancipation—took too much champaigne, and fell in a ditch on his way home—he wore a fashionable red waistcoat, and a turkeycock seeing the red colour, flew to him in the ditch, and commenced blubbering over the head of the juror. (Loud laughter.) He fancied it was Lord Norbury who was still inveighing against Emancipation; and whenever the turkeycock paused in his blubbering elocution, the old juror would exclaim "Quite true, my lord; these are noble sentiments, worthy of your lordship, and highly honorable to the Crown." (Roars of laughter.) Here the turkeycock would again resume, and cry out "blubber, blubber, blubber," to which the old Brunswicker would reply—"I agree with your lordship; your remarks proceed from true Protestant principles worthy of a bishop; and they eloquently defend our holy church; I always admired your language as the ornament of the bench, and we both shall die sooner than retract one word of your brilliant speech, or emancipate these Catholic rebels." (Roars of laughter, which burst out again and again for several minutes.) Now, here was an old fellow so drunk that he could not distinguish between Lord Norbury and a turkeycock, and yet the devilment of bigotry was so much in him that he would not agree to unchain the very men, who, perhaps, sat by his side on that day, and for whom he had pretended to entertain feelings of friendship and toleration. (Loud cheers.)

Up to the year 1846, the office of a British Minister seemed to be revolutionizing the neighboring States, and making royal matches. They have attempted to place a Coburg in all the royal palaces of Europe, and to transfuse the influence of England into the blood of several royal houses. Not a revolutionist in Europe, who was not the intimate friend and correspondent of the English Foreign Secretary. The very men most abhorred in their own country, were received at all the English embassies; and there could be no mistake that England advocated their cause, approved their schemes, and assisted their machinations. Every rebel foreigner appealed to England for advice, and in his difficulty flew to her for protection. (Breathless emotion chained the entire audience.)

Concomitantly with this political scheme, the English Bible Societies, under the protection of England, sent their emissaries into all these countries; and by misrepresentation of the Catholic doctrine, by lies of the grossest invention, and by bribery, they opened a campaign of proselytism in every Catholic city in Europe, and united their efforts against Catholicity with three resident conspirators against monarchy. The lodging-houses, the hotels, and the watering places, were everywhere filled with a swarm of Soupers and Biblemen, Tourists, novelists, naval officers, military men, young lords, correspondents of the London press, were to be found at every town of the European continent, all pressing forward to carry one point—namely, the slander of the Catholic priesthood. Stories about convents, lies about priests, anecdotes of monks, filled thousands of nicely bound small volumes, and sold at all the railway stations in England; and no less a sum than five millions pounds were annually expended by these societies through Europe in this flagitious work of calumny, lies, profanation, and perjury.

Not an ambassador, an *attaché*, a *chargé d'affaires*, a messenger was employed in our diplomatic circles who was not as unprincipled a writer as Sir Francis Head, as conceited a historical libeller as Macauley, as great a hypocrite as Sir Stratford Canning, as ridiculous a Souper as young Peel, and as mean a bigot as Sir Henry Bulwer. Not a man would be accredited to any Court who had not the kidney of Shaftesbury, the rancor of Palmerston, and the intolerance of Russell. It was a strange sight, indeed, to behold other names, which I shall not mention, teaching sanctity by corruption, publishing faith by infidelity, propagating truth by lies, enforcing purity by profligacy, and really worshipping God by the devil.

(The whole audience here again, after a long pause of silence, burst out into the loudest acclamation.)

Fortunately for the cause of religion and of order, this doubly infamous conspiracy has been wholly detected and laid before the gaze of mankind: most propitiously, Louis Napoleon has succeeded in rescuing France from an abyss of national disaster, and most providentially every Catholic country has escaped an awful catastrophe; and they all now, by a united reaction, have detected England's perfidy; have banished her spies from their respective territories; have degraded her diplomatists; insulted her name; banished her from their international councils; and at this moment, she hangs her head like a convict, in the presence of foreign courts—the detected assassin, the perfidious enemy of the religion and the liberties of Catholic Europe. (Loud and enthusiastic cheering.)

All these men are now defeated and degraded: Russell is a discarded hanger-on, waiting at St. Stephen's behind the chair of a successful rival: Palmerston, like an ill-conducted servant, has been reduced from Foreign Secretary, to a detective superintendent of police; and like an old jaded actor, who once took a first part in the performance, but being ultimately unable to act, still clings to the stage, and earns his bread in a minor office; we behold in pity the Foreign Minister, once the terror of Louis Philippe—once sweeping the Mediterranean with an invincible fleet, now reduced to be a Crown prosecutor against his former companions at Old Bailey by day, while at night he receives a precarious employment, snuffing the candles behind the scenes at Lord Aberdeen's benefit. (Vociferous and wild cheers.)

Lord Palmerston's fate reminds me of a man in the County Leitrim—a terrible bigot—who, during one of the paroxysms of a brain fever, fancied that one of his legs turned Catholic. (Loud roars of laughter.) In his indignation at seeing Popery contaminating his Protestant person, he jumped out of a window to kill the Catholic leg, but he unfortunately fell on the Protestant leg, and he limped on the Protestant leg all the days of his life after. (Continued roars of laughter.) Poor Palmerston, I think, will have an unbecoming halt during his life on his Protestant leg. (Immense cheering.)

In what a proud contrast does not Lord Aberdeen appear in reference to his Whig predecessors. The friend of the Catholics, the advocate of justice, the enlightened and consistent supporter of toleration, he has won our willing veneration, and has earned the respect of Christian Europe. No bigot, no hypocrite, no persecutor, he has already gone far to heal the wounds of former administrations; and by perseverance in his honorable career, he will succeed in due time, in removing the contempt, and suspicion, and the hatred in which the British Government and the Protestant creed have been held during the last few years, by the Catholic Sovereigns and people of Europe. Many a million of money this British fanaticism will yet cost England in the maintenance of an army to defend her shores against the numerous enemies she has made: and the Protestant church will soon learn to her cost, that her lies and infidelities will yet concen trate upon her the just indignation of mankind, and, at no distant period, will sweep her tenets and her name from the map of Christian Europe. (Cheers.)

When I use the word "England," I do not mean the noble, generous people of England; no, I mean the mean, the perfidious, the persecuting Government of England. And all Europe now understands this distinction as well as we do; we thank God, that England is at length detected, convicted, and degraded all over the world. At this moment, whenever she speaks of civil liberty, all the world call her liar, tyrant, assassin; whenever she talks of liberty of conscience, all Europe scouts her as a persecutor, a hypocrite, an unblushing slanderer; whenever she attempts to introduce the name of God, and to talk of sanctity, and of English Christianity, all Europe bursts out into an immoderate fit of laughter, and cries shame at her, and points to her treachery, her scandals, her murders, her suicides, her blasphemies, her infidelities, her crimes, her enormities; and mankind considers Sodom and Gomorrah, and Babylon, as so many earthly paradises in comparison of the multitudinous sinfulness of England.

She is met in every market place in Europe at this moment, and called liar, and demon; her ambassadors are jibed at this moment at every Court in Europe, and called hypocrites, Soupers, infidels; and her travellers, tourists, correspondents, are watched in every corner of Europe, as so many burglars, assassins, and demons of naked infidelity. The Lord be praised, she is caught at last, and poor Ireland shall soon be free. (Loud cheers.) Yes, Ireland shall soon be free from English persecution, and from the oppression of the Protestant establishment.

Two curses have been inflicted on Ireland—namely, the rackrenting landlords, and the accursed tithes. These two embodiments of malediction, have bent Ireland to the earth, and have crushed her body and soul; and, like a swarm of locusts, they eat up every green and living thing, and left nothing behind but the flint of the land.—After centuries of this oppression, it suddenly pleases our rulers to make a law of Free Trade. No one, more than I do, advocates the principle of cheap bread for the working man, and of employment for his children in the mechanical arts of commerce. But the principle has introduced a scene of woe, which no pencil can paint. The poor are exterminated, the ditches are crowded with the weak and aged; the poor-houses are charnel places of pestilence and death; and the emigrant ship, like an ocean hearse, is sailing with her flag of distress hoisted, moving slowly through the waves, as she throws out her putrid dead; and, like the Telegraph Company laying down their submarine wires, the crews of the emigrant ships have learned, by long practice, to tell off a line of the Irish dead along the bottom of the deep, and, at the same time to sail six or seven knots an hour. (The deepest sensation.) England has practised them in this ocean sepulture, so that, before the end of the year 1849, they could smoke, tell off the winding sheets, and sail, all at the same time, from this dexterous, nautical, cholera practice.—(Death-like silence pervaded the entire assembly.)

Men there are, who assert that the Government could not avoid this catastrophe. I answer, it is a cruel lie. If there must be a change in the laws of trade, well, then let it be made; but let the law-makers bear the responsibility. (Loud cheers.) If they must have a new law, well, then, let them pay for their whims; let them make compensation for the damaging results of their own free, deliberate acts. They say the law is good in principle; I answer, but bad in detail. They say it has healthy premises; I reply yes, and a deadly conclusion. They say, it is perfect in argument; but I assert, it is murder in practice. They assert, it is the law; but I resume, and say, so much the worse—it legalises and authorises the public massacre of the people. This is a legal mockery, to hear the legislators tell the dying, starving, rotting peasant, that he ought to be quite content with his lot, since he dies a constitutional death, he will be buried according to law, in a Parliamentary churchyard, and will sleep till the day of judgment in a logical grave. (Here the whole assembly cheered.)

I am no politician; all I know is, that the English laws have killed the people; and what care I for the principle of Protection, or the logic of Free Trade, if the triumph of either party murder the poor. And I reply to the Freetrader, and to the merchant, and to the Cobden's school, by saying, if you will and must have your way, then be prepared for the consequences, meet the consequences, pay for the consequences—if there is to be suffering, then let the guilty suffer—punish the landlords—afflict the money lenders—exterminate the House of Commons—murder the English Cabinets—extirpate the Protestant church—yes, punish the guilty who produced the catastrophe: if there will be a famine, then buy bread for the dying, give them the twenty millions of gold you have in the Treasury; add twenty millions more to the National Debt if necessary—treat the Irish with the same justice as you have treated the slaves of Jamaica—do pay for your own acts—do punish the guilty—but in the name of honor, truth, justice, humanity; and in the sacred name of oaths pledged and ratified at the foot of the throne, do not punish the innocent poor—spare the unoffending peasantry—shield the defenceless tenantry who trusted you; do not massacre the millions who confided in your former laws—(here the gifted orator lifted high both his arms, with clenched hands,) and as you have done it—and massacred all Ireland trusting in you, I swear, before high Heaven, that you have mixed up a curse with your bread, which will eat into the marrow of your bones; and you have awakened in the swelling bosom of Irishmen, a flame of legitimate anger which will never be quenched, till you shall have made satisfaction for the sufferings, the extermination, the expatriation, the death; and, I shall add, the massacre of the unoffending children of Ireland. (Any attempt to describe the wild enthusiasm that followed this sentence, is totally vain.)

Ladies and Gentlemen, after a very happy sojourn of nearly two months amongst you, I must say the sad word farewell. I am impressed with many struggling feelings at this moment: sorrow, pleasure, gratitude, enthusiasm, pride, are strangely mixed up in my bosom; they are all your work; you have remoulded me. I came from London to Glasgow, and in parting from you, I proceed to Derry in Ireland. You gave me a warm welcome on my arrival, and I must bid you a sorrowing farewell till our next meeting. I can well understand now the words of the ballad familiar to you in Glasgow :—

"If England were my place of birth,
I'd love her tranquil shore;
If bonnie Scotland were my home,
Her mountains I'd adore;
Though pleasant days in each I've passed,
Still I dream of hours to come.
Then steer my bark to Erin's Isle,
For Erin is my home:
Oh, steer my bark to Erin's Isle,
Old Erin is my home."

LETER OF REV. DR. CAHILL TO THE REV. J. BURNS OF WHITEHAVEN.

Rev. Sir—Your letter published yesterday evening in the *Cumberland Packet* reached me last night. Many thanks for the kind expression of your good wishes for my salvation, and for desiring the eternal welfare of all Catholic souls. I hope the public voice of this town will learn fully to appreciate the sincerity of those feelings, and to make you a suitable acknowledgment.

I beg to tell you, with great respect, that you are *probably* unacquainted with our doctrine of the Eucharist! we do not "create our Creator." If this language were uttered by any other person but by one of your known liberality and acknowledged education, I should designate it as the lowest form of vulgar bigotry Such words, coming from you, are simply a mistake; and your only fault in the present case is, your writing on a subject which avowedly you have not studied.

The editor of the *Whitehaven Herald* will not keep his columns open for my reply to you longer than twelve o'clock on Friday; and hence I shall conclude this short note, and reserve any further observations on the subject for my public answer.—I have the honor to be, Rev. Sir, your obedient servant,

D. W. CAHILL.

" Feelings of unmingled love and compassion for your soul, and the souls of those who are misled by the Romish priests, constrain me to use every effort in my power to awaken in you and in them the dormant feelings of common sense, and to arouse you and them to attend to the voice of reason and the voice of God. I believe your religion to be false, and truth and justice compel me to publish my conviction. I seek to gain your soul and, therefore, I write plainly, and let none of my fellow-men judge me an enemy because I tell the truth. * *

" Every hour you consecrate a bit of bread you create your Creator!

" Grant me, sir, as a common ground of argument, that God Almighty made you, and gave you the faculties you possess, and I will undertake to show, by self-evident truths that the doctrine of transubstantiation is subversive of the foundation of human belief, and therefore incapable of being proved by any evidence, or being believed by any man under the influence of common sense. If God made man, then the testimony of the sence, is the testimony of God. To seek to support this testimony is absurd, and, to doubt it, is to be mad. * * *

" Now, Sir in all controversy, the proof rests on him who takes the affirmative side of the question. If you wish me to receive your doctrine you must furnish me with the grounds on which to rest my faith. To justisfy me in rejecting your dogma, I am not even obliged to produce direct proof of its falsehood. It is enough if I can show that the proof you allege is not sufficient.—The doctrine is overturned if it be not proved. If I can show that every passage you bring forward is according to the usual laws of language, fairly capable of another sense, I have overturned your doctrine ; and if this principle be just, then the battle is won without firing a single shot of direct disproof at all. * * *

I think the soul can no more feed on flesh and blood than on bread. If, then, the body of Jesus be food to the soul, it must be so, not literally, but figuratively. The soul cannot eat His flesh in any other way than by believing in Him. It eats by faith, and not by teeth. See how hard it is to force Scripture to sanction what is false and absurd

* * * * * * * *

" I beseech you, Sir, to put all your trust in the blood of Christ which cleanseth from all sin, and renounce the vain effort of adding to its perfection. Cease that blasphemy that represents the work of Christ even yet unfinished, and keeps Him continually a sacrifice on the altar. Come to Him and He will give you salvation without money and without price. "—*Vide Letter of Rev. J. Burns.*

WHITEHAVEN *Wednesday Dec. 7th.*

REV SIR :—I have selected a few passages of your courteous letter to me, to which I shall more particularly direct my reply ; and if I were not made acquainted with the profession of the writer, I should have never supposed that the author of these extracts could have read even the elements of theology or moral philosophy ; but above all, I could not have believed that a clergyman of high character and station, could make a statement exhibiting such a deplorable ignorance of the fundamental principles of our common Christianity.

Firstly, then, since you set up in spiritual things the the evidence of the senses (as you call it) as the infallible standard of your faith, you will tell the world how can you believe in God, who is a pure spirit, and therefore cannot possibly fall directly within the domain of the senses ? Secondly, will you say by what evidence of the senses you discover three distinct persons in one God?

Do, Rev. Sir, say how you arrive at the conclusion by the senses, that trinity is unity, in *essence*, and unity *essentially* trinity? Thirdly, will you kindly inform poor forlorn Catholic souls, how you detect the presence of divine grace by the senses; that is, how can you see, feel, taste, smell, and hear divine grace, which St. Paul describes as " the emanation of God, " and " the charity of God poured abroad?" Fourthly, will you say, Sir, how you can even know you have a " soul, " by the *evidence* of the senses ? Fifthly, will you tell the Romish priests, where did you learn the existence of eternity, of heaven, or of hell, from the evidence of the senses ? St. Paul tells us, that "neither the eye hath seen, nor ear heard, or the heart of man conceived, this place," and therefore, will you be pleased to tell us, how it has happened that the air of Whitehaven has so elevated the action of your senses, that you and your congregation can behold, with an unclouded vision, what the tongue of St. Paul could not utter, or the heart of St. Paul could not conceive ? We poor Romish priests educated at Maynooth, always fancied these things were known by " faith, " and not by the senses; and we have foolishly believed faith to be "the gratuitous gift of God," and not at all the philosophical result of the most perfect examination of the senses. Sixthly, will you be pleased to inform the senseless Catholics how you discover the original sin, in a newborn baby, by the aid of the senses ? I venture to say, that even a Whitehaven baby appears to the senses the very same, self same child before and after the sacrament of baptism? If therefore, Rev. Sir, you will believe nothing but what can be proved by the senses, your act of faith must, beyond all dispute, deny every single word of the creed which you publish on every Sunday from your pulpit to your unfortunate congregation.

You seem very fond of employing the words "common sense" while speaking of faith. They are not accidental terms in your mouth; they are scientific, official, professional phrases; and you so jumble together logical, theological, and elocutionary language, that, in almost every sentence you have written, there is a scientific mistake, a mistake of words, and a clear incongruity in theological terms. You reject everything which you cannot conceive is your common sense. This is certainly your statement.

Firstly, then, will you therefore prove to us Romish scholars, how does your common sense understand and explain that God has no beginning? Our Popish common sense cannot conceive any existing thing without a cause. Now, as you admit nothing which you cannot understand, pray tell us on what principle you understand an effect, which is not an effect, a generation without being generated; motion, life, and power without a beginning.

Secondly, the earth cannot be as old as God, as it would then be God; nor can it be made out of the substance of God, as matter would then be composed of spirit, and inanimate clay formed of the essentially living God. Hence the earth must come from nothing, and called from this nothing by a mere act of God's will. Will you say, in your science of your common sense, if you understand the natural mystery? If you do not understand it, of course, as you have said, you cannot believe it; and therefore you are bound, in vindication of your system, to state publicly, for the salvation of the Romish priests, and of all the Papists, whose interests are so near your heart, that, as you cannot conceive by common sense how matter was created, or how man was formed, that therefore there is no such thing as Protestant tithes; that the Scottish kirk is a public delusion; that the sermons in your church are baseless visions; and that the public letter lately addressed in this town to Dr. Cahill is a dreamy image and a fantastic, ideal, deceptive sound.

Thirdly, will you again explain the incarnation by your system? I have learned in the schools, that divine faith cannot be tested by the rules of logic, much less by the common sense of the world. I have been taught, that although there are three persons in the Trinity, each distinct, and each God; still, it does not follow from these defined premises, that there are three distinct Gods.

Fourthly, will you be pleased, Sir, to explain to me, by common sense, how the *two distinct natures* of God and man, have only *one person* in Christ? how can there be nature without a person? how can a finite human nature fill an infinite divine person? or how can an infinite divine nature be confined within the figure of a finite human person? Will you kindly say whether the spirit was human or divine, or a mixture of both, half finite, and *half infinite*?

Fifthly, pray explain again, how God could become

man, the incarnate unembodied Word could become flesh; how the eternal person could be torn; how immortality could die; how an immaculate God could assume human guilt; how the mockery, the agony, the cries of the beloved Son of God could please the Father ? Sixthly, will you say how it is, that, although God is whole and entire, in the million and tens of million of places in space, there is but one God ?

Ah ! Reverend Mr. Burns, your loose assertions and unscientific statements, convince me of the truth of Lord Shaftesbury's report on the lamentable deficiency of Protestant clerical education; demonstrate that you can malign a creed without having studied its tenets, and circulate wounding mis-statement under the cover and the imposition of religious zeal. Finally, will you explain the justice of God, in charging on a child born 1853 the crime of Adam's desobedience committed nearly six thousand years ago ?—It was metaphysically impossible that the free will of this child could enter into this act of Adam as an accomplice, the soul of the child being not created at the time ; and it was equally impossible for the same will to prevent or avoid this fault of Adam—Now the common sense and the common laws of Englishmen, to which you appeal in matters of faith, will not charge one man with the guilt of a third party, who was not, or could not possibly be an accomplice.

You have, Sir, to account for this fact by your system of common sense, and thus settle this most vital question. The plain palpable result of this absurd and fatal misapplication of reason to faith is, that you have made your creed a mere worldly system; and you have forced even your friends to regard your religion as a human constitution, sustained by the same kind of principles as you smelt iron, spin cotton, form railroads, and conduct commerce. Your public, perfectly understand this system, and hence they have lost confidence in all your spiritual ministrations, and all respect for your profession. The laboring classes seldom enter the Protestant churches, Their common sense, they think, is as good as yours; and as they can read the Bible, and " eat faith " at home, they generally sleep till two o'clock on Sundays, and never listen to the parson until he has invented a story about a priest, a monk, or a convent, or the bones of a child being dug up, some time ago, somewhere, by somebody, in some nunnery. The total absence of all religious instruction in these churches, added to the constant teaching of doubting the entire evidence of antiquity, has converted the finest nation and the most generous people into a ferocious multitude of bigoted infidels.

Lord Ashley's Report (which I have not read, but of which I have heard,) reveals a state of religious ignorance in this country beyond the most exaggerated powers of credibility. His description of the factories and collieries, awakens thrilling feelings of pain and shame in the bosom of every honest religious Englishman. Think of hundreds of grown girls, who could not tell "who was God, or Christ, or the Holy Ghost," and who were sunk at the same time, in the lowest state of immorality, too extended and too gross to be named in this letter. Hundreds of colliers were never even once in a church—had never learned one word of their catechism, and perfectly ignorant of the cross.

One man being asked who made him, answered, "My mother:" a second being questioned as to the number of Gods, replied, "That there were *seven*, and that he was able to fight any one of them:" a third, being pressed to tell who was Christ, said, "He did not know him, as he had never worked in his pit: a fourth being asked if he was afraid of God, replied, "Na, na, but that it was the *other b*—— he dreaded," (meaning the devil): a fifth, being interrogated if he was afraid oi the punishment of the next world, appeared quite surprised at hearing of future punishments, and replied that, "If his friends would bury his pickaxe with him, there was no place made, even of the hardest rock, could keep him confined."

Why, Sir, the history of the Snake Indians, or of the Bosjesmen, does not reveal such hyper-barbarian ignorance as can be met with in some districts, callings, and trades in England. How can the Protestant clergy, who receive annually eight millions sterling, look men in the face, with the crimes of this barbarity on them? And how can the acute English nation continue to be gulled by the notorious lies of Irish conversions, invented by hired calumniators, in order to divert the public mind from beholding the annual millions of this overgrown robbery, or canvassing the flagrant hypocrisy, and the antichristian slander of this infidel conspiracy? The brutal murders, the wife-killing, the infanticides, and the avowed spreading of infidelity, and the thousands of children whose deaths are daily concealed, are the frightful fruits of your system of the doctrine of the senses, and your hu man faith. Was there ever heard such insane audacity, as to assert that God could reveal nothing which the Protestant conventicle, or the Scotch kirk could not understand? It is the same kind of rampant and ridiculous silliness, as if a congregation of oysters or frogs denied that there existed such things as the truths of algebra, music, or photography, merely because some *few elders* of these tribes could neither see, hear, feel, nor understand the subject. This system will soon make all England infidel.

Hired lecturers, are now publicly delivering lectures on the opposition between what they call "the *secular* creation and the gospel creation,"—that is, on palpable open fidelity. Depend on it, that your teaching will, at no distant day, sap the very foundations of social order in this country; that you will call into existence a generation of men, who, if not checked, will threaten the very existence of English monarchy; and the throne of Great Britain will yet have to rely on Catholic allegiance and Catholic fidelity for its preservation and security.

You seem much captivated with the reasonableness (as you call it) of the figurative sense being applied to the words used by our Lord at the Last Supper. Now, Sir, I look on the Protestant doctrine of the Last Supper, to be such an aggregate of incongruity, that, if one were not certain of its being believed by a large section of persons in this country, it could never be supposed that such an opinion could be seriously held by men who believed Christ to be God, and to have uttered intelligible language.

That doctrine states, that "the Last Supper is a memorial of Christ's sufferings and passion: where bread and wine being taken in faith, Christ is spiritually received." The four terms, therefore, within which this doctrine is included, are the words "memorial, faith, (bread and wine,) and the spirit of Christ."

As you, therefore, appeal to the standard of the Scriptures, and the standard of language on this point, I shall, *for a moment*, meet that appeal, by quoting some texts from the Gospel of St. John, chapter the sixth:—

"v. 52.—If any man eat of this bread, he shall live forever, and the bread that I will give is my flesh, for the life of the world.

"v. 53.—The Jews, therefore, *debated* among themselves, saying, how *can* the man give us his flesh to eat?

"v. 54.—Unless you eat the flesh of the Son of Man, and drink his blood, you shall not have life in you.

"v. 55.—He that eateth my flesh and drinketh my blood, hath everlasting life, and I will raise him up in the last day.

'v. 56.—For my flesh is meat indeed, and my blood is drink indeed,

"v. 57.—He that eateth my flesh and drinketh my blood, abideth in me and I in him.

"v. 58.—As the living Father hath sent me, and as I live by the Father, so he that eateth me, the same shall live by me."

In the foregoing texts our Lord uses the words "*eat my flesh*" five times; and it must be well remembered, that these words were employed four times after the Jews *debated* among themselves "how *can* this man give us *his flesh to eat*." He heard their objection ("how CAN he;") and, of course, according to all the rules of a public speaker to his audience, he replies to the difficulty which they proposed; and in place of retracting his words, or altering them into other clearer words, or making any change or explanation in his expression, he, on the contrary, becomes more emphatic in his manner, and repeats four times, with evident increased energy, the self same words.

And it must not be forgotten, that, in thus re-asserting these words four times, in the teeth of their contradiction, he also adds some new circumstances of vital interest to the question under debate; namely, in v. 53, he threatens *damnation* to the man who merely *omits* what he orders; in v. 55, he offers *justification* to the man who *fulfils* his statements; in v. 56, he asserts twice, that what he has said is a *literal* statement (*alethos;*) in v. 57, he again declares, that the man who corresponds with the conditions named, is *intimately identified* with him; and lastly, in v. 58, he utters TWO OATHS—namely, "by his mission and by his life," that what he stated would give eternal life; and finally, in all these assertions, threats, promises, and rewards, he uses the word "eat his flesh" with an unvarying consistency in reply to their objection. Now as the whole Jewish religion was made up of types and figures; and as a matter of course, the Capharnites were perfectly acquainted with this fact, can any man believe, that Christ would hold out threats of perdition, and would *swear* twice, in order to make them believe the most known fact of their country?

Now, Sir, by what authority do you, who seem so much attached to the word of God, take it on yourself to change *the clear, expressed words* into a meaning certainly not *asserted*, or affirmed in the *written* or *spoken* language?

You reply that it *must* be received in a *spiritual* or *figurative* sense, from the impossibility, as your common sense asserts, of understanding these written words in their literal sense. You, therefore, assert that flesh means "faith," means "figure of flesh," means "spirit," means "metaphor," means "image or memorial." In the first place, this is, on your part, a most unwarrantable assumption, it not being affirmed in the words: and secondly, it may turn out, as I hope presently to show, that your meaning must end in an *absurdity of idea*, and in an *incongruity* of language, such as would deprive Christ of all future confidence in the expression of his thoughts; and convert the language of the Testament into an unmeaning or incongruous symbol. If, then, your meaning be correct, it follows, of course that, that mode of expression must be just, which describes a man, as "eating a spirit, eating an image, drinking a metaphor, eating an allegory, and drinking a shadow."

Now, Sir, if all this language be perfectly just, and the ideas congruously expressed, it follows, of course, *all the other cognate words* of "the verb to eat," can be similarly used, with equal justice and equal correctitude: hence, Sir, we can employ with equal truth the words "to wash a spirit, to weigh a spirit, to bleed a spirit, to boil a spirit, to roast a spirit, to salt a spirit," as well as we can say "to eat a spirit." The words are decidedly of the same *cognate* character, and if one of them can be used with precision, so can all the others. Then, it is perfectly correct to say, "to wash an image, to bake a metaphor, to boil an allegory, to salt a trope, to eat a shadow, to wash a shadow, to bake a shadow." And then, again, Sir, it will follow, that the image of a thing can justify the soul, and the metaphor of a thing can feed the soul. And again, Sir, you represent Christ as swearing by *two oaths* that these are his words, and that this is his meaning !!!

You have, therefore, adopted the most incongruous and ridiculous form of words, such as no rational human being has been ever known to use; you have, in the face of heaven and earth, translated the word "flesh" into "spirit, image, shadow, metaphor;" and you have done all this, forsooth, because you could not understand how "He could give us his flesh to eat." But if you will reflect on the crib, on next Christmas night, and ask how can a trembling, poor, naked, abandoned child, be the eternal, consubstantial Word, the King of Kings; your common sense will be shocked, till you see the heavens opened, and *hear* the angelic choirs rend the blue vault of His Fathers skies, saying, "It is he." How can you understand a word to be flesh, a God to be a man, infinite dominion to be weakness, infinite power to be destitution, infinite riches to be poverty, infinite majesty to be slavery, immortality to be death, and infinite sanctity to stand charged with human guilt. Now, all these mysteries are placed in the very alphabet of Christianity, in order to level all human reason on the very threshold of the New Law. Our doctrine is just the same kind of mystery; and while we are astounded at the statement contained in the words, we at the same time *hear* him re-assert it over and over again, and we bow and believe. And I could no more consent to believe the absurd, ridiculous, the incongruous, the newly invented meaning of *your altered text*, than I could consent to believe our blessed Lord to be an idiot or a maniac. You, therefore, perceive Sir, how absurd is the novelty, how ridiculous is heresy.

In order to see more fully the consistent language of our Lord, I shall again quote some texts from St. Mathew, chap. 26

"v. 26.—And whilst they were at supper, Jesus took bread and blessed and broke, and gave to his disciples, and said, take ye and eat, this is my body.

"v. 27.—And taking the chalice, he gave to them, saying, drink ye all of this.

"v. 28.—For this is my blood of the New Testament, which shall be shed for many, for the remission of sins."

Now, Sir, according to your assumed meaning, Christ said "this is my body," meaning that this is my *spirit.* Now, Sir, since the invention, improvement and perfection of human language, have you ever seen, read, or heard of any human being, in any age, or any country, use the word "body" to mean "spirit?" It is precisely the very opposite, and cannot by the rules of language, be employed *even as a metaphor,* as there cannot be any resemblance between two things which are metaphysically opposite. And when we come to apply your meaning to v. 28, it is hard to say whether one feels a greater amount of ridicule, or pity, or contempt, for the teachers of a doctrine which would go to say "that the blood of the spirit was shed, the blood of a metaphor shed, the blood of a shadow shed, the blood of an image shed, the blood of faith shed, the blood of a memorial shed!!"—Now, Sir, in your own language, do you see how ridiculous is error, how absurd is human novelty in Revelation?

I shall, in conclusion, quote by your standard of the Bible, and the criticism of language, some texts on the subject from St. Paul to the Corinthians, chapter the eleventh of the first epistle, v. 23:

"v. 23.—For I *have received* of the Lord that which also I delivered to you, that the Lord Jesus the night in which he was betrayed took bread,

"v. 24.—And giving thanks, broke and said, 'take ye and eat, this is my body, which shall be delivered for you; DO THIS in commemoration of me.'

"v. 25.—In like manner, also, the chalice, after he had supped, saying this chalice is the New Testament in my blood; THIS DO YE as often as you shall drink, for the commemoration of me.

"v. 27.—Wherefore, whosoever shall eat this bread, or drink the chalice of the Lord unworthily, shall be guilty of the body and of the blood of the Lord.

"v. 28.—But let a man prove himself: and so let him eat of that bread, and drink of the chalice.

"v. 29.—For he that eateth and drinketh unworthily, eateth and drinketh damnation to himself; not discerning the body of the Lord."

You see, Sir, in these texts, that St. Paul keeps up the same consistency of word and idea as our Lord; and that he asserts his having received the above communication, not from the Apostles, but from *the lips of Christ himself*, after his resurrection, in order to stamp that communication with an importance beyond anything he had to tell them. Here St. Paul clearly speaks of the GUILT of the body and blood of Christ. Now, Sir, be candid with me: has any man, in any age or any country, ever heard of "spilling the blood of a spirit, murdering bread and wine, killing a metaphor, sheding the blood of bread and wine, killing a shadow, bleeding an allegory, taking the life of a trope, and murdering a shadow?"

But, above all, can you have the cool hardihood to preach before any assembly of rational beings, that Christ would pronounce a *double damnation* against a man for not "discerning a BODY in a spirit, a body in a metaphor, a body in faith, a body in a shadow, a body in bread and wine?"—that is, he has pronounced double damnation on a man for not discerning what cannot be discerned, for not discerning an absurdity, an incongruity, an impossibility:—that is, he damns a man in double torments for not seeing a part greater than the whole; for not seeing a square as a circle; for not seeing the colour of white as black. What Christian acquainted with the life of Christ, could seriously believe that his last will, (which David foretold in reference to Melchisedeck, and which he himself foretold in his disputation with the Capharnites,) contained the bequest of metaphors, figures, and shadows, to *feed* and *nourish*, and *strengthen* the life of the soul!!—This is theology with a vengeance!! May God, Almighty God, forgive you, Sir, for teaching such insanity to your poor dupes; and may HE in his grace open your eyes, and the eyes of the poor creatures who are doomed to listen to such absurd, and ridiculous, and degrading doctrines as England and Scotland have adopted since the days of Luther and Knox.

Your church has never ceased to publish through the world her great respect for the Scriptures, and to express her horror at any robbery, as she calls it of the Word of God. Will you, then, tell me why you have, with such palpable shamelessness, mistranslated, subtracted, and added to the most important passages of both the Old and New Testament? I shall, therefore, select one text in reference to the present subject—namely, the 26th verse of the 26th chapter of St. Mathew. As it happens that I have not a Greek Testament with me, I must quote from memory; and as your journals here have no Greek type, I must write in the English character. You will, of course supply the long vowels where they occur.

Your Greek original of the text alluded to, is :—

Esthionton de auton, labon o Iesous ton arton, kai eulogesas, eklase, kai edidou tois mathetais, kai eipe : Labete, phagete, touto esti to soma mou.

Your translation of this text, taken from an edition in 1846, printed by Mr. Spottiswoode, Fleet-street, London, is: "And as they were eating, Jesus took bread, and blessed *it*, and broke *it*, and gave *it* to his disciples," &c. Here you introduce the pronoun "*it*" three times, in order to carry the antecedent "bread," as it were, through the whole text, and therefore show that it was this said bread the Apostles eat. Now, the pronoun "it," is not found in the original; and thus the Protestant church with a palpable and a shameful interpolation, corrupted the Greek text, in order to make out a lie to meet their absurd doctrine on this vital point. I have taken the trouble of comparing with the original text the gospel of Saint John, the epistles of St. Paul to the Corinthians and to the Hebrews;

and I have found one hundred and eighty-four texts mistranslated, being either interpolations, or new meanings, opposed to the philology, the genius, and the received construction of the Greek language.

There are upwards of sixteen hundred errors in translations and additions or subtractions, or interpolations in your Bible. The Protestant church can lie in print as well as in speech: the pen can lie as well as the tongue. I freely admit the honor and truth of their clergy in social intercourse: there is, however, no lie however dishonorable; no misstatement, however discreditable, to which they will not stoop in matters of Catholicity. I should be sorry to say one word hurtful to you personally, as I can have no cause to do so, and as I can have no feelings towards you but those of respect; yet, considering the shameful forgery of the Protestant Bible, I would prefer that a Catholic should read the worst books of immorality, than this forgery in God's Word—this slander of Christ. Old age can check immorality, but the forgeries of God's book, the lies told of Christ, the wicked perversion of the inspired volume, the base substitution of words, the flagrant robbery of the text of life, are so many hideous crimes of Protestantism, that, in vengeance for such blasphemous interpolation, the curse of all crimes, and of all errors, and of naked infidelity, seems to be inflicted on your entire nation. And this is the Bible, this public forgery on the name of the Holy Ghost, this libel of God the Father, this slander on Christ, which you wish to give to the poor children of the Irish.

You seem to smile, in what you are pleased to call

"indignant sarcasm," against the follies, "the nonsense" of transubstantiation. If, Sir, you have any sympathy to spare, may I beg you will reserve it all for yourself, in order to console yourself in the midst of the indignant sarcasm to which your clear unacquaintance with this question, will expose you even before your friends.—Transubstantiation, though a stupendous, mysterious fact, and beyond the power of men, is yet, Sir, a very common occurrence with God, and, indeed, may be called one of the most general laws of nature, and may be seen among the very first evidences of His omnipotent will towards the race of men on earth.

First, then, he created man by changing "the slime of the earth" into the flesh and bones of Adam, in his first official act of transubstantiation—that is, by the word of God on matter. His second official act, of changing the bony rib of Adam into the flesh and blood of Eve, was also transubstantiation, by the Word of God the Father on bone. The first official act of Christ on entering on the three years of his mission, was performed when he changed the water into wine at the wedding of Cana, by the word of Christ on water. The food, Sir—that is, the bread and wine, which you, and all men may have eaten on this day, has been changed into flesh and blood on your own person, and on the persons of all men, by the word of God on the vital action of the stomach. The universal crop of wood and grasses, and flowers and vegetables, and human and animal food, which the earth actually produces, is an animal evidence of transubstantiation of clay by the word of God the Father, on the productive energy of the entire earth. The hat on your head, the silk in your cravat, the linen on your back, the cloth of your wearing apparel, the wool or cotton in your stockings, the leather in your boots, the Whitehaven coals in your grates, the gas in your lamps; the bread, the butter, the cream, the sugar, the tea-leaf on your breakfast table, the mutton, the beef, the bacon, the fowl, the wine, the brandy, the ale on your dinner table; in short, almost every object the eye beholds on earth, is one vast aggregate of evidence of transubstantiation, by the word of God on matter.

Beyond all dispute, all these came from clay. Even the paper of your spurious Bible, the leather on the back, the Indian ink, are such evidences of transubstantiation that one can scarcely conceive how you could read that very Bible without being burned with scalding shame at the stark-naked nonsense, and incongrous maniacm you have written to me on the subject. God has supplied us, during four thousand years with this mighty, universal, constant evidence, in order to prepare us for the more mighty, infinitely more stupendous evidence of the same principle in the New Law, by the power and the word of Christ. The Father has given life and preserved life in all living things on earth by this principle of nature, in order to make us behold the uniformity of action in the Trinity, when Christ at his coming will give life to the soul and preserve it in grace on the self-same principle, "the bread that I will give is my flesh *for the life of the world.*" I would undertake, as a chemist, to prove, that there are more, far more mysteries (but of course of a different kind), in a *handful of clay*, than are contained in the entire code of the Christian Revelation.

You will reply to me and say, that while God has done all I have said, yet that *man could not do it.* You mistake; a man can do it, when commanded to do so, by the Word of God. Moses changed a rod into a serpent, and changed a serpent into a rod; he changed the waters of the river Nile into blood, and the same river of blood into water, by the word of God on his lips. And do you not think, Sir, even in your common sense, that a man in the New Law could do the same thing as a man in the Old Law, if he were commanded to do so? The word of God will certainly have the same power in every place, in every age, and in every man on whom that word will descend. Now, Sir, you have seen in St. Paul to the Corinthians the text where St. Paul, in an ecstasy of astonishment, told them that he heard from the lips of Christ how he changed bread and wine into his body and blood, and concluded by also informing them that in the same breath, Christ had ordered the Apostles, by two distinct commands, to mark its importance, to DO THE SAME in remembrance of Him.

And lest it should occur to your common sense that the Apostles had not the power to execute the command, will you hear, Sir, the words of Christ to them? "*All power* is given to me in heaven and on earth; RECEIVE *ye*, therefore, the HOLY GHOST." This text, therefore gives not only the gifts of the Holy Ghost, but the third person of the Trinity himself, as an official resident, with the Apostles and their successors, in order to communicate the per manent official presence of the Holy Ghost, equal to the Father and Son. I think, Sir, your common sense must yield at length, and acknowledge with candour that our case is complete, our warrant of office in this great act most decided, and, of course, efficient exercise of our power beyond the reach of cavil or contradiction.

But you will say that such a fact has never occurred in the New Law. This is a mistake; it happened in the Incarnation. When the archangel (a creature,) announced to Mary the will of God who sent him to wait on her, and to tell her that she would bring forth a son, "she replied HOW CAN IT BE, as I know not man:" he resumed, "it will be done by the power and operation of the Holy Ghost." Here, Sir, is a position which *might be argued* as a clear case of transubstantiation in the very first act of the New Law—namely, the blood of Mary, the relative of Adam the criminal, changed into a human body for the second person of the Trinity by the power of the Holy Ghost. Thus, Sir, if the redemption and the perfection of fallen man commenced by an act of transubstantiation in the Incarnation, why not continue the same principle among all future men by the power and operation of the same Holy Ghost?

But you will certainly re-assert, as you have done in your illogical, untheological letter to me, that a thing must be always essentially what it appears to be. You are generally right, Sir, in the laws of nature; but in the laws of grace, the senses must be silent under your most favorable position, whenever the word of God makes the contrary statement. Thus the dove, which alighted on the shoulder of Christ at the Jordan, had all the appearance of a dove to the sense of seeing; and this sense was not deceived, because its domain is entirely confined to appearances. But, Sir, it was not a dove: it was the Holy Ghost under the appearance of a dove to point out the spotlessness of Christ. Again, the twelve tongues of fire, which descended on the apostles, were not tongues of fire, but " the form of tongues of fire; " but they were really the Holy Ghost, in order to express the new burning zeal and gift of language given to the apostles. Will you say why cannot Christ appear under the appearance of bread and wine, as well as the Holy Ghost under the appearance of a dove and tongues of fire, in order to point out how he feeds the soul, and thus carry out the promise he has made, when he said—"the bread that I will give is my flesh, for the life of the world."

Why do you not tell your congregation at Whitehaven not to believe that "the dove or the fiery tongues," were the Holy Ghost? You are bound to do so in your system of the infallibility of your Protestant eyesight. You ought to tell them that you consider the testimony of the senses, as the senses of God, and therefore the eye is right! You ought also to inform them, when you are alone in your drawing room, and neither see, smell, taste or feel the air, that therefore there is no air, Whitehaven; tell them, also, that as the eyes of the Jews did not see the Godhead in Christ, that therefore he was not God; tell them also, that as he appeared a criminal, it must therefore be a fact (founded on the senses and God) that he was a melefactor; tell them, also, that the ascension of our Lord is a mere fable, because from the laws of gravitation (to which the senses bear unerring testimony) no body can ascend upwards composed of flesh and bone as His was—"The senses are God's own law, and he cannot contradict himself." Tell them, also that as fire cannot burn a man's thoughts, that therefore it cannot reach the soul; that the senses tell you that the fire can only reach matter, and consequently you have the testimony of the senses and God, that there is at present no hell, as the body has not yet risen. Do, Sir, tell the world all this Whitehaven theology, and let nothing be believed unless it is as *palpable* as a railroad, and can be seen *working* like a steam engine!

You also ask, how can His body be present on our altars *unseen?* and when I reply, "by the sacramental mode," you cannot comprehend me, and you have recourse to your "indignant sarcasm." Now, Sir, as you are perfectly acquainted with the coals Whitehaven, will you be pleased to see *hard coal* going into the furnace of a gasometer : see it very soon bituminous, tarry, *liquid* coal —that is to say, it is palpable in the furnace, impalpable in the gasometer: that is to say, again, invisible in the tubes, and *visible* in the jets; that is to say again, darkness in the tubes, and light in the lamps; that is to say, opaque in the furnace, and transparent in the tubes—will you kindly tell us, how can the *same thing* be palpable and impalpable, visible and invisible, darkness and light, opaque and transparent? Now, Sir, if all these modes, apparently contradictory and even contrary, belong even to the ordinary forms of matter, will you tell us, why cannot Christ assume any bulk, or any form in any mode of existence He pleases, and still be the self-same Christ, but in a new mode of existence? This, Sir, is the case on our altar; it was the case when, after His resurrection, when He entered the closed doors and stood in the midst of the apostles.

I am now done with the mere cursory view of this question, with one additional remark on the words you have used, namely, "that we create our Creator" This phrase does not become you; and your bigotry will gain notoriety by this phrase, at the expense of your education as a theologian. You are clearly palpably ignorant of our doctrine, and it is distressing to reflect how a gentleman could not have honor to spare the Catholics, and discretion to spare himself, by publicly writing on a subject which decidedly you have never studied as a scholar. No, Sir, we do not create our Creator!

Hear me. We just do what we are commanded to do; hence, when He took bread and changed it into His body He commanded us to do the same, and we believe we do change it into *His body.* In like manner he changed the wine into His blood, and told us to do the same, and we believe we change the wine into *His blood.* But He has not said "this is my divinity, do this," and therefore, we do not do that; and hence you malign and calumniate when you say "we create our Creator." Our office is changing the bread and wine into the humanity, not the divinity of Christ; but as the humanity is now, since the resurrection, essentially united with the divinity, therefore, wherever the humanity is present there also must be the divinity, not by our creation, as you are pleased to write to your dupes at Whitehaven, but by the essential concomitance of the two natures of Christ, which, since his resurrection, can never be separated, standing before God for ever as the living triumph of His mission, as the eternal pledge and security of man's unchanging justification.

I have the honor to be, Reverend Sir, your obedient servant,

D. W. CAHILL, D.D.

P. S.—You cannot retort on me, and against my belief on the Eucharist, the same *cognate* words which I have applied to your new interpretation. The retort would only prove that my belief may subject the host to be profaned—I admit it; it may be profaned by *sinners*, but adored *by all the good*. But even so, that profanation, since the resur rection, cannot be accompanied with shame, or sorrow, or agony, and when the infidel asks you, can you belief in a God who was mocked, blindfolded, spit upon in the hall of Pilate, flogged naked at a pillar, crucified between two thieves, and his blood spilled and profaned ; will you say, Sir, what is your reply ? You admit the whole charge, and answer that these facts, so far from destroying your belief, only confirm it, and prove beyond all other facts that he was our Saviour. If your reply to the infidel be valuable and invincible, the same reply from me to you must be equally valuable and invincible. If his retort on you would be foolish in Christian faith, yours would be equally foolish against me. You cannot make an argument serve two opposite points —an argument cannot be urged *pro* and *con*. If your retort against me possesses force, the infidel triumphs over you. Therefore I admit that the Sacred Host may be profaned by sinners—and if everything in faith must be rejected which is or may be profaned, you must on this principle reject the Father, the Son, and the Holy Ghost, and grace and faith, and the entire Christian Law.

All the objection you can raise to our doctrine is, that it exposes Christ to be *sacramentally profaned*, a fact, which he once *borne in his natural form*; what *happened* once can never, therefore, be deemed absurd or incongruous; whereas, our objection to your interpretation is, that it stands before the mind, if I may so speak, an evident absurdity, a plain impossibility. Our doctrine may therefore end in the profanation of Christ from sinners, a position which, I presume you frequently put forth, in reference to the conduct of sinners, before your congregation; but our creed can never be charged with a metaphysical absurdity, such as eating an image, boiling a ghost, bleeding a spirit, salting a metaphor, and baking a shadow; and feeding the soul with the nutritious spiritual food of metaphors, tropes, allegories, figures, and ideal resemblances ! ! !

REV. DR. CAHILL AND "THE RAMBLER".

In consequence of the former letter, an anonymous article was published in the London Monthly Rambler, under the title of "Dr. Cahill's Letter on Transubstantiation," and a friend of our author wrote to the Editor, asking a convenient space in the next number of that Journal in order to answer to the misstatements, gross falsehoods, and calumnies of said article, "which," he added, "did produce what may be called a wide-spread feeling of dissatisfaction amongst the clergy and laity." He proposed "to show by a single reference to the letter of Dr. Cahill, that his arguments were misrepresented; and that an unjustifiable meaning has been attached to his words."

This the Editor refused to do under several pretexts, and Dr. Cahill thought proper to address himself *to the Editors of Catholic Journals*, relating these facts, and stating, that "in every paragraph—indeed, in almost every sentence—gross falsehood is asserted, palpable calumny is uttered, my clearly-expressed meaning is distorted, and *whole sentences are carefully suppressed.*" After a full preliminary notice of all these incidents, the Rev. Doctor came to the controversial part of his letter, as follows:

NEW BRIGHTON, *February*, 1854.

In approaching the theological part of this letter, I feel unusual pain in being compelled to expose the want of truth on the part of the *Rambler*. God knows, I cannot rejoice in a triumph over the writers—victory in this case is defeat. Exposure of those who have joined my Church, at much personal sacrifice, is, to me, the bitterest pain; but they have forced me into this unwilling course by an inevitable necessity.

Before criticising my letter at Whitehaven, one should suppose that the writer would, as a Catholic, have sent to me a private letter, stating his objections, and demanding an explanation; but no such prudent letter came from the English Vatican, No. 17 Portman-street, London—or, at least, one should imagine, that this model of logic, criticism, and grace, would have read the original letter of the Rev. Mr. Burns, to which my reply was directed, and he could then understand the line of argument adopted against the objections made. Yet, strange to say, this eminent censor has not read that letter: and, hence I shall, beyond all dispute, prove to the reader before I shall have concluded this letter, that this clique have mistaken their case, and that they have earned the crushing expression of public ridicule and public censure. Hear them on this point:—

"Of the letter of Mr. Burns, which has called forth this reply from Dr. Cahill, *we know nothing more than is to be gathered from the extracts* which the latter has prefixed to his rejoinder."

Now, if he had read that letter, he would have earned the direction of my answer, and have avoided the imprudent article he has penned. Hear Mr. Burns,—"I ask you, Sir, what can be the reason that Mother Southcott was thought crazy for pretending to give birth to the Messiah? and that you, a priest of Rome, can, without exciting ridicule, make a Messiah every time you celebrate Mass?—What is the extravagance of Joanna Southcott to the extravagance of the priests of Rome? * * * If God made man, the testimony of the senses is the testimony of God: if the senses deceive me, then God, my Maker, is the deceiver. And thus your doctrine is incapable of being believed by any man under the influence of common sense."

In order to meet his appeal to his common sense, I ask him, how he can apply the rules of common sense, and of his senses, to the doctrine of the Trinity, Grace, Original Sin, the Incarnation, the Existence of the Soul, or even the Immortality of Man: and I conclude by inquiring how he could even explain the *Transubstantiation* which is every day elaborated by nature through almost every substance by which we are surrounded? Although my meaning could not be misunderstood by any one outside No. 17 Portman-street: and although my words are clearly applied to the *modal* changes in nature; and although I have adduced this section of my reply, as a *mere illustration, a mere comparison sub uno respectu,* and not at all as an argument of demonstration, the writers in the *Rambler,* by introducing *words of their own forgery,* by suppressing *whole sentences* of my letter, and by an evil-designed ingenuity seldom surpassed, have devoted nine pages of deliberate falsehood and scandal to the palpable distortion of my clearly-expressed meaning. In order to convince the reader of the truth of my statements, I shall select only two extracts from my letter.

The first is as follows:—"God has supplied us during four thousand years with this mighty, constant, universal evidence (*i. e.,* of nature), in order to PREPARE US for the more mighty, the INFINITELY MORE STUPENDOUS evidence of the same principle in the New Law, by the power and the word of Christ."

Now, I ask any candid, any honest man, if I have not in this extract pointed out the changes in nature as a *mere preparation* for a change INFINITELY MORE STUPENDOUS in the New Law? Surely one thing *infinitely* more stupendous than another thing, cannot be the *same* thing. Now, gentlemen, hear the writers in the *Rambler* on this point so clearly expressed:—

"What, then, must we think of the snares which beset the 'popular' controversialist when we turn to the next paragraphs of Dr. Cahill's letter, in which he asserts that *the miracle* of Transubstantiation is 'a very common occurrence with God, and may be called *one of the most general laws of nature?*' Again we say that we acquit him of *intending* anything approaching to that which his words imply. He is carried away by that unfortunate desire to bring down the ineffable mysteries of faith to the level of human capacities, which is the bane of some minds; and which has here led him into statements, which, viewed merely as rhetorical illustrations, are inaccurate and worthless, but *if looked upon as a declaration of Catholic doctrines,* are shocking to the last degree."

In the quotation just made, Gentlemen, there are two cases of grievous injustice :—firstly, it is clear that I have *not identified* the changes in nature with the mysteries of the Eucharist; I have clearly stated these two things as *infinitely distinct:* and yet, the Reviewer would fain make me say, that they *are identified.* But mark his hesitation while he writes: he says he is sure I do *not intend* it: that it is a mere *illustration:* and yet observe his dishonesty, where he insinuates again, in the same hesitating style, that I have put forward these changes in nature as *declarations of Catholic doctrines!* On this point I shall leave the public to judge of the prudence, the candor, and the justice of the writers. But I have a heavier charge still to bring forward against this last quotation of the Reviewers. They have uttered a palpable falsehood in the extract adduced—they have *forged a word* which I did not use; and I therefore brand them before the public with the most dishonorable trick which I have ever experienced from the veriest characterless bigot of the enemies of the Catholic Church. The forgery is as follows, as you will soon see. Their words are: "Dr. Cahill asserts, that the MIRACLE of Transubstantiation is a very common occurrence with God, and may be called *one of the most general laws of nature.*"

Gentlemen, I have not used the word "MIRACLE:" this is a plain forgery: any reader can see the truth of what I say. I was speaking, beyond all doubt, at that time of the laws of nature: they wish to distort my words as applied to the Blessed Eucharist: I was not speaking then of the Eucharist: *I did not write the word* MIRACLE in that or any other place. Although it is but one word, it is *decisively* applied to the Eucharist: it fixes irrevocably a particular meaning: *I did not use it:* they *forged it:* and introduced it, where it is evident I could not have employed it: and I have thus caught the malevolent clique in their own snares, from which, and I say it with sorrow, they can never extricate their honor as Gentlemen, or their honesty as Catholics, as long as they live. But, Gentlemen, I have still a far more weighty charge against the ecumenical trio of Portman-street. What will the public think of them when I shall quote extracts from their anonymous article, where they ask whether *my meaning is such as they describe,* and where they palpably distort it, and fix to it a *sense of their own construction* the very opposite of mine? And, Gentlemen, what will the public think, when I shall prove beyond all contradiction, that these good Catholics, these pillars of the council of Portman-street, have—with a duplicity, a perfidy, of which there is no parallel outside their former theatre of Exeter-hall—*suppressed the very section* of my letter, which is a perfect categorical answer to the questions they put? Firstly, then, hear their own quotation—their questions:

"For ourselves, we would ask Dr. Cahill whether he really means to insinuate that the change produced by the consecration of the sacramental elements, is of *the same nature* as the chemical changes to which he has likened it; a mere natural growth from one form to another, an aggregation of additional particles of matter to an original substratum? *He cannot mean it. We will not wrong him* for a moment by the supposition. Why, then, does he employ this series of most profane and irreverent *illustrations?*"

In this passage, again the writer utters his *contradictory hints:* he asks, "Can't I mean a certain thing?" then he says again, "I can't mean it:" and yet he leaves the clear impression behind, that *I do mean to say* that the change in the Blessed Eucharist is of the *same kind* as the chemical changes of nature. Now, Gentlemen, will you hear me while I make the extract from my letter, and while I inform the reader, through you, that this clique of parsons have *suppressed the entire extract,* which follows the very extract which they put. Gentlemen, when you will have read over again the above quotation from the Reviewers, read the following extract of my letter: "I undertake to prove, as a chemist, that there are far more mysteries, but, of course, of a different kind, in a handful of clay, than are to be found in the entire of the Christian Revelation."

This extract was the concluding sentence of my illustration from nature; it is a perfect, direct answer to the questions put by the Reviewers, and *this extract they have* suppressed. As I conclude this section of my reply, I charge the writers so far as I have gone, with an undeniable forgery, with a dishonorable suppression of the truth, with the hostile publication of a calumnious and scandalous article, and with the cowardly injustice of refusing to an English gentleman, and accomplished clergyman, the opportunity of making a defence for his slandered friend. But depend upon it they shall not calumniate me with impunity: and I finish this sentiment by exclaiming, "Oh, would mine enemy should write a book!"

In reference to these passages, in which the Reviewer

speaks of "illustrations and metaphors," one is amused by the hesitations and contradictions which occur almost every sentence. It is evident, that he would fain find fault if he could: it is clear he comes prepared for censure, at all hazards, but not having sufficient data, he hesitates, advances, withdraws: says and unsays the sef-same thing, in the same paragraph.

"Many and many are the *false and pernicious impressions* which have been conveyed through the medium of illustrations,—*powerful* and *beneficial*, as is the effect of metaphors in theological writing, when they are critically correct and applicable—*harmless*, as they may be when employed uncritically on trifling subjects; and *delightful*, as the *charm* they convey when springing from a deep, clear, and vigorous imagina tion, we cannot but think that the *greatest caution is needed in their use* when employed to illustrate those ineffable mysteries;" and in page 172 the same writer calls "illustrations *profane* and *irreverent*."

I have read the passages quoted over and over again, to learn what is really the opinion of the Reviewer with regard to illustrations: and I have been unable to glean any accurate idea from the half-smothered sentiments of the writer except a wish to express a censure which he cannot justly make, and which he is afraid plainly to utter. The reader can see that in the same paragraph, he calls the same thing "false, charming, profane, irreverent." The only thing required in the use of them is "caution," which of course, no man or set of men living can employ to perfection, except the three parsons of Portman-street ! ! ! Be it known, therefore, to the church of England, Ireland, and Scotland, that, whenever any one wishes to employ an "illustration" in religion, the incautious and illiterate English, Irish, or Scotch preacher must write a polite note to the ecumenical triumvirate of Portman-street to learn the precise use of metaphors, and after waiting for a reply from these models of learning and good breeding for nine days, perhaps they may be favored with "a hearing," as to whether they will be permitted, in the judgement of these profound theologians of Oxford (where theology is less than half taught), to read the following Gospels without the presence and instructions of "the three tailors" from Tooley-street:—

The kingdom of Heaven is *likened* a treasure hid in a field.–*Matthew.*

The kingdom of Heaven is *likened* to a merchantman seeking pearls. —*Matthew.*

The kingdom of Heaven is *likened* to a householder going to hire laborers.—*Matthew.*

The kingdom of Heaven is *likened* to a certain king, who made a marriage-feast.—*Matthew.*

The kingdom of Heaven is *likened* to ten virgins with lamps, going to meet the bridegroom.—*Matthew.*

The kingdom of Heaven is *likened* to a man travelling in a far country.—*Matthew.*

The kingdom of Heaven is *likened* to a sower going out to sow seed. The seed is the word of God.—*Mark.*

"*As* the body without the spirit is *dead*, so *also faith*, without good works, is *dead.* "—*St. James.*

In the whole course of my experience, I have never read anything that can even approach the sickening conceit, exciting a smile of pity, of the writers of the above paragraph on illustrations, where they clearly set themselves up as the models of criticism, the teachers of the priesthood, and the infallible guides of the whole church of these countries.

On that part of their Review, where they cavalierly

avow that they had *not* read the original letter which called out my reply at Whitehaven, I have one remark to make, in order to prove the reckless imprudence of the writers. Every theologian recollects the trouble and vexation which the Popes Leo and Gelasius endured from the Manicheans of their day, who *refused* to admit the doctrine of the church in reference to the consecrated wine in the chalice. Hereupon the Popes refused to admit these persons to Communion, unless they received Communion in *both kinds*, adding " that they could not permit them to *divide the Sacrament* and thereby *render it null.*

If these words are read in a mere logical and theological point of view, and detached from the case of the Manicheans, it would seem as if Communion, under *both kinds* were *essential* to the *integrity* and *validity* of the Sacrament. Protestants constantly quoted these Popes on this point. But when it is recollected that the language of the Popes is directed against persons who *deny the chalice,* it will then be evident that the command of the Popes to drink of the chalice, is imposed (in this particular case), *not* because *both kinds* are *essential,* but in order to uproot at once the growing heresy, and to silence perfectly the objection that Christ is not present in the chalice. If the Reviewers had the prudence to understand the objection against which my illustrations were employed, they would not have now to defend themselves against the reckless falsehood they have uttered of me; nor would the public have to deplore the scandal they have given to the faithful.

I have seldom read the sermons of Catholic preachers, or studied the doctrine of the Church, as laid down by the Fathers, in which are not to be found abundant illustrations such as the Scriptures themselves present; and so accustomed are the public to these illustrations that not one individual amongst the most illiterate of our communion would ever think that these illustrations are to be taken as strict *declarations, sub omni respectu,* of doctrine. In the Gospels already adduced, what man would ever think that the kingdom of Heaven was "money hid in a field:" or "the captain of a ship:" or "a farmer hiring labourers;" or "a king:" or "ten young women:" or "that faith *died* like the body, and was buried and grew putrid;" or "that the word of God was an ear of corn, made of potash, phosphorus, and sulphur?" Every one knows the value of illustrations; and hence the readers of my letter have perfectly understood my views. I have received communications from Bishops, thanking me for the letter: and one of the first Theologians in England, a Professor of twenty-one years' standing, wrote to me to say, that he CONSIDERED that letter "a masterpiece of controversy, both in matter and manner."

There is in nature a *change* from one substance to another, from natural, chemical, and mechanical agencies; but there is no "*total conversion*;" according to our idea of the difference of substances, the wool on the sheep's back is different from the turnips on which it feeds: but *this change* is *modal*; and except under the *one solitary illustration* of "change," has no relationship whatever with the change or "conversion" in the Eucharist, which firstly, is of a *different kind,* and secondly, is NOT a *modal* change but "a *total conversion.*" While on this point I would suggest to the Theologians of the *Rambler* to forbear their *explanations* of the manner *how* this change is effected. Their words, ARE it is effected by the *annihilation* of one substance, and the *substitution of another.*" It would be much more prudent in them, to read the Catechism of the Council of Trent, and adopt the old words, "A *conversion* is made of the whole substance of bread, *into* the substance of the body of Christ, and of the whole substance of wine, *into* the substance of his blood." These words *annihilation* and *substitution,* are unnecessary words, and at present I shall merely call the attention of Theologians to these phrases, but shall not utter one word more on this point of my subject.

Gentlemen, I have at this part of my letter, met *half* the objections made by the Editors of the *Rambler;* you will therefore be kindly pleased to keep your columns open to me in your next publication, for a second letter from me of the same length as the present one. In that part of their Review, where they speak of the Protestant Bible, I will fill with bitter sorrow the Catholics of this country, with the views of our infallible council of Portman-street. In all my life, I have not read anything to resemble the combination of glaring falsehood, and palpable Protestantism, rampant Protestantism, to be deduced from their assertions in this part of their Review.

I also demand from you, Gentlemen, that you will not permit any opponent to reply to me, till my second letter shall have been published: that is, till my full reply shall be given. This request I demand, as an act of justice. I should be very sorry, indeed, to identify these three writers of the *Rambler* with all the converts. God forbid! Their conduct is the act of individuals, and not of the body. Oh, no! And their motives cannot be mistaken. It is a small movement on Puseyite principles—it is a little imitation of Tractarianism. It is the old idea of progress. The Lord knows where it will end. Perhaps it may terminate in a new Puseyism, as far beyond old Catholicity, as the first Puseyism is on this side of it. The Lord protect us, the old fashioned Priests, from the genteel theology of Portman-street! The motives of this movement are clear: I wrote to Rev. Mr. Burns, Dec. 7, 1853: and although weeks and weeks elapsed after that letter, yet not a word of censure from Portman-street—not a line in the *Rambler* of January, 1854. But some few weeks ago I wrote a letter to Prince Albert, and I mildly quoted the Oxford Commission, when instantly one convert from Bayswater, in connection, as he stated, with other converts, wrote to me a letter, with which the public are already acquainted. He again received a letter from another convert, thanking him *for his falsehood;* and, lastly, the three converts of Portman-street, in an article embodying the word "we" in every sentence, made the unjustifiable attack, which is the subject of this reply. These simultaneous, combined, and coincident letters, look very like a malignant spirit, proceeding from men, who should more appropriately be consigned to the position of learners, rather than assumingly usurp the office of oppressive dictation.

They have mistaken their case: they have built their spite too high, and it will fall: and what I regret most, is, they have ruined their once useful periodical. It will in future, be called the Parsons' Hornbook. These gentlemen, remind me very much of the old fable, where a boy being once very fond of his cat, prayed to Jupiter, that the cat might be changed into a woman. Jupiter granted his request; but some time afterwards this lady having heard a mouse at night making a noise behind the curtains, forgetting she was a woman, jumped out of bed, and pursued the mouse with the former instinct of the cat. The application is not inappropriate: our Reviewers of Portman-street, although changed into Catholics, cannot divest themselves of the old instincts of the Protestant alliance; and, in some instances, would, if they dared, pursue the Priest, their old victim, with the same malevolence, trick, and misrepresentation, as when they formerly stood on the hostile platform of Exeter-hall.

Gentlemen, I am now done for the present. Your readers must recollect who have commenced this painful controversy, and no man of candor, can complain of me, if I repel gross falsehood, and gratuitous misstatement by public exposure.

I am, Gentlemen, your obedient servant,

D. W. CAHILL, D.D.

THE REV. DR. CAHILL AND THE "RAMBLER."

SECOND LETTER TO THE EDITORS OF THE CATHOLIC JOURNALS.

NEW BRIGHTON, *February* 21, 1854.

GENTLEMEN—Within the last two years, an opinion and a feeling have been extending through almost every rank of Catholic society, that some few converts have been erecting themselves into a sort of inquisitorial tribunal; in these coteries the habits of the old clergy have been rather too freely criticised, and an unbecoming assumption and an ill-concerted dictation gave much pain to numerous Catholics, who were too respectful to check and too confiding to notice, this now almost universal impression. When the heart is full of anything, the mouth cannot long keep the secret enclosed within the gushing bosom; and hence our new critics are not ashamed to tell the public, that they themselves are henceforth the infallible guides and the sole teachers of Catholicity in Great Britain and Ireland. Let us hear them in page 176: "There is no foundation whatever for the prevalent Protestant notion that he (Dr. Cahill) is to be taken as a chosen champion of the faith."

It is the first time during my three years' residence in England, I have heard of the championship of England in Theology even talked of; it is to me quite a new idea; and it appears to me to be a phrase, rather borrowed from the old London Ring than from any modern rumor. I have never heard that phrase applied to my humble labors; I have asked several clergymen if they had heard it; and all have declared the idea to be quite a new thing lately promulgated from Portman-street. But, although the public have never conceived the bright topping idea referred to, not so the three Parsons in Portman-street; their indignation at any one occupying any place, however humble, becomes so irresistably consuming that they cannot avoid telling all whom it may concern, that Dr. Cahill, or any priest, , or the most eminent ecclesiastic in England is not to dare to light a farthing candle in the Church without their kind permission; that Portman-street is the great ecclesiastical gasometer of the nation; that no lamp can be fed from any other source; and that they, (not Dr. Cahill, or any other priest, not having undergone the double-milled training of Portman-street), are the sole importers of theology into this country and the redoubted champions of England. Let any candid reader review the page quoted from their malicious article, and it is impossible not to see the absurd affectation and the killing self-sufficiency of these blind half-bred zealots.

But the public will be much surprised at the next quotation from these models of Christian teaching. In page 176 they say: "Why do the Bishops and Clergy permit him to write and lecture as he does?"

What will the reader think of the constant, the unbroken falsehood of these men, when I now tell them, that, since I came to England, I have written only four letters on religious subjects; and these letters were answers to challenges, repeated challenges from Protestant clergymen. Hear me. Up to March, 1853, I never even acknowledged the receipt of the numerous and insulting letters of challenge which I received from all quarters. Having made a rule to give no offence in my duties as a priest, to any human being in his consciencious belief, I did not even reply to these challenges. But, an English Bishop, second to none in his lofty position, having heard me utter these sentiments at his own table, where I had the honor of being invited, suggested and requested that in future I should reply to all these letters of challenge. Accordingly I sent my first reply to a clergyman in Glasgow. My second reply was made in Letterkenny, in the house of the venerated and beloved father of the Irish Bishops. My third reply, at Birkenhead, was written in the house, and with the cordial sanction of an English Canon and Dean, a gentleman most decidedly equal to any clergyman in England of his years and station, and who, I fondly hope, will yet add an expected ornament to the English hierarchy. And my fourth and last letter was penned while travelling in the company of the Bishop of that diocese, whose consent (on my own responsibility) I had previously obtained to answer any of the numerous challenges I had received in his diocese.

Gentlemen, I have here explained an important point in the letter of the veracious Parsons of Portman-street. Their language is an unmitigated falsehood; and affords an irritating instance, that while these parsons have changed their faith they cannot change their logic; and that in furthering an ungenerous and an ill-founded feeling, they can have recourse to the self-same bare-faced misstatements as their former companions—the calumniating mountebanks of the Protestant Alliance.

But this is not all; let any one read pages 176 and 177 of (what I am *now* justified in calling) their lying article, and he will read about as impertinent a lecture to the Bishops and Priests of England as could securely be penned by any man, outside of Bedlam—read it, Gentlemen. The Bishops are there taught what their rights are, and what they are not. They are informed to temper their authority with prudence; that much of their authority is a mere moral influence, not a right; and, of course, as the superior teaches the inferior, the English hierarchy must in future learn Canon law, and above all they must learn to behave themselves well while under the ecumenical tuition of "the three tailors from Tooley-street." Nor is this all, on this long homily, "*ex sermonibus sanctorum Redactorum.*" Not at all; the English priests are also informed that the only reason why Bishops do not more frequently reduce them to the proper sense of their duty, is for fear they would "recalcitrate hopelessly." The English clergy are, therefore, placed in the position of eternal gratitude to these sleepless sentinels, for putting them on their guard under their perilous circumstances, and warning them with such timely prudence, in their conciliating periodical, of the fate that must await them, if they trespass too far on the endurance of their Bishops. While on this point, I gladly here seize the opportunity of expressing in an enduring public letter, what I said in Ireland with undying gratitude, in reference to the English Priesthood.

As I am leaving England in a few weeks, perhaps never again to return; and as I have made a final engagement to visit America in some months hence, I can now freely indulge my own heart in giving utterance to feelings which just now, at my departure, cannot be liable even to a suspicion of flattery or selfishness. During the three years I have been in England, I have lived exclusively with the clergy; and from the moment I entered under their roof, I was placed entirely under their control. I never delivered a lecture or moved one step without their command or sanction; and their courtesy, their kindness, their affection to me, cannot be expressed in any one form of words which I can here employ. They all, without even one exception, received me as their nearest friend; I made their house my own; and if I were to add any one feature more remarkable than another in their attention to me, it is, that I always felt they accumulated on me the distinguished compliments because I was an Irishman. I wish to repeat this idea over again, that my countrymen may read this letter in Ireland; and that whenever they shall have an opportunity (when I am far away from them), they will ever express to an English Priest, wherever they meet him, for my sake, some token of the vast amount of the gratitude which I owe them, which I shall carry with me to the grave, but which I can never hope to repay.

In reference to the article of the Reviewer, therefore, where they ask: "Why do the Bishops and Priests permit me to lecture?" it furnishes a sad instance of the folly, the pitiful, exasperating folly—and I will be excused now, when I add the lies of these three self-sufficient inquisitors; and on this point I would venture to offer one remark to the Bishops, whom they presume to lecture; and this is, that these prelates would in common charity, take their mad lying pens out of their unsteady hands and close the new shop in Portman-street, where they have erected their forge, for manufacturing culpable falsehood and public scandal. Their remarks in reference to the clergy, in the extract quoted above, do not press on me so much as on the gentlemen who have invited me to their churches; and before the expiration of a month hence, it may be, that they shall find it necessary to retract their foolish offensiveness. I have said, in my last letter, that I should surprise the Catholic public with the rampant Protestantism of these writers; and hence I proceed to fulfil my most unwilling promise; at the same time believing that my remarks on this part of their article will give an additional warning to Catholics against the Protestant Bible.

Those half-converted gentlemen, are so unconscious of their want of biblical and theological knowledge, that they undisguisedly, but disedifyingly utter sentiments in reference to the Protestant Bible, which are the appropriate expressions of the Soupers of Connemara—misstatements, genteel Protestantism, and rank heresy are contained in almost every word they have written on this subject.

In page 170, they say:

"The Protestant Bible has abundance of errors, and some of them of very serious importance;" and in a few lines further on in the same page, they call these errors "mistranslations."

Here we learn from our superiors at Portman-street, that clear, decided additions, subtractions, suppression of whole books, denial of the inspiration of the whole books, alterations, in facts, in words, in tenses, and consequently in doctrine, are things of rather "serious importance;" that is to say, they are things not to be laughed at. Has any one ever heard of serious heresy—a term, which, I suppose, these teachers employ by way of contrasting it with "jocose heresy." And has any Catholic work ever described sins, as sins of "importance!" this word so offensive to "ears polite," makes the crime of heresy look rather a respectable thing. The old priests who have not had the advantage of being brought up and educated at Portman-street, would call these wilful perversions of the Bible, according to the example of St. Paul, by the names of grievous, soul-killing, damnable, subversive of authority, and giving the lie to the Holy Ghost: but now, the Lord be praised, we are informed that these mistakes are merely like the fluctuation in the funds or the cotton-market; or like an increased duty on tea, they are rather serious and important; and they are to be described in the same language, as when we speak of the improvements in our shipping interests, or the casualties of commerce; they are things not quite a joke, and therefore are matters of importance. The very phrase proves that our Reviewers do not know the ordinary language of our ancient Catechism.

But they go further, where they call these heretical declarations of false doctrine by the genteel name of "mistranslations." Indeed! Upon my word, we have a right to be proud of the masters of the *Rambler*, when the omission in the Protestant Bible of two books of the Maccabees, containing thirty-one chapters, is only a "mistranslation!" We have splendid teachers, indeed, when we learn from our superiors in Portman-street, that six books of the Old Testament, declared apocryphal by the Protestant Bible, against the supreme authority of the Church, is a fault merely amounting to a mistranslation, and is just a sort of thing that a man ought to think of before dinner, when he is disposed to be serious.

And when any of the old-fashioned priests (who have not read the genteel Theology of our new masters,) charge the old Protestant Bible (still adopted by the Lutherans) with throwing out of the Canon, the epistle of St. Paul to the Hebrews, the epistle of St. James, the second epistle of St. Peter, the second and third of St. John, and the epistle of St. Jude, the Lutherans and all Protestants can quote the Theologians of Portman-street, as superiors, and the champions of all England and Wales and the Colonies, by observing that these trifling things are indeed rather "serious" and are "mistranslations!" And when any poor persecuted Catholic from Dingle, Kells, Achill, or Connemera will ask our infallible Theologians of the unfortunate *Rambler*, if there be any harm in purchasing, keeping, and reading a Bible, which throws out books declared canonical by the authority of the Church, which despises therefore that authority, which substitutes facts, which adds prepositions, and in fine which changes the word of God at pleasure, how happy must that poor Catholic feel, when he has the superior advantage of learning (the Lord be praised) that this kind of a THING, is indeed rather a "serious" consideration; that the thing is of some "importance," and that the whole weight of the thing may be classed under the head of a "mistranslation." Only think of the accomplished and respected parish priest of Connemara, Rev. Mr. Kavanagh, exhorting his flock against the Soupers and Bible-readers, telling them that the danger of receiving Bibles from these wolves, was rather a "serious" thing; but that the guilt of their receiving these Bibles, amounted to an important literary fault, namely, mistranslation.

But, as these gentlemen are so finished in Greek and Hebrew, I shall take the great liberty of daring to ask them some few questions, touching this case of "mistranslation," and concluding this section of my observations by calling their learned attention to the view taken of the point at issue, by the Council of Trent in its serious declarations, called "Anathemas."

I shall now proceed to examine the facts of the case, to see if our masters of the *Rambler* have critically told the truth, in calling the errors of the Protestant Bible by the name of "mistranslations." One of our proofs of the doctrine on the official right of the Church to impose temporal punishment, or penance for sin, is taken from the first epistle of St. Paul to the Corinthians, chapter the 5th: "*Ede kekrika os paron ton outo touto katergasamenon.*" Our translation is: "I have already judged as though I were present, him that hath done so."—The Protestant version is: "I have already judged concerning him," &c. Our translation, which any one can see, gives St. Paul the power to judge the man—"*ton katergasamenon*:" while the Protestant translation makes St. Paul only judge the case, not the man: and this palpable corruption is done, not by a mistranslation, but by the introduction of a preposition not contained in the original text.

In Matthew, chapter 3rd, the Church translates the word "*metanoeite*," "do penance;" whereas the Protestant Bible has it, "repent ye." Their meaning is founded on the philosophical derivation, "*metanoos*," change of mind. On the same principle might they translate our word "collation" (viz., our fasting meal,) into the word "conference." And hence, if they use the words "repent ye" in the case before us, with philolo gical accuracy, it can be said with the same propriety, that on fasting days, the Catholics at their breakfast eat a conference; as every scholar knows that the philosophical meaning of the word "collation," is "a conference." But there is more mischief in the two cases adduced than the genteel fault of "mistranslation." These two gross additions and perversions involve a greater crime than this delicate Protestant phrase: they go to invalidate the Sacrament of Penance: they not only insinuate, but palpably deny the existence of penitential works; and they ascribe the justification of the sinner, to mere internal sorrow, to the exclusion of the works of penance. Now, in order to convince the readers of the *Rambler*, of the false guidance of the three Parsons of Portman-street, I shall quote the Canons of the Council of Trent on this point, which will show these readers that these mistranslations are not quite so jocose as our masters have stated them:

Canon the Twelfth: "If any one saith, that God always remits the whole punishment, together with the guilt: and that the satisfaction of the penitents is no other than the faith, whereby they apprehend that Christ has satisfied for them, let him be Anathema."

Canon the Thirteenth: "If any one saith, that satisfaction for sins is nowise made to God by the punishment inflicted by Him, or patiently borne, or by those enjoined by the priests, let him be Anathema."

Canon the Fifteenth: "If any one saith, that the satisfactions by which penitents redeem their sins, are not a worship of God, but traditions of men, let him be Anathema."

I undertake to say, gentlemen, that before I shall have concluded the genteel doctrine of "mistranslations," the public will learn that curses upon curses, Anathemas heaped on Anathemas, will fall upon the unfortunate dupes who may be induced to follow the palpable ignorance, the undisguised Protestantism, and the heretical teaching of the Parsons' Hornbook. But I proceed:—

In the Epistle of St. James, where the sick are commanded, in the imperative mood, to bring in the Priests of the Church to annoint the sick man, and to forgive him his sins—the Church translates the words, "*Proskalesastho tous Presbuterous tes Ekklesias,*"—"Let him bring in the Priests of the Church;" whereas the Protestant Bible has it, "Let him call for the Elders of the church." Now, in reading Cicero, if any schoolboy, meeting with the words, "*Patres conscripti,*" translated them, "O conscript married men having children," the world would laugh at the stupidity of the boy: and his master would tell (not the paragons of Portman-street,) that the word "fathers," did not critically mean married men with children, but men of official, senatorial, legislating, governing dignity. And precisely on the same principle and historical fact, (independently of the authority of the Church,) the word "*Presbuterous,*" does not mean any old man in the Church, but it means the men invested with official, judicial, governing dignity: it means authority, not years: and hence the Protestant mistranslation substitutes one fact for another in this case, and is a clear, decided, obvious declaration of a heretical doctrine.

But let us examine the Council of Trent on this thing, which is not a joke, or a thing rather serious: *vide* Homiliam de Portman-street:

CANON THE FOURTH—ON EXTREME UNCTION:

"If any one saith, that the Presbyters of the Church are not Priests, who have been ordained by a Bishop, but Elders in each community . . . . let him be Anathema."

Now, it is clear from these Canons, tnat the Anathema of the Church are pronounced on any one who saith the doctrines referred to; but our Protestant Bible expresses these doctrines as clearly as words can express them; and hence, I feel, their own imprudence has placed them in a difficulty from which not all their stratagems can extricate them.

But, I shall proceed: In Genesis, chapter 14th, "Melchisedech," king of Salem, bringing forth bread and wine, for he was a priest of the Most High God, blessed Abraham." In this text, the *causal* Hebrew particle, "for," is introduced, in order to show that Melchisedech brought forth bread and wine because he was a priest: and that therefore his office was to offer bread and wine. But the Protestant Bible takes away the particle "for," and substitutes the propositional copulative conjunction "and," in order to make the words "bread and wine" be a mere casual occurrence, and not a thing necessary to be offered: and thus laying the foundation of denying the Priesthood in the New Law.

In Malachy, chapter 1st, we find the words:

"From the rising of the sun to the going down, my name is great among the Gentiles, and in every place there is sacrifice, and there is offered to my name a clean oblation."

In the Protestant Bible, the words are:—

"And in every place incense shall be offered to my name: and a pure offering.'

In this text, the very sense is not only mutilated: false words are not only introduced, as any one can see by reference to the original text; but the word incense is substituted for sacrifice. It is putting the thing which accompanied the sacrifice, for the sacrifice itself: as if Protestant writers would put the candles that are lighted on the altar during Mass, or put the bell that rings during the Elevation, for the Mass itself; and then tell the world, that the Mass is a mere ceremony of a bell and a lighted candle.

In the same way, in all the Prophets, wherever any remote or covered idea of sacrifice is hinted or expressed, the Protestant Bible, in all these passages, always substitutes the word "prayer."

In order to show how exceedingly incorrect and mischievous it is for any untutored tyro, in our Church, to call these gross corruptions and misstatements by the name of "mistranslations," we have only to read the Council of Trent on this point, in reference to the sacrifice of the Mass

Canon the Second: "If any one saith, that the sacrifice of the Mass is only a sacrifice of praise and thanksgiving; or that it is a bare commemoration of the sacrifice of the cross, and not a propitiatory sacrifice . . . . . let him be Anathema."

I have thus, Gentlemen, taken pains to prove that the plain miswording, the additions, the corruptions, the entire removal of whole books, the denial, and the contempt of the authority of the Church, involved in denying the authenticity of other books of the Holy Scriptures, constitute an awful amount of guilt in the Protestant Bible; and I trust I have demonstrated that this guilt is expressed in such clear language, that no reader can mistake it; and I have added to this indictment against the Protestant Bible several Anathemas of the Council of Trent, in all these points at issue: and hence I shall be enabled, in the remaining part of this letter, to place before this nation (what I now am justified in designating) the ignorance, the assumption, and the impertinence of the article of the *Rambler*, proceeding from the half-bred, half-converted clique, who have written such calumnies of me, and who have deliberately penned the following most gross misstatement, and which at the same time evinces such a decided leaning to the Protestant Bible: Hear their words:

"Take, for instance, the astounding assertion, that he 'would prefer that a Catholic should read the worst books of immorality,' than the Protestant Bible! If any of our readers have not already seen Dr. Cahill's letter, they will lift up their hands in astonishment, and question the accuracy of our quotation; nevertheless, we assure them that we are giving the exact words."

In the whole course of my life, I have never met anything like the undeviating falsehood, the reckless disregard for common honesty and of truth, which appear almost in every sentence of these malignant Parsons.

In the following quotation from my letter, you will see at a glance, whether they have given my exact words, as they have emphatically "assured" their readers. My words are as follows, in answer to Mr. Burns's appeal to his Bible:

"Considering the shameful forgery of the Protestant Bible, I would prefer that a Catholic should read the worst books of immorality, than this forgery in God's Word, this slander of Christ. Old age can check immorality; but the forgeries of God's book, the lies told of Christ, the wicked perversion of the inspired volume, the base substitution of words, the flagrant robbery of the text of life, are so many hideous crimes of Protestantism, that in vengeance for such blasphemous interpolation, the curse of all crimes, and of all errors, and of naked infidelity, seems to be inflicted on your entire nation. And this is the Bible, this public forgery on the name of the Holy Ghost, this libel of God the Father, this slander on Christ, which you wish to give to the poor children of the Irish."

Could it be believed possible, that any man, pretending to the character of common decency, could write such a gross falsehood and trick, as are contained in the quotation which he calls my "exact words." I need no greater revenge over this wretched clique, than the indignant contempt which they must receive from the decision of any man who reads even this one shameful misstatement. And now let us read their next paragraph, which follows:

In speaking of Protestants they say:—

"What story of Catholic wickedness will they not henceforth believe? What tale of priestly licentiousness will from this time, be too monstrous for their credulity? The Protestant Bible has abundance of errors, it is true, and some of them of very serious importance; but is it not a violation of all common sense and decency, to pretend that a Catholic had better read the filthy productions of obscenity, than the book in which these mistranslations occur? Is there a priest in the United Kingdom who would bear out Dr. Cahill in such a notion? Would not all, with one accord, denounce it as a perfect portent in the domain of morals and casuistry?"

Here any one can behold the wrathful resentment of the Parson, at my denunciation of the mistranslations.—Could any speech at Exeter-hall surpass the malignant spirit detectable in this quotation? But I repeat again the same sentiments; and I again declare, in spite of these advocates of the Protestant corrupted, forged Bible, that I would prefer (between the two evils,) works of immorality to works of infidelity; and I shall forthwith state my reasons:

Firstly, then, old age, of itself, cools down the immoral heart, while infidelity and heresy gains strength over the enfeebled intellect. Secondly, immorality is scouted in all society of every creed, and must not dare to lift its head except in secret; while Protestant infidelity is lauded, encouraged, rewarded, and therefore confirmed by the very society that condemns immorality. Thirdly, immorality stands opposed only to the ten commandments of God; while infidelity adds to this crime, the opposition to Christ and the authority of the Church. Fourthly, immorality practices vice, but dare not teach it in public; while infidelity not only practices deadly, mortal guilt, but teaches it, declaims it, demands honor for it; and can command large audiences to learn it. Fifthly, immorality has generally but one accomplice at a time, while infidelity can have ten thousand. Sixthly, all the infidels of Christian countries are apostates from the Church, and St. Paul tells us that, "it is impossible for such persons to be renewed again to penance;" whereas there is no such impossibility pronounced against immorality. Seventhly, the immoral man can repent, and be prepared to be forgiven in a short time: but the infidel man has to repent also, and to learn the Christian doctrine, which requires time and perseverance. Eighthly, the immoral man merely injures himself and a few accomplices; while the man who adopts the Protestant forgeries, in spite of the Church, joins the Soupers, encourages the Protestant Alliance, betrays the Priesthood, sells his country, and is the enemy of God and a perjurer to man. Ninthly, the immoral man acknowledges his weakness and his crime, and so far pays homage to God's law and judgments; while the infidel refuses homage, makes a profession of opposition to inspired teaching, and opposes an obstacle to the success of the Cross. Tenthly, the Canons of the Council of Trent, have pronounced several Anathemas against the man that saith any of the clear infidelities of the forged Protestant Bible; while the immoral man is left to the ordinary denunciations of the Gospel. I therefore repeat the proposition I have advanced, and which has so much offended our masters the Convert Parsons ot Portman-street. Lastly, one act is on moral principles more grievously sinful than another, if in its "end, object, and circumstances," one contains a larger amount of guilt under these three heads than the other: and hence as infidelity, for the reasons already stated, opens an extent of guilt indefinitely larger than mere immorality, it strikes me, that the Converts have read as little of our moral treatises, as they have of Mr. Burns' letter; and that they have, with all their other qualities, a matchless effrontery, of which the public will soon form a correct opinion.

I have thus given my reasons for the statement which

I made, and I undertake to say, that in place of denouncing the casuistry of Dr. Cahill, the whole nation, lay and clerical, will say of the clique who praise the Protestant Bible, that if they were alive in the days of Elizabeth, they would be found near Tom Crammer's grave praising the new parliamentary prayers, and trying to patch up a piebald Puseyite gospel, in order to suit the genteel Protestant taste of the day.

Gentlemen, I am not done with Portman-street as yet. I have not reached as yet, the lowest depths of their folly, their uncharitableness, their malignity, and their calumny. I beg to assure the public that I have charges still more grievous to put forth, on the subject of their articles in the *Rambler*, which will still more surprise the public; and hence, while I ask the favor of a *third* and LAST letter in your columns, I think I can with truth convey to you the thanks of the clergy and laity of these countries for your kindness to me in the present instance. The Reviewers, of course, will answer me in their anonymous periodical; but give me your impartial columns, and, depend upon it, that their conduct to me will not leave ten readers to the Parson's Hornbook within three months from this date. The public know me too long to encourage a book of falsehood and calumny against me: and I feel my humble name has been stamped with too flattering partiality by the public approval to permit any man living, or set of men, be he or they who they will, without putting forth whatever power I possess, and covering my gratuitous calumniators with universal and well-merited censure. In all this exposure they must blame themselves: when they joined us, we clothed them in the lion's skin, and admitted them to our society, begging of them to be *silent*: but if they foolishly begin to bray, and imprudently raise their voice and show their *long ears*, the fault is entirely their own.

I am Gentlemen, your obedient servant,

D. W. CAHILL, D.D.

REV. DR. CAHILL'S SPEECH

AT A GREAT MEETING IN LIVERPOOL.

On August 30th 1852, a large and important meeting of Catholics took place in the Concert Hall, Liverpool. The secretary having read an address to the Rev. Dr. Cahill on his appearance amongst them, and then having detailed the happy results exhibited by the absence of a procession on St. Patrick's Day last, stated that the people were resolved in future to abstain from all processions. The celebrated Divine came forward, and delivered a speech, of which we copy the abstract given by the journals; and as it was pronounced amidst the most rapturous enthusiasm, and immense cheering, we will omit the frequent exclamations which did interrupt at every moment the orator. The multitude dispersed after adopting a resolution to the effect that the Catholics of Liverpool were deeply grateful to the Rev. Dr. Cahill for the magnificent address he had delivered, and that they were resolved in future to do all in their power to carry out the views expressed by him and the venerated clergy of Liverpool.

The Rev. Doctor said:

He could assure them, that in the whole course of his life, he never beheld a more important and influential meeting—none but an Irishman could understand it. And what was he to say to that great meeting? He had it. He was a "chip of the old block" himself, and as such he stood before them. He was glad to hear them praise him so, for he was sure he must deserve something when they did so, for if he did not, such applause would not come from that great meeting. He would, if he could, contradict them in what they had said, but, if he did so, he would be contradicting himself. If he were anything in their sight, it was they who made him so—they had created him something. They had given him strength in Liverpool, and that proved their own power. He had something to tell them—he had got a new suit of clothes since he last saw them. He wished to appear before them as respectable as he could; and who did they think was his tailor? Why no less a personage than Lord Derby. It was a fact. Lord Derby had made the coat he wore; and he believed they would think it a good fit. He begged of them also to look at his vest. It was cut precisely after the fashion of the 4th Victoria—the Processions Act—by Lord Derby, who had become tailor and general barber to the Pope. Yes, it was Lord Derby who made his clothes; and as that Noble Lord had turned tailor and barbor to the Pope, and as he (Dr. Cahill) was a Popish priest, he thought it right to patronise Lord Derby; and so now he appeared before the meeting in his new parliamentary dress, and if any one in that meeting had garments to make, he would advise them to take such, for manufacturing to Downing-street. He had been writing a letter to Lord Derby, and they would find it in the Dublin papers of Saturday next. It was that letter which made the clothes he now wore. When he looked on that great meeting, and saw such a number of people present, his point was gained in Liverpool. What could he say, or how could he thank them? They had followed the advice which he had given them, to observe peace, law, and order, and if they wished to continue in that brilliant course for the future, he would ask them to hold up their hands as a pledge for the future. Before he quitted the subject of Lord Derby's tailoring, he must observe that although he was long aware of the dexterity exhibited on the thimbles by that Noble Lord, yet he was not aware that his Lordship was so expert at the needle as he proved himself to be. They had told him that it was he who instructed and guided them on the late occasion of their having given up their annual procession. Well, if he were their guide and instructor, he would do something in return for them for their obedience; he would therefore tell them some news—news from the Continent, and even other places in the world, and he was much mistaken if they would not be pleased with what he had to tell them. He would begin with Austria. When it trembled and shook with revolution—when Hungary raised up Kossuth in order to free his native land, that miscreant committed suicide on his country. Yes, he did, but who were the prime levers in that murder?—the English Government.

Mark, not the English people, for it should be always borne in mind that he made the most emphatic difference between the English Government and the English people. To illustrate that, he had never yet met an Englishman who did not cry over the misfortunes and the misgovernment of Ireland—sigh for the advancement of the trade and commerce of that country, and longed to see her free and happy. Therefore, let no one connect the English Government with the English people. It was now on record, that the English Government were the engines which deluged the Continent with blood, and made the whole fabric of European kingdoms tremble with revolution. It was by the machinations of that Government, that Lombardy, Sardinia, and other countries were left tottering on their unsteady foundations. He need only refer them to the manner in which poor Charles Albert was treated and betrayed by one Howard—they were all pretty well aware of that, and now that unfortunate monarch was rotting in his grave, the victim of English perfidy. Let them again look at Rome—Rome, that belonged to the Popes—a few Italian States, about half the size of Connaught in Ireland.

These States were given as presents by the emperors and kings of Europe to the Popes, and no power in Europe had a right to interfere with the government or management of these States. In fact, they were private property given to the Popes, but England's Government cast its eyes towards Italy, and sent a Lord Minto there. They had heard of Lord Minto. He (Lord Minto) said, he was asked to go to Rome, but he was not; yet he did go, and by his vile conduct he involved the whole country in a state of frightful confusion, and attempted to upset the very foundation of the Vatican itself. The King of Naples trusted in the English Government, and the English Ambassador at that court supplied a torch that nearly destroyed that poor country. Let them go to Spain, and look at the English work there in 1832. The English Government promised to place a usurper on the throne of that kingdom, provided they got in return the Church property of Spain—and they did get it, and placed the usurper on the throne. They demolished the Convents and Nunneries—turned out the Monks on 1s. 3d. a day, and the Nuns on 10 1-2d.—they left but one Convent standing in the kingdom—broke down the religious establishments—destroyed the dynasty of that country, and committed the most awful acts the world ever beheld—and were guilty of the most perfidious cruelty ever heard of in any country on the face of the earth.

Again, let them look at Portugal--the English Government entered into a conspiracy there, against the Catholic Church property, and in that country there was another instance of the murderous hand of England in the spoliation of Church property. He now came to France. The revolution of 1830, (he saw it, for he was there at the time,) was fomented and got up by the English Government. The English Government was at the beginning and end of the revolutions that had taken place on the Continent, and which shook the foundations of the empires. They almost annihilated Catholic education in those countries he had mentioned. The Cross—the emblem of man's salvation, was trodden under foot. Morality ceased, and all those horrors were committed by a clique of the English Government for the purpose of extinguishing the Catholic Church. However, he was glad to tell them, that the aspect of affairs had lately changed, and that Austria, Sardinia, and Naples, were not now cursed with such iniquity.

And as for France, just now, she had it all her own way. Austria, Italy, and France, had seen the machinations practised towards them; and they had driven the usurpers from their territories; and these countries were now free in religion, politics, and Catholic education. The English Government had fired the Church with the torch of infidelity; but he (Dr. Cahill,) had come to tell them, that the Catholic Church had recovered part of its property on the Continent. In Austria, the Emperor had placed the Catholic schools under the Jesuits—and could the youth of any country have such perfect instructors? The King of Prussia had given a full and fair extension to Catholic education. Rome had maintained her ancient name for religion and education. The King of Naples had discovered his mistake; and now all the schools in Naples were under the control and vigilance of the Catholic clergy. The best of all remained to be told—France—glorious France—had recovered her long lost rights, and now enjoyed the blessings of Catholic education. He then alluded to the College of France at a former period, when the students were ordered to read the Catechism, but so far had infidelity worked there, that they refused, ran out of the College into the streets, shouting out, "Long live the Devil, but no Catechism for us!" Look at France now—the oldest daughter of the Catholic Church, which can date as far back as the renowned Charlemagne—at least one thousand years.

He next alluded to the conduct of France, who drove seventy-three thousand plotting miscreants from Switzerland—fellows who were bribed to foment rebellion and revolution all over the Continent; but the Prince President, soon made them walk about their business. In 1846 and 1847, the Catholic colleges, the monasteries, and nunneries in Switzerland were overthrown by the miscreants whom he had spoken of. And they even penetrated so far as the monastery of Mount St. Bernard, and committed ravages wherever they went. No country on the earth presented such scenes of murder and bloodshed.

He would now tell them the object he had in these matters, in order to contrast such horrible atrocities with peace, law, and order. The workings which he had mentioned, were the workings of the British Government, but Ireland, amidst surrounding nations, preserved peace, law, and order, and loyalty to the throne of England. But Lord John Russell was not satisfied with that, he sent out his missive to create a revolution—he did not succeed. How has he been answered? He (the Rev. Dr. Cahill,) would tell them how Louis Napoleon had answered him.

The other day, at the ceremony of blessing the eagles,

the imperial eagles of France, which belonged to his uncle, Prince Louis Napoleon, with an army of three hundred thousand fighting men—in presence of the Archbishop of Paris, had a throne raised for that celebrated prelate seventy-two feet high, and above that throne, a cross one hundred and forty-four feet high. The Archbishop celebrated solemn High Mass, in the presence of three hundred thousand French soldiers, armed in steel—and at the elevation of the Sacred Host, 100 pieces of French ordinance were discharged in thanksgiving to God.

That was not all; the 300,000 soldiers of France, drew their swords, knelt on one knee, (as is the custom in all Catholic countries for soldiers,) and amidst the clang of three hundred thousand swords, and the thunder of one hundred cannons, the Holy Host was lifted to Heaven—the grandest spectacle ever witnessed in Paris, since the days of Charlemagne. That was the answer given by Louis Napoleon to Lord John Russell, who incited the people of this country to trample on the Cross, and burn the effigy of the Blessed Virgin Mary. It was a good reply on the part of Louis Napoleon. When his (the Rev. Dr. Cahill's) tailor, Lord Derby, issued his proclamation against a religious procession which took place at Ballinasloe—the Irish name of that place was "*Kylena spithogue,*"—he liked the Irish names—Louis Napoleon answered him as follows:—Riding in his carriage the other day along the Boulevards, the Prince saw a religious procession headed by a number of clergy, who carried a Cross, and when he saw it, he bowed to the Priests, raised his hat, and when the Cross appeared, he stood up in the coach, took off his hat, and remained uncovered, bowing his head all the time until the procession passed on. That was the answer he gave Lord Derby. He answered John Russell one way, and he replied to Mr. tailor Derby in another.

The Reverend Gentleman went on to detail the proceedings which had recently taken place on the Continent, in reference to the expulsion of English incendiaries; and, attributed such to the firmness, good sense, and determination of Louis Napoleon, who was a good Catholic, and loved the religion in which he was educated, and in which he would die. He (the Rev. Dr.) would call another witness in the shape of America; and the Sultan of Constantinople, who assisted a short time ago, at the marriage of a Catholic lady and Greek gentleman in that city, the ceremony being performed by a Catholic Bishop. The Sultan attended and remained uncovered, and expressed himself in terms of admiration for the Catholic Church; and observed, that no man should stand covered in the presence of God, and while assisting at a most sacred rite of the Catholic religion.

He then summed up his observations, and said he had thrown them out for the consideration of the English Government, if they still wished to pursue the persecution of the Catholic Church. He then referred to Greece—the late intended quarrel, which arose about the loss of some Englishman's breeches and a cabbage garden; and after dwelling in a happy strain on the return of an English fleet crowned with victory from Greece, (after making the above conquest,) he went on to state the difficulties of England with America, China, India, Kaffirland,

&c., and said that England was not at present able to fight an American tom-cat. And as to prevent the Americans from going where they pleased, he was sure so far as any opposition that England could give to America, the boats of the latter, might sail into the bay of Galway, and catch as much fish as they could. China, the Burmese Empire in India, Kaffirland, America, Canada, the latter only waiting for a favorable opportunity to shake off the English yoke. France, with nearly a million of soldiers—but no one could tell what France would do yet; and they should remember that in England alone there were two millions of Chartists only wanting to put their hands to their staves, for they all had staves; and the Manchester factory people, who if deprived of cheap bread, and the import of eleven million of pounds worth of cotton from America, would assuredly starve if the supplies were stopped—they would have nothing to eat unless they devoured brick or the Established Church. The latter, he thought, would be more agreeable picking than baked clay. All those things were pressing on England at the present moment, and yet she was the only country in the whole world that persecuted her subjects for their religious opinions. Yes the government of England was the solitary one on the earth's surface that persecuted her own people for the sake and in the name of religion. Let him again not lay this crime on the people of England— it was the Government. If England only knew her duty, she would hold out the right hand of fellowship to her subjects in Ireland, and that hand would be met in affection and harmony.

He drew a picture of the desolation to which Ireland

had been reduced, and gave, amongst others, an instance of where a poor widow woman in Mayo (her name was Byrne,) had to carry her seven sons to the grave, which she dug with her own hands, and when the last of her boys was deposited there, she died herself, and was burried in the same grave, shroudless and coffinless; two poor women having borne the body wrapped in hay, to its final resting place. All this, while there was nineteen million of money in the Exchequer of England, a great portion of it having been plundered from Ireland. He gave several instances of where the dead bodies of the people were dragged from the holes into which they had been thrown, by dogs.

He knew an educated man in Dublin, an apothecary, who had to go into the South Union Workhouse. The poor of Ireland had sunk into the grave—the middle classes had descended to the vacant place of the poor, and the landlords had been swallowed up by the infernal law made by themselves and the Government. Emigration was now sweeping away the bone and sinew of Ireland, and whatever money was left in it. And was it for hatred of the country the people were flying to glorious America? No, it was hatred of the English Government; and who could tell, in the course of a short time, what that hatred might not eventuate in? In the midst of all Ireland's misfortunes, she lost one of the greatest patriots that the world ever saw—the burning flood of whose eloquence made tyrants tremble? Oh! if he were alive now, with what a meteor voice would he not fly through the country, comforting the afflicted, and seeking redress for the people of his glorious native land!

He need not tell that meeting that he alluded to the immortal O'Connell. Oh! when he was called to the reward of a well-spent life—liberty gave a departing sigh in Ireland, and patriotism's sun set in the land of his nativity. Such a time did the enemies of the country take upon them to renew persecution. And yet during seven centuries there was not one act of disloyalty ever proved against the faithful clergy of Ireland. On the contrary, the people of Ireland had suffered and died in defence of the English throne.

He then went on to show how the Irish had acted in the case of Charles the First, and from him down to King James—that they had suffered for their loyalty; and the only return they got, was persecution, insult, and death. He then proceeded to thank the Irish people in Liverpool for their cheerful obedience to his request, and the request of the venerated bishop and clergy of the town and district, with whose co-operation he had been successful in preventing a procession on St. Patrick's Day last.

He told an interesting anecdote about a man, (to show what feeling the Irish entertain for anything belonging to the country,) whom he saw leaving Dublin and taking a dog with him to America. The man told him the dog cried so much when he saw the house pulled down by the landlord, that he could not leave the poor brute behind him. At this moment the dog began to bark, when the man said, "Sir, he hears us talking of the landlord now, and he knows all about the way he treated us, as well as myself!"

The Reverend Speaker then drew a comparison between the adventures of Lord John Russell, Lord Derby, and others, and the travels of Gulliver, in which he was most happy, and loudly applauded. He then impressed on the assembly the necessity of their strictly adhering to the principles of peace, law, and order, and to continue in the good resolve they had formed—to abide by the advice of their excellent clergy, and that they would be happy in this world and the next. He next alluded to the determination of the Irish Members, and said, although the Government might vapor under their weakness, yet the resolution of a steady band in St. Stephen's, would soon wring justice from them. He implored all, to be united in bonds of peace and charity, and to take the hand of the English and Scotch, and identify themselves with these people; and for their cheerful acquiescence to his request last year, he promised them an excursion to Wales next May, when they would renew their friendship, and invite even their enemies to accompany them, in order to show that they were the preservers of peace, law, and order. It was by such conduct as this, that they could conquer their persecutors, and defy the world. He then passed a well-merited compliment on the chairman, for his honesty, patriotism, and love of religion ; and said, while the people had the wise counsel of such a man and the clergy, they need not doubt of their success. He sat down amidst the most rapturous and prolonged cheering.

REV. DR. CAHILL'S LECTURE.

SOCIAL CONDITION OF IRELAND.

In accordance with announcement, the Rev. D. W. Cahill, D. D., delivered, for the benefit of St. Augustin's Schools, four Lectures at the Concert Hall, Lord Nelson street, Liverpool—three on Natural Philosophy, and the fourth, which is reported as follows, on the Social Condition of Ireland. The Hall was crowded to excess, there being not fewer, perhaps, than 2,500 persons assembled. On the platform were several of the well-known Catholic Clergy of Liverpool and neighborhood. Upon the Doctor making his appearance, successive rounds of the most enthusiastic cheering greeted him.

As soon as the enthusiasm had somewhat subsided, he commenced by saying:—"Ladies and Gentlemen, I have again to repeat my sincere thanks to you for this most ardent reception which you have given me. Though somewhat accustomed to receive those hearty demonstrations, yet, I must confess, that on this occasion, you have outdone yourselves. (Cheers.) Several nations are very remarkable for music, others for drawing, others for sculpture, others for eloquence; but I don't think there is a nation in the world able to shout with the Irish. (Loud cheers.)

I assure you, Ladies and Gentlemen, I have a most difficult office to discharge to-night. The statement of Lecture is worded in this way—"The Social Condition of Ireland." There never was a heavier or more responsible task; yet, to an Irishman, it is a somewhat easy task, as it is his constant study. (Hear, hear.) I don't appear here to-night to inflame your feelings with animosity, to introduce amongst you national feelings. No, I appear here to-night as Counsel for Ireland, and you shall stand over me as a jury. (Cheers.)

In the present instance, I have a two-fold object in view—I wish to inform the Irish about our country, and to the Englishmen, to give a clear and impartial apology for the condition in which my country is placed, on account of the constant and horrid discord into which misgovernment has plunged it; and the terrible poverty consequent upon this mis-government, which, so pressed the yoke upon the finest country and the finest people in the world. (Cheers.) The charges brought against us, are: that we are lazy and won't work; that we are improvident, and won't accumulate capital; that we have no enterprise, and would not engage in commerce; that we are discontented, and would not be propitiated; that we are rebellious, and would not submit to the laws; that we are disloyal, and would not be content with the throne.

Now, my business here to-night is not to make a speech, for my language would be unable to do justice to the subject: but, as a Reverend Counsellor, to lay bare and uncover the wounds of Ireland. And, as I know that several wounds have been inflicted upon the body of Ireland since I was born; and my father said deep wounds had been inflicted upon the body of Ireland since he was born; and my grandfather told him wounds deep and ghastly, had been inflicted in his days; my great-grandfather had said the same. I found myself taking off the bandages for the last three hours before I came here. (Cheers.)—I only point out to you the grievous distress our poor country has suffered. I have to go back, not for a century, nor for two centuries, but very near 700 years, before I can do justice to this most distressing case of Ireland, which I promise to lay before you. I should be exceedingly sorry if any English gentleman should think that I was guilty of stirring up any anti-national feeling, or giving any expression unbecoming the sacred profession which I hold. (Cheers.)

First: Therefore, I begin with the years 1172–7, when Henry II. conquered Ireland through the dissension and treachery of our own countrymen; and from this time down to 1570, for nearly 400 years, there was continued struggling between England and Ireland; and during these 400 years, they could never conquer Ireland—never able to pass Leinster, so that three other Provinces were never conquered. And in these times the most barbarous cruelties were practised on the people. (Hear.) It is scarcely sinful to say, that never was the Protestant cruelty of England surpassed by the Catholic cruelty of Ireland. Amongst other instances, he would mention that the English soldiers were not allowed to deal with us—not to spread even what civilization they might boast. Never were the conquered treated with greater cruelty than from the reign of Henry II. to that of Henry VIII. The execution of Clare he would allude to, when the British soldiers outraged the wives and daughters of the Irish before their faces, and shot them, or tossed them over the rocks if they complained. Five hundred lashes was the punishment if a British soldier married an Irish girl; and I am happy to say to you, to the credit of the gallantry and taste of some of those men, the beauty of the Lasses of Limerick tempted them, in spite of five hundred lashes. (Cheers and laughter.) I could point out to you, if I pleased, several instances of the most blackened cruelty; but it is not necessary, since I look upon them as dreadful stories; and it is more to the credit of a lecturer to moralize on fact of history, than merely recount them.

Now, I ask, what agriculture could have been successfully pursued in a country like ours, which, during the four hundred years we have now in view, was a scene of perpetual struggles between the oppressing conqueror and the poor conquered? (Hear.) How could commerce be entered into, while the enemy's camp was at their gates, and they were nearly all occupied in repelling the invaders? (Hear.) Every honest Englishman will bear me out in these conclusions. In England, at the very time commerce was beginning, the crusades had begun, and all their opening and kindling influences of chivalry. During these 400 years England was cultivating learning and the arts and sciences, with the most important characteristic—combination amongst themselves: while poor Ireland was learning war, and feeling its fury, which made it a theatre of animosity and dissension. (Hear.) To you, Ladies and Gentlemen, my jury, I now appeal, and ask whose fault was it that our country was so wretched? Was it the fault of the Irish? (Cries of no, no.) No, Gentlemen, it was the fault of fate; a strong and foreign enemy was against us, and pressed us down. (Applause.) And after this, next came the disastrous period of Henry VIII. He found fault with his queen; dismissed her;

quarrelled with the Pope, because he condemned him; and married a subject in 1553. He was succeeded by two or three young princes, whose career lasted, including Elizabeth, until 1603.

Those years were the most disastrous in Irish history. England had changed her national faith, but failed in changing the Irish. The conquerors took every acre of land, as the law said: "An Irishman must only have an acre of arable land, and half an acre of bog. The laws of Elizabeth were levelled against the three most important things in a nation's welfare—property, education, and the religion of the people (the Catholic faith.) During the seventy years we have now in review, persecution raged to the greatest extent; and Elizabeth contemplated the entire subjugation of Ireland. About the end of her reign, by dint of the cruelest warefare, and the banishment of 70,000 Irish, she subjugated that country, leaving behind her the most withering, burning destruction, and heart-rending cruelty that have ever been recorded against any nation.

Look, now, at the position of our poor country—no agriculture, no commerce, no learning, no education, no homes, no property, no position! And don't you think, now, that succeeding historians behave very wrongly, when they charge and upbraid the Irish with want of education, when all education in it was by law extinguished? And don't you think that the English historian is a villain to so charge them. But I will say, to the credit of the generous frankness of the English, that I never sat with an Englishman for an hour, that would let me go on with my statements, before his generous disposition swelled with indignation at the injustice and iniquity of the treatment of my country. To the glory of my country I tell it, though so persecuted, even the seventy thousand banished Irishmen never gave up their faith. England gave it up—but all Ireland remained faithful. She never flinched, but perished at the block sooner than forswear one shred of her ancient faith.

I give you an idea of the fidelity of Ireland. I will give an instance: in 1654 nineteen Catholics were seized in old Leighlin, on account of their faith. They were promised extensive landed property, if they would change their faith. Three days were allowed them in prison to think upon the subject; but when asked on the first day, they all replied, "No." The second day, and again the same answer. On the third, when told to prepare for the block; they all answered as one man, "The sooner the better." One of the company, a young lad of eighteen, when brought before the executioner, requested to see the Governor; his request was granted, as something important was expected. He humbly asked pardon for being so bold in soliciting the Governor's presence, and then begged that he might be beheaded first, as his father was among the others, and he could not bear to see him put to death. The youth's request was granted, and then followed the decapitating of the rest, the nineteen heads being cut off upon the block, sooner than say they surrendered the faith of their fathers! And so terribly was the persecution carried on in these days, that to shoot an Irishman was only £5 penalty. I will give you an instance. Some soldiers were passing an hotel, into which they entered. In some difference or frolic they shot the waiter dead. The landlord, deep in grief, made a statement of the grievous murder to the colonel. This gentleman treated the matter quite coolly, saying that he must have given some reason, and jocosely said, "Oh, never mind; put him in the bill; I'll make it all right." So, Gentlemen, the waiter was put in the bill, which ran as follows: "Breakfast, 1s. 6d.; dinner, 2s. 6d.; shooting a waiter, £5." And shooting a waiter was only £5!

And now, as I have gone over the events of these seventy years, will you allow me again to moralise? How do you think Irishmen could preserve their property, be educated, and maintain their faith under such trying circumstances? Their heroic conduct under these oppressing times, was far better and more glorious than was that of the noble Greeks under Leonidas, at the pass of Thermopylæ; for they stood bravely under it for seventy years. It was in these times, that the Irish priest and the Irish people became first perfectly acquainted with each other. The people only knew us before as the heads of the Church; knew us in our rich vestments, gorgeous ceremonials, golden croziers—the Irish Church being rich and powerful in these times. The people knew the Priest only by the great superiority of his learning, by his religious counsel.

But the days of persecution came; the Priest had to put off his vestments and assume the freize coat; had to leave his altars and preach by the hedges; had to rol' about himself the chains that bound the people, live in the forest with them, and descend with them into caves; and still more, if necessary, to perish with them. And from that hour to this, the people venerate the place called the "Mass bush," or the "Mass rock." For the poor Priest, at the risk of his life, would privately attend at these places; and perhaps, as the morning sun arose, he would uncover the Host of Salvation to the people and to God.

You know, that I am acquainted with the inmost chords of an Irishman's heart, and can touch them when I like; and none but an Irishman can know how to speak to you. No persecution, no events since, not the most refined tyranny, have been able to break these bonds of sympathy between the Clergy and the people, which will go on, and strengthen in Ireland to the very end of time.

And now, we go on to the third period of Irish history, from the reign of James I., 1603, until the beheading of Charles I., in 1649; and how did we fare now? Worse. Poor Ireland was conquered; and now we might naturally suppose that there would be an end to it. But no; we were again subjected to the fresh evils and cruel persecution by our conquerers under the Scotch Monarch. And again, I ask, how is it possible, with such evils to contend against, for Ireland to have advanced in those arts which would make her happy, prosperous, and free?

In the troublesome time of Charles I., we fought for our King, the King of England; and yet, the English historian calls the Irish rebels, because we did fight for Charles I. and the same historian calls the English loyal, though they fought against him. But it is one of those cases which the Catholic historian puts forward as a proof of Irish loyalty. Catholicism is eminently monarchical; the loyal Catholic throughout the world has ever died at the foot of the throne; and it is the only religion in the world which stands without a stain as the tried friend of monarchy. We now arrive at 1649, when Charles was beheaded.

And what sort of a period now follows. If the devil himself ever came upon earth, he came in the shape of Cromwell. He came to Ireland, wrote to the ancesto. of the present Marquis of Ormond, to the following effect. "Ormond, I command you, under the penalty of death, to surrender to Cromwell; and if you surrender, you shall have £30,000, and do so, I advise." I saw the manuscript of this letter in Trinity College, Dublin. Ormond did surrender; but the Irish Catholics, to the last man, fought for their King. And when the greatest persecutor that ever lived came to our country, we resisted him, and yet we got the name of rebels. Tipperary was the most violent in the defence of their King. Tipperary previously had been very wealthy, and the most religious people in Ireland. They had more to lose, more to fight for. These two things taken from them—their property and their religion—have made them the most violent of all Ireland from that day to this. Cromwell, in order to curb them, made a plantation here; yet, not a man would volunteer to face the Tipperary boys, excepting the most reckless and depraved. So, the earliest settlers were the wickedest of the troops; and these becoming landlords, had been the most tyrannical; whilst the people had been the most furious in opposition to them.

Now, it is pleasing to me to read the history of the struggle, as it shows how nobly they fought for the defence of their country and their faith. As an instance of the condition of Ireland, and the opinion formed of us at this time by the English; there was in 1654, a wonderful bear exhibited in London, which could tell the age of the moon, tell what o'clock it was, and could tell who was the biggest rogue in the room. It was so clever that the whole audience took it to be a Tipperary man. And, one day, the population actually came to the theatre, to insist that the manager should bring out the bear, to show it was a bear, and not a Tipperary man. Such were the results of misgovernment. And while I look upon the government of England as being the most diabolical and the most infernal on God's earth, I look upon the English people as the most honest, and the most noble. I have travelled Europe over, and I must say, if the English people were Roman Catholics, there never would be a finer people upon earth. I have only just to mention their earnest exertions in having fifty-three Bible Societies, and spending one and a half million a year in religious works, which may be regarded by them as exponents of their deep religious feeling, although I differ from those societies.

Again, in reviewing the last period—sixty years of cruel war. I ask what could we do? Could we carry on agriculture? advance in science? engage in commerce? Don't you see I am going on year by year, and minute by minute, to lay bare to you, as my jury, the deep wounds I have alluded to? Was there a moment for Ireland to breathe in the midst of all this? Some people would ask, how do you account for the remaining at all, under these violent persecutions, of any Irish in Ireland? I will tell you. When James I. made his first plantation in Ireland, he said to his men, "You must take as much land as you can keep." So these soldiers and adventurers invited the poor Catholics from their hiding places, and let them small parcels of land by the year, at high rents; and, by this means, from a desire to make the Irish subservient to his aggrandizement, the Irish people and Irish religion, were preserved in Ireland. From this began the idea of tenure in Ireland. Notwithstanding the gross misrepresentation of the English historian, they could see that the only two faults of Ireland are the defence of her political rights to the very death.

To this day, you will hear men talk, how the Irish hated the English. And why not? Would any man smile if a dagger was stuck in his bosom? How could a nation respect laws which deprived the people of their lands, robbed them of their religion, and deprived them of education? Yet, I am not depreciating the English of the present day. I am proud when abroad of being addressed as an Englishman. Much as I love France, I would rather live in England a thousand times than in France. If England would only give us laws, as she has herself, we would do well. There never were any such laws before, or elsewhere. But Ireland was subject to every persecution, and from none did she suffer more than from Orange Irishmen. We have a story in Ireland about one of these Irish Orangemen, called Tom Smith, a bailiff of

Leinster. He was a remarkable man, being blind of one eye and lame. Nature closed one of his lights, and he could not see much with the other, which he always kept half shut, as if afraid to see, or be seen. He was also an appraiser, in connection with Orange authorities; and as persons would not pay tithes, Tom Smith was called in to take the goods in payment. He was so excessively conscientious, that when called upon to testify that he had only taken goods to the value required, he would put his little finger through his waistcoat button-hole, and declare upon oath, that it was *through* (true.)

Another instance of legal justice. A man was tried for murder; and after the jury had found a verdict of guilty, and the Judge had put on his black cap, to pronounce sentence—the man alleged to have been murdered walked into court. The Judge thereupon took off his cap, and addressing the foreman of the jury, said, they must reconsider their verdict, as the circumstances of the case had been altered. The jury did retire, and after a long deliberation, returned with a verdict of guilty. The Judge, in astonishment, asked how that was, when he was told, 'the prisoner at the bar stole an old grey mare eight years ago from one of the jurymen, for which he was not caught, and so we'll let the verdict stand as it is.'—(Groans and hisses.) Now, all such abuses were carried out under sanction of law.

The Reverend Lecturer again reviewed the historical period down to William III., Prince of Orange, who overcame James II. at the Battle of the Boyne. He is usually taken as the representative of Orange principles, but he was far from any such low character. This king was a most worthy man—he had many excellent qualities. He was very imperfectly appreciated and misunderstood in Ireland. He was a man of wide and tolerant principles, and Orangemen did him much injustice. However, the moment he succeeded in his conquest, his party were let loose upon Ireland, and the people never suffered such tyranny. (Hear, hear.)

From George I., 1714, to George III., 1760, Ireland was still persecuted. The Catholics were deprived of all their rights, except what was given to them by stealth. But George III. was a good man; but a stubborn old fellow. He sat on the throne for fifty-three years, with his judgment matured, but he never could spell the word emancipation without the letter '*s*,' instead of '*c*.' When George IV. and the Duke of York were boys, under tuition, the old king heard them crying. He asked what was the matter, when the master said, it was the Latin Grammar they were averse to. 'Pho, pho,' said his Majesty. 'What do they want with Latin?' There's plenty of fellows about them that will know plenty of Latin for what they will want. (Laughter.) The year 1760 is a most important period.

George III. came to the throne in perfect peace, and having nothing to do, they were determined to tax the American people. The Americans remonstrated, and sent Washington to London to state their grievance. He waited on the Prime Minister several times in the Court, to get a hearing. He was treated so lightly, that at last, he said to the Minister: 'I call here frequently, and yet I get no conclusive answer; what shall I do?' The Minister laughed at him; and when Washington got into the street, with his hat off, he vowed vengeance before God against England. (Rapturous cheering.) He returned home, fired the zeal of his countrymen. In battle after battle, he was victorious over the English, and in 1782, he lifted the flag of American independence. (Applause.) I intend going to America shortly, and I will take a bottle of Irish poteen, and when within the nearest distance of Bunker's Hill, I will drink on deck to the American flag. (Cheers.)

After these reverses, you never saw anything in your life so agreeable as England became to Ireland. Again, the French Revolution began in 1789, in which she overturned her altar and her throne; and England, in terror, then gave us the privileges we now enjoy, and which gave us leave to worship God. Maynooth College was founded about this time, 1795. Carlow College, 1799. And we also got leave to vote at elections. England yielded through fear, what she would not give to justice; and the heads of our party said they did not thank England for what she had done. England gave a paltry £9,000 for the College of Maynooth, and £30,000 to the Lock Hospital in Dublin, for the encouragement of vice. In the language of those great men, Shiel and O'Connell, England's difficulty is Ireland's opportunity. As Shiel said in one of his parliamentary speeches—"Ireland is like a convicted felon in a convict ship, his only hope of escape and relief is the wreck of the ship."

From the year 1793 to 1830, when the Irish were allowed to have property, and vote at elections, they acquired two twenty-fifths of the whole property of Ireland, by which the industry of the country was encouraged; a clear proof that if we had accomplished so much under a tolerant Government in a few years, we should have done very much under a propitious Government.—There is no other nation under heaven, that has accumulated money with more honesty, more industry, and more frugality than the Irish. Again, look at the illustrious names, that like stars, burst forth in the firmament of literature, when the ban upon education was removed.

We have Milner, Lingard, Shiel, O'Connell, Dr. Doyle, and many others, who stand before all Europe, as the most ēminent men who have graced the annals of any country. On the contrary, from 1622 to 1793, we had not a single individual to write in our favor, and represent our grievous case, in opposition to the lies of English historians, which, like the pediments of a bridge, are the foundations upon which succeeding historians have built their bridges; so that there are lies lying beneath the very depths of the structure.

The 40s. freeholders, were created about this time, to carry out a deep laid plan for the destruction of our National Parliament. In eight years, by bribery and intimidation, England succeeded in taking away from us our National Parliament. It was a remarkable time; it was on a first day of a first week, of a first month, of a first year, in a new century; on a Monday January 1st, 1801. They succeeded, by spending four and a half millions, and have left Ireland without a Parliament from that day to this. Our Parliament gone in 1801, what more did England do? She took away our Linen Trade, by putting a duty upon them : she discouraged our trade, beggared our commerce, and made that verdant, beautiful Island a desert. Yes, it was the Irish landlords sold our birthright, and by their treacherous conduct has come upon us, the greatest curse Ireland has ever sustained. Between the years 1793 and 1815, land rose cent. per cent. in Ireland; provision rose in equal proportion; the wealthy left it; clothes became dearer, and the young men entered the army; so that the Irish could live no longer in their own country; they had to leave Ireland, come to England, and go abroad. The gentry lived upon their incomes, in luxury and waste, so that they sank Ireland into still greater depths of poverty—14-25ths of the landed property being mortgaged.

We now come to 1830, and look at our position. We have cruel middlemen upon our lands, exacting the highest prices, and the poor tenantry rent-racked, the landlords spending their money, and living out of the country; corn cheap, and no money; no manufacture, not a chimney in Ireland except in Belfast. Catholics then got the Emancipation Bill, but what did that do? It introduced elections, but yet, when they elected Roman Catholic friends, they were ejected and turned out of their homes the next day. Awful times followed. Mr. O'Connell began to agitate for another Parliament, but his professions were doubted; as it was alleged, they wanted to separate Ireland from England. A new spirit arose amongst the young men of Cambridge and Oxford, the nursery of statesmen, to look with suspicion upon the movements of Ireland. The press headed the outcry, and scarcely a newspaper in England, but what contained something to the discredit of Ireland. The Protestant church in Ireland was consolidated by law. English feeling was never more jealously manifested. So what did we get by Emancipation? Thus we see we have only had about twenty three years, in which it may be said Ireland could advance in improvement.

And now for the charges brought against us. We are idle. Idle! Where is the work to do? There is no work. We are improvident and beggarly. Yes, like a story I heard the other day of a poor fellow that was going to America, by one of the emigrant ships at the Waterloo Dock, when he was accosted by a German, who sold boxes, with—'Buy a box, Sir.' What for? said our friend. 'To put your clothes in,' replied the German. 'Bedad if I do, then, I'll have to go naked on deck.' We have no enterprize, and not a single chimney or manufactory. We are dirty—but give us the price of razors and soap, and we will show you that we are clean.

I'll tell you a story of a party of Cromwell's soldiers, who went into a cabin in Ireland, and demanded the second best bed in the house. "That's bad news for Morgan, Sir," replied a poor fellow, sitting at the fire. "Who the deuce is Morgan?" asked one of the party. "Morgan, Sir," answered the owner, "is no other than the pig." Not contented; when able-bodied men are laboring for 4d. a day, and some girls, young women, for 1 1-2d. a day. I dined with a Scotchman lately, near Limerick, who recently invested much money in Ireland, and this gentleman said, speaking of laborers, "I never saw such men; I had no idea of them before I came. I will give them 1s. 1d. a day, with a kind word, and they will lay down their lives for me. I never saw such men." Idle they are called, when there is no work to do. What! Lazy upon 1 1-2d. a day! Would it not be better to starve by a ditch rather than work for 1 1-2d. a day?

And now, will you allow me to ask you, as my jury, who is to be blamed for all these evils? I don't want to blame the English solely. We call upon the Irish landlords to open the rich and varied mines that are beneath our feet; to open manufactories; to amend their laws of land-letting, and stimulate Irish commerce. Look at our kindred in America; don't we see them there, free from the vices attributed to them here? We have been much maligned by the press and Protestant Church during late years, when our only crime has been, we have fought for our political privileges and our religious creed. But yet, he was proud, notwithstanding, of the English character. Just look at a company of ten gentlemen, none speaks before the other is finished; how bland, how graceful, each listens, and none obtrudes. Get ten Irish gentlemen, just as well bred, and you will hear them a mile off, all speaking at once at the top of their voices, and each beginning his speech ten minutes before the other ends, so that he may come in at the finish; but if you get into the company of ten Irish ladies, you would hear them two miles off. But I must certainly say, that the English are always grumbling, because they have too much to eat, and an Irishman grumbles because he can't get enough to eat. There was a fine little fellow lived down in the west of England, he was the son of a nobleman, and one day he was sitting on the garden wall, enjoying himself with a large piece of plum-cake; when all of a sudden, he alarmed the whole household by most heart-rending and piteous moans. His poor mother flew to him and clasped him to her bosom, inquired most anxiously, "Johnny, dear, what is the matter?" Johnny, with big tears in his eyes, exclaimed, "Oh, Mammy, I can't eat any more!"

I will now sum up as counsel for Ireland. I only wish

I might have a week's discussion with Lord John Russell or Lord Palmerston, and you know you would have the better side of the question. You that are in England, I would charge you not to think of returning to Ireland, but identify yourselves with this country, and try to place yourselves in respectable positions. There is no work for you in Ireland; there is in England. I congratulate you upon the good use you have made of my letter of counsel to you from Scotland, last July. It has saved you from many broken heads, and breaking the peace. I wrote to Sir George Grey, who thought I was a fire brand. But I was no firebrand, but a peace maker. The only firey trick I ever did, was to bring the blush into Lord John Russell's face. I am in correspondence with every Court in the whole world. I have just had a letter from Vienna, which says there will be no war, though Russia depends upon the perfidy of England. By this right hand, and by my influence with you, I have laid the basis of permanent peace in this city, and when I come to Liverpool, the merchants of Liverpool ought to acknowledge the debt they owe me. At your soiree—at my soiree—you did not mention the name of Dr. Cahill, then in Scotland. I did not forget it, and I do not forgive it.

I will conclude with the year 1847, when the potato-rot famine, and fever staggered the living and scourged the land. The poor Priests lived by your side at the time, they did not neglect you. In Liverpool, thirteen Priests, in their black shrouds, lie buried under your feet. Then came the cholera. The poor tenantry, turned off their farms, and under the burning heat of July, might have been seen without shelter—290 persons living in the fields, lying dying in all the horrors of wretchedness. The famine and plague were not sufficient, but the exterminating landlords levelled the cottages of his poor tenantry to the earth, and sent them out in emigrant ships, packed so that it became almost a floating funeral hearse over the broad waters of the deep. Ten thousand of these poor persons perished in America, and others perished through ague. But Ireland, now, is getting better; she is getting free from all her poverty and ailments. The green grave is closing over her wounds, labor now begins to look up in Ireland. Manufactories are springing up in large towns, the people are spreading over the earth to improve their condition, and in America, in every village may be found and Irish home. Irish abound from the shores of Canada to the forests of Mexico.

A lamentable scene was mentioned a few days ago, of a poor Irish woman in New Orleans. In one of the chief streets was to be seen at noon-day a poor woman, raving in sorrow, with her hands to her eyes, and clinging to her on each side was a child. Before her, in a cart, driven by a negro, was the corpse of her husband, carried off in the yellow fever. She pitifully exclaimed, "Oh, Jack, dear, was it for this I came to America, to lose my poor husband! Oh, that I had never crossed the salt seas. Here I am and nothing to eat, and nowhere to go." A gentleman, overhearing her, kindly gave her a sovereign, but her grief was so heavy that she scarcely recognised the gift.

Such were the hardships our people pass through. I perceive now there is no slander or articles against us in the *Times*. And do you know why? Because Napoleon III. stands at the head of 150,000 men. The Emperor and Empress lately attended a review in France, where 100,000 men were present. They attended High Mass in the field, and in the sight of the whole troops, knelt down humbly before the Priest. One hundred and ten cannons were discharged when the Priest lifted the Sacred Host to the blue vault of Heaven, and 100,000 men bent upon their knees and adored their Lord and God. When Prince Albert was in Dublin, I thought to write a letter to him upon the grievances of Ireland. I shall do so yet. The Governments of Europe are beginning to stir. Austria has turned the *Times* newspaper out of her dominions; the Queen of Spain has prohibited it also. Bulwer was turned out at forty-eight hours' notice from Spain, in consequence of his interference with the Catholic worship. We have now seven Catholic thrones; and when Leopold dies, his son having married into a Catholic family, we may expect an eighth. So, as God is just, we may expect the triumph of the true Faith. And, as all nations come to an end, there may be a time when England shall fall, and receive that retribution attending all injustices. To use the words of Macauley, whom I don't like to quote, there may be a time when a New Zealander will stand upon London bridge, sketching the ruins of that great city. Nineveh, with all her beauty, perished; Palmyra, the great seat of learning and architectural splendor, is now crumbling into dust. Babylon, the great terror of her time, is now punished for her cruelties. Scarcely a vestige of ancient Rome is now standing—all gone—ruined; and I wish England to take my warning in time, and beware of the wrath of God, in persecuting his Church, and the faithful Irish people, for in the words of the Scotch poet—

"By oppression's woes and pains,
By our sons in servile chains,
We shall drain our dearest veins,
But we shall be free"

The Rev. Gentleman then retired amidst the most enthusiastic cheering.

DR. CAHILL'S REPLY TO AN ADDRES OF THE CLERGY OF BEVERLY.

The members of the clergy of the diocess of Beverly, availing themselves of the opportunity of a second visit of the Rev. Doctor to their neighborhood, tendered an address, testifying their admiration and gratitude for the services rendered to religion ; and wondering "that men calling themselves the children of the Church, should have stood forward to misrepresent his arguments, to deny his right to be considered as an exponent of the Catholic Faith and to stigmatise him." Dated February 27th. 1854.

Very Reverend and Reverend Gentlemen— The regard, the affection, and the kind condescension which breathe through every line of your most valued address render it impossible for me to make a suitable reply in any form of words at my command. This public document is, under existing circumstances, a most necessary rebuke to persons who, from being treated with courtesy, and perhaps flattered, seem to have lost sight of all prudence, by putting forth their crude knowledge without sense, their blind zeal without charity, and their offensive criticism without learning. They appear to have conceived the possibility of converting their old friends, by praising Protestantism and by abusing Catholicity; they seem to think that they can reduce their present position to a happy mean between our Gospel and the Book of Common Prayer; and it would strike any penetrating observer, that these gentlemen have joined us, more because they try to scape the contradictions of Protestantism, than to embrace the convictions of Catholicity. This liberal compromise will never succeed, "No man can serve two masters."

But it is fortunate they have been checked in this early stage of their Tractarianism: no one could volunteer to give the public correction which they compelled me most reluctantly to administer; and if proofs were wanted to show the untamed tone of their minds, it can be found in every sentence they write in reference to me, where, in place of making an apology for their gross misstatements, they are still struggling to defend their foolish conduct in the face of the indignant public.

Gentlemen, just read that sentence in their article, where they say that the word "Transubstantiation" was created by Catholic Theology to express "the annihilation of one substance and the substitution of another" Here they identify the questionable opinions of some few theologians with the unquestionable dogmas of faith; and if they read Bellarmine and St. Thomas, instead of Vazquez and Perroni, they would pause before they exposed themselves to the just criticism of the scholars of the Church.

Again, hear them while they tell the faithfull, in page 173, that the "Accidents in the Eucharist (the only portions of matter, which are, as far as we know, cognisable by the senses) remain unaltered."!! Here we are informed, firstly, that our sensations are "portions of matter;" and secondly, that although the Council of Trent declares that there is a total "convertion of the substance of bread," yet here it is stated that "portions of matter" remain unaltered after the consecration.

In reference to the shameful observations made by the writers in the *Rambler* on your "English Choirs and Church Services;" there can be but one opinion. These gentlemen have carried into our Church, all their former antipathies against everything Catholic, without adopting the charities of their new faith. Only hear them designating the English Church by the name of "Anglo Catholic;" calling the sacred music performed at the Holy Sacrifice of the Mass by the name of "Mass Music." They speak as lightly of it as of a Scotch reel or an Irish hornpipe. Listen to their description of the English Choirs, where they use the words — "gross irreverence, pitiable ignorance, scandals, concerts, offensive exhibitions, the congregation smiling, the performance, some of the

Choir kneeling in mockery, the confusion, the disorders, a system, the church converted into a concert room, irreverence behind the gallery curtains." Gentlemen, you have done well to call the public attention to this distressing article; and I hope it will be at once the means of discontinuing the further scandalous publication of the lamentable Periodical, till the Bishops and Priests, in their own defence, will place it under the guidance of some person who has solid learning, who can write the Catholic sentiment, and who understands the Catholic doctrine.

I might regret having taken so much notice of these imprudent persons if I had not received this address; but now I am pleased that any circumstance has occured, which has placed before me a precious document, which makes my heart so happy, and which I shall bind up with my choicest and warmest feelings, as long as I live.

I am, Very Rev. and Rev. Gentlemen, your for ever attached,

D. W. CAHILL, D.D.

P. S.–The third letter, which I promissed on next Saturday, I shall reserve; and I shall, if necessary, publish it in some future occasion.

DR. CAHILL'S SPEECH IN LIVERPOOL.

The following speech was received with great applause at a meeting of the Irish residents of Liverpool to express their sympathy for Mr. John O'Connell, as the son of the Liberator, and to open a subscription for him.

The orator commenced with a brilliant sketch of the political career of O'Connell: the injustice inflicted on his country did not rouse his energies so much as the wrongs perpetrated on his creed; he was the impersonification of Ireland's own child; he was the master of all ages, the patriot of every nation; his name is raised higher in the national history than the Irish eternal mountains; he has rivalled Cicero in classic eloquence, has equalled Demosthenes in patriotic fire, and has surpassed both in national virtues; he placed himself at the head of ideas, not soldiers; all the nations were his people; all mankind are under an obligation to him, which they never can repay, and Ireland stands at this moment charged with the whole debt due to the imperishable success of O'Connell, who has descended to his honored tomb without a nail in his illustrious coffin purchassed with the money of Ireland. John O'Connell can show his own achievements in the field, to prove his claims on his country; he has never betrayed the cause of his countrymen, as many recreants have done; he has avowed the noblest feelings for them.

When the speech was over, a number of subscriptions came in, and several persons called for collectors' books. The meeting shortly afterwards separated, cheering most vociferously for John O'Connell, Dr. Cahill, Mr. Levingston &c.

Mr. Chairman, Ladies, and Gentlemen—There is not a nation under the sun, able to shout with the Irish

Catholics. Being bound hand and foot so long in national chains and penal servitude, and being prevented from speaking by the Attorney General—the eternal, undying Attorney General—of Ireland, there was no way left to express our feelings, except by national shouting; and hence, there is an eloquence, a poetry, a patriotism in the Irish cheer, which is more tragic than Shakespeare, more burning than Demosthenes, more inspiring than Milton—and if ever that cheer rose up into the regions of divine fancy itself, it is when the Irish soul is stirred up from its deepest recesses of feeling by the magic sound of the immortal O'Connell. (Here the entire assembly rose again and cheered again and again for the immortal name of O'Connell.)

When, in the beginning of the present century he commenced his political career, he could procure only thirteen persons to attend a meeting in Dublin, to petition for Catholic Emancipation. He was then, if I may so speak, a mere ensign in politics; but he rose from rank to rank with a brilliant name, and with unexampled success, till he took, by universal consent, the supreme command of the national force, and in numberless skirmishes and one hundred battles, he met the foes of Ireland foot to foot, and shoulder to shoulder, and by courage that never quailed, a perseverence unsubdued, and a genius without a comparison, he struck off our national chains, conquered ancient oppression, and won the Emancipation of Ireland. (Wild and rapturous cheers, which lasted several minutes.) And when we throw ourselves into his mind and examine his heart, we learn that the injustice inflicted on his country did not rouse the great energies of his being in half the mightiness as when he concentrated his power against the wrongs perpetrated on his creed.

No one ever heard him address a jury who did not find his feelings enlisted for his client; it was impossible to listen to him for five minutes in an assembly of his countrymen, as he poured forth from his burning bosom his own flood of melting eloquence, over the woes of Ireland, without resentment for our national degradation; but when the insults to his religion awoke his passion into legitimate anger, his whole soul glowed with brilliant fire, and as he directed the flashing torrents against the opponents of his Church, his consuming words resembled the rapidity and terrors of the lightning. (Tremendous cheering.)

He was the impersonification of Ireland's own child; he was the son of Ireland's own heart; he possessed the tongue and the soul of the true genius of his country. Other men have had an evening in life, he had none; other great characters were seen to ascend to the horizon of their career and gradually set, his sun stood fixed in the meridian in full dazzling splendor, without a motion to the west; and when he departed from us, it was the whole span from mid-day to night, leaving his country covered with a sudden darkness and mourning, after burning skies, during half a century of patriotism that never has been surpassed, and a national fame that perhaps never can be equalled. (At the conclusion of this sentence no words could describe the enthusiasm that followed.) But if ever a memory could be said to be palpable, it was his—and if ever the instructions of a master could assume a living form, his lessons are still breathing and alive all over the world. He was not merely the teacher of Ireland and of his own age—he was the master of all ages, the patriot of every distinguished nation. (Loud cheers.)

When the present representatives of Ireland defend our country and our creed in the British Senate, I think I hear his words in their mouths. They are children, to be sure, compared with the aged father of Ireland; but when they speak with energy, and honor, and patriotism, I think I recognise the accent, hear the voice, and feel the enthusiasm of the ancient orator of my country. (Loud and continued cheering.) I fancy he is still alive in Ireland, when I read in the newspapers the success of the poor Irish tenantry to return to Parliament a friend to the poor; when I dwell on the speeches at elections, the orations at the public dinners, given to the tried advocates of our national rights, I recollect well that they are only repeating the language they once heard from him, retailing his arguments which he once flung from his great mind, and rekindling the fire which once blazed on his electric lips. (It is quite impossible to describe the enthusiasm of the assembly at this moment.)

And the fire burns in America at this moment with a brilliancy that will yet send its glorious illuminating beams back again across the Atlantic, to the poor old mother land—many a fervid heart along the rapid St. Lawrence and the swollen Mississippi, who have learned patriotism at the feet of Ireland's orator—many a patriot out there who has been trained in the lessons of national independence in our popular assemblies in poor Ireland—and many a thousand hearts in time to come will be ready, when necessary, to lend a suitable aid (when Ireland shall most need their succors,) to the cradle of their faith, the scene of their patriotism, and the theatre of their national struggles. (Wild cheering, and waving of handkerchiefs.)

Wherever an Irishman is placed, all the world over, he boasts of the name of O'Connell; that name is raised higher in our own national history than the eternal mountains of our country, and it will last as long in imperishable existence; and when the Romans talk of their Cicero, and the Greeks of their Demosthenes, we point to the Irish forum, and the British Senate, to a name that has rivalled the one in classic eloquence, that has equalled the other in patriot-fire, and that has surpassed both in national virtues. (Any attempt to describe the emotion of the meeting is impossible.)

And not alone has Ireland learned from him the science of freedom, and the art of national independence: he has taught all the nations of the earth, by the science of reform, by a moral and peaceful combination. He placed himself at the head of ideas—not soldiers; he took the command—not cannon; and by the triumph of reason, he gained victories such as no conqueror ever achieved by the flashing sword, or the thunders of the artillery. (Loud cheers.) Twenty-three French peers, with Count Montalambert at their head, presented to him an humble address, in which, after offering to him their homage, they acknowledged that he had invented a new political stratagy; that he was the author of a new principle of national reform; that he had discovered a mighty plan, by which the greatest advantages to man could eventually be acquired by the steady application of the primary laws of God, and that, by carrying out his ideas, the combination of men's hearts would be in the end more successful than the united terrors of the sanguinary steel. (Loud cheering for several minutes.)

From Ireland, as from a professor's chair, he delivered his lessons to universal mankind—all the nations of the earth were his people; and his voice was heard from East to West, from North to South, and for half a century along the boundless horizon. No man can ever again take his place. He filled the whole world with his fame—he was the light of our skies, the undying creation of our age, the ornament of our race, and the imperishable monument to the name and character of Ireland. (Loud cheers, waving of hats, handkerchiefs, &c.) There can be no doubt that he has placed all mankind under an obligation to him which they never can repay; and his name will go down through each successive generation of his countrymen, gathering accumulated honor, as it is heard through coming time. The poor Irish did endeavor to give their devotion to him while living; the poor man contributed his mite, in his yearly duty to the national gratitude.

But whatever the nation gave, the nation received back again; their national devotion was annually repaid; what they bestowed on the patriot, the generous patriot refunded the same year; and thus our nation stands at this moment charged with the whole debt due to the imperisha ble success of O'Connell. (Loud cheers, and cries of "it's true, it's true.") If Ireland purchased an estate, in fee for O'Connell, and that his children's children inherited it, and lived on it, I could place a graven plate on the gate of the family mansion, to commemorate the sciences of the departed orator, and the honor of my grateful country.—But I protest, when I consider the disinterestedness which returned the gift each year to the poor who bestowed it, I place the nobility, the honor, the pride of this act alone, the highest point of the patriot's fame; and his memory stands before me unsullied in its purity, by retaining for himself not one penny of the money of the nation. (Here the audience rose and expressed their feelings of delight by a loud burst of applause.) Mr. O'Connell died without being indebted one shilling to our nation; and consequently we still owe to him the full amount of her services.—He lived in comparative poverty on our account, and we therefore stand indebted to him for his sacrifices. Not one of his sons or family wear a single glove or ribbon purchased from the donation from Ireland; and hence, while I value his success, while I am grateful for his sacrifices, while I venerate his patriotism, while I admire his genius, and worship his eloquence, there is one point higher than all, and that is the lofty pride of his heart, by which he descended to his honored tomb without one nail in his illustrious coffin purchased with the money of Ireland. (Loud and rapturous cheering.) The only act of his glorious life with which the future historian will find fault, is that he deprived his family of the large resources of his profession, and that in fact he robbed his sons of their just hopes, their expected fortune and merited position, in order to devote his whole life and resources to the services of Ireland. (Loud cheers.) But when Ireland has followed his example for fifty years, there is one part of his character in which our nation will not take part in his career, and that is, Ireland will not rob John O'Connell of that just debt which Ireland owes him. (No one can describe the emotion of the meeting at this time, amidst cheering, &c., all standing.) No, I thank you for this rapturous enthusiasm. No, no, Ireland is too honest, too grateful, to rob John O'Connell, on his own account—and on this evening, and in this place, shall begin our instalment of the debt which Ireland will certainly discharge. (Here loud cheers were given for John O'Connell.)

John O'Connell need not point to the statues of his ancestors to prove his claims on his country; he can show his own achievements in the field, already the tried champion of nineteen years. In every battle for Ireland during this eventful period, he stood by his father's side, and whenever the heat of the fight raged most violently, there might be seen the unflinching, fearless son, with his sword drawn, standing in front of the lofty plumage and glittering armor of the giant father, as he repelled the advance of the enemy. (Loud and rapturous cheering.) I am delighted to find that you are in such good humor. (Loud laughter.) They tell a tale of an Irishman once in France, and being asked by a Frenchman what kind of a looking man was the great O'Connell? The Irishman paused for a moment, and then said: "Why, then, I'll tell you that he is, for all the world, like the Lakes of Killarney."—(Roars of laughter.)

Now, if any one here has not seen my friend Mr. O'Connell, I must tell them that he is descended of the Lakes of Killarney; and that if you remove the father out of view, while you are looking at him, his political honesty and national fidelity will not suffer by a close comparison with any one of his age or standing. Since he commenced his political career, many a recreant betrayed our cause—John O'Connell never (cries of never, never;) many a man left our ranks and sold Ireland for gold, but John O'Connell never: and if the creed of St. Patrick, and if the religion of Ireland be maligned, listen to the rising voice, observe the boiling anger, and look in his face and see his passion, as it mantles his indignant brow, while with all his mind, and with the whole of his father's heart, he defends his country's faith against the malignant assaults of its continued enemies. (Loud and long cheering.)

But this meeting is not a political assembly; if it were political, I should not have attended, lest one word might escape my lips that could give offence to any one of the advocates for the rights and the liberties of Ireland.—(Cheers.) I like every one who struggles for Ireland; I love all who maintain the political interests, and defend the religious creed of Ireland. One man may labor to advance the civil rights of my country, another person may strive to strike off the chains that bind the cross of Christ, but give me the man who labors for both; I respect all the others—but I love with my whole heart, and all my sympathies are with the poor—the poor abandoned, persecuted Irish peasant.

When I go on board your emigrant ships, (which I do whenever I am in your city,) and when I see the poor old grandfather, with his worn frame and haggard look, and white scattered locks of tangled hair, carrying his little grand-daughter on his back; and when I behold the poor tottering old grandmother, without a bonnet or a cap, with her little grandson on her back; when I look at them carrying the children to the ship, my heart melts to see the miserable looks of our poor Irish children, their little bare legs hanging in front, in the pelting snow and the biting frost—I weep for those poor little exiles, when I think of their being wrenched at such a tender age from the fostering care of a mother and kind home. It is a heart-rending sight to see three generations, the grandfather, the son, and the grandchild, crawling in hunger on the gangways of the emigrant ship, doomed never again to kiss the Irish primrose, and lay their feet on the green turf of their country. (Here the meeting was affected to tears.) I always bid these poor exiles a last farewell, with my eyes full of tears, and my heart bursting with unmingled feelings of Irish sympathy, and legitimate political anger; and when I take my place on the shore, and see the ships weighing their anchors, swell their canvas, and move slowly on through the foaming deep, I hear my heart foretelling as she clears the river, that she is a large ocean hearse, and that before the sun sets twice, she will bury her living cargo in the foundations of the sea, amidst the crashing horrors of the yawning abyss, and the moaning terrors of the midnight tempest. (The entire audience here felt deeply affected.)

How grateful I felt, on reading the speech of Mr. John O'Connell, to see the feelings he entertains for his poor countrymen. It is what I expected from his generous heart, and gives an additional credence, if such were wanted, of his devotion to his country. But I must say, that as all my sympathies are with the poor banished, persecuted, exterminated tenantry, I feel all my soul engaged in the plan that can give to Ireland such a law of tenant right, as will protect her poor from the cruel law of wholesale extermination; and the men who struggle to procure such a law for the poor, deserve the admiration of their country, and the gratitude of posterity; (cheers) and I feel great pleasure in stating here, that in a communication I have had in London with one of the first (I may say the first Catholic Irishman,) of our present Irish party in the House of Commons, he stated to me that if a national testimonial of ten thousand pounds were decided on for Mr. John O'Connell, he would be found at the head of the list, and, by his fortune and exertions, carry out the work to its fulfilment. (Loud cheers for Mr. Moore.) I did not name Mr. Moore, but I suppose as I said he was the first, you have selected him. (Cheers.) Well, as you have named him, I shall leave it so, from my respect for your opinions. (Cheers for Mr. Moore.)

You all recollect the tale of the Queen having, during her stay at Balmoral, asked a Scotch girl what o'clock it was? The girl replied, "Whatever you please, Ma'am." (Roars of laughter.) Now, I say to you, in reference to Mr. Moore, "Whatever you please;" but when I have a good thing to say between friends, I like to say it. I wish I could make up the breach in the ranks of our gallant Irishmen; I would willingly go on my knees to implore of all our friends to bury private opinions, and unite in one compact body for the protection of the poor. (Great cheering, and cries of "You are the man who can bring them together.") I have only one more word to say—namely, that Dr. Yore, the Vicar General of Dublin, is the treasurer of this O'Connell tribute—an additional reason why I am here this night; and, as I act under Dr. Yore, and Dr. Yore under his Grace the Delegate Archbishop, and so on, you have a regular pyramid of living ecclesiastics as a model for your conduct in this national testimonial. (Loud cheers.) Mr. Chairman, Ladies and Gentlemen, I am now done; I thank you exceedingly for your overwhelming kindness, and your warm enthusiasm. We shall reward Mr. O'Connell for his past honest political career, and his faithful services in the cause of Ireland, and we shall do an act of justice which we owe to a tried patriot, which we owe to the cause of our country, and which we owe to the feelings of our own hearts. I thank you on my own part as the private friend of the O'Connell family—I thank you on the part of John O'Connell, and I thank you with all my heart on the part of my country. (On bowing and retiring the Reverend and eloquent Gentleman was greeted with a degree of heartfelt applause quite indescribable.)

DR. CAHILL TO THE RIGHT HON. LORD JOHN RUSSELL.

Upper Gloucester Street, Dublin.

My Lord—I make no apology for the liberty which I thus take in addressing so exalted a personage as the first minister of the most powerful empire in the world. On this point, your Lordship must recollect that I have not presumed to go up to your place; it was you, who, by your most unexpected letter, came down to mine; and if your Lordship find yourself now in my presence, you must see, it was you who have approached me, and not me you. As you have attacked—in a letter which will yet surprise yourself, as much as it has astonished all Europe—every Catholic in the whole world, from the Supreme Pontiff down to the "heathen" Irish, it follows, as a matter of course, that, in this large and incomprehensible insult to two hundred millions of Catholics in the old world, your Lordship must necessarily have included me; first, as being a countryman of the heathens, and secondly, as being one of the traitors, whom (as Hume hints) you pretend to be afraid of, as aiding the Pope in his sole and undivided sway over the realm of England. Your Lordship's late letter I consider, therefore, as partly directed to me, and therefore do I feel myself partly bound to send your Lordship an answer to certain passages which appear to me not noticed by any of those persons who have already replied to you.

There can be no doubt at all that your Lordship intended to fill all England and Ireland with the cry of no Popery, and to pelt the Catholic Priesthood with the old degraded slander of being traitors to the Throne. The Pope could not assume "sole and undivided sway over the realm of England," unless the Catholic Priests and people withdrew their allegiance from the Queen, and gave it undivided to him; nor could his sway be sole over the realm, unless the Priests and the Catholic people entirely ignored the Queen's supremacy, when able to do so, and transferred their entire allegiance to him. This, then, I take to be your decided meaning—to inflame the English mob, if English words have any decided signification. Although this ungenerous charge has been already made ten thousand times, it ought—as Cobbett used to say—to be again refuted with scorn ten thousand times; and this is the point which I shall presume, first, to discuss with you. Your Lordship knows better than I do that the history of all Christian time over the world has but one page in reference to the allegiance of the Catholic Church to the throne—and that page is, an unbroken, unshrinking fidelity to legitimate monarchy, to legitimate power, in every country, and in every age, even to chains and death. Let us examine the various countries, and come to facts and dates:—

Firstly—Is not the French revolution in 1789, written in the blood of the Royal Family and the French Priesthood? They lived united, and they fell together—they were the faithful servants of their Royal Master, and hence the streets of Paris ran red with their blood, and thousands died in exile in a foreign land for their fidelity.

Secondly—In Spain, when the ancient constitution was changed, and when [as the English Cabinet knows?] the succession to the Throne was altered, the Priesthood clung, with fidelity to the legitimate heir to the Spanish Crown, and suffered trials and persecution—from what is still called there the English party—which makes the blood freeze. In one day, the 17th July, 1833, upwards of one hundred Priests were butchered in Madrid alone; in Toledo, thirty-three Convents of Nuns and Friars were closed, and the aged inmates pitchforked into the streets, and left to die of hunger and cruel treatment on the public highway. They were attached to Don Carlos, and therefore became the objects of plunder and assassination to the enemies of order and to the conspirators against the ancient laws.

Thirdly—When rebelion broke out in the Canadas—what is termed the Papineau insurrection—the Catholic Priesthood there received the thanks of the Legislature for their distinguished allegiance; and all Catholics, are, since that time, admitted to a full share in the offices, emoluments, and honors of the State. Sir Francis Head states, that the Catholics of Canada are the best support, there, of the English Crown.

Fourthly—When Norway was taken from the King of Denmark, and given by the allied powers to Bernadotte, for his services to them, and his treachery to Napoleon, the Roman Catholics—few in number—offered their roperty and their lives to their King to resist the encroachment, and, as Beere's narrative states, gave a noble instance of fidelity to their Lutheran King.

Fifthly—In the various revolutions which have convulsed Europe since 1847 in Lombardy, in Naples, in

Austria, in Hungary, and in France, the Catholic Clergy have not been so much as named for any disloyalty in these eventful times; and when the whole populations of whole kingdoms, such as Hungary, have been hurled along in one tempestuous revolution, in a perfect hurricane—when prince, ministers, and generals, and armies, yielded to the storm, will you point out, my Lord, the kingdom, the province, the parish, the town, the village, in all these countries, where the allegiance of the Priest has been violated to the Crown? Tell me the place, the name, the date, the office of the Priest who has been a traitor to the King, in this European phrenzy, when monarchs fled from their capitals for fear, when their friends abandoned them, and when almost half the Thrones of Europe were nearly crumbled beneath the violence of popular fury?

Sixthly—Did not the Pope himself, who now seeks the sole sway over the realm of England, did he not fly from his capital sooner than declare war against Austria? And yet, my Lord, are all these Priests, and this Pope, now leagued in England to rob our Queen of her realm! and claim undivided sway in her empire alone, where we have the most perfect constitution that ever the world saw, and where we are governed by the most exemplary, the most illustrious, the brightest, and the most beloved sovereign that ever sat on the throne of Alfred? Are they the men who bled at the foot of all the Thrones of Europe in defence of their Kings—are they, my Lord, seeking the sole sway over the realm of Victoria? Shame, my Lord—I will not retract the word—shame, shame, Lord J. Russell, to have made such a charge of attainder against the most faithful subjects of the Queen, and to have inflicted a deep, deep, and burning insult on millions of your former friends, and nearly one half of the entire human race.

Seventhly—When I turn from Catholic Europe, and come to Protestant England, let me ask you, when revolution raised its horrid head in England, 1649, who was it, I ask, who sold a King, who fled to them for protection? who was it who bought that King with a national oath to spare his life? who was it, who, in the teeth of these national engagements murdered that King in midday, before the gaze of mankind; and before God and man, committed an act of national baseness, national perfidy, national dishonor, and national cruelty, of which there is no parallel in the history of the civilised world?

Eightly—Who again were these men, who, in the year 1688, joined an unnatural daughter in her disobedience to her royal father? who were they who conspired with an usurper, and expelled their legitimate monarch, and left him to die in a foreign land, a beggar at the gates of the French Court? who were these men, therefore, who, in your own country, overthrew the realm which you now pretend to be in danger? who were they? were they Irish or English? echo answers English! Aye, and the heathens, poor faithful fellows, clung to these Kings and suffered from Cromwell, the foul monster, a cruelty which can never be known, till the eight hundred women, whom he murdered at Wexford, will stand before God, on the last day, and cry for vengeance. These are your black pages, my Lord; and before you ventured to raise a state rebellion in England, in 1850, as your Cabinet did in Ireland, 1798, you should have weighed the difference of times, and have seen that what a Prime Minister could do in the end of the last century, your Lordship cannot effect in the middle of the present; therefore, it is the half century in advance, and not the intention of Lord John Russell, which has defeated the state trick.

Your Lordship has been pleased to designate the creed which I profess as the "mummeries of superstition."—This phrase is certainly not very courteous, although coming from the fountain of toleration; and, in making a reply, one is little disposed, even to you, to speak in language too highly perfumed. The Rev. Mr. Bennett, who styles himself "your Parish Priest," asserts, that you profess three distinct creeds—"that you turn your back in the evening on the principles which you professed in the morning;" and that, "when it suits your purpose, you gladly ignore all the laws and obligations of every church whatever." You are a Presbyterian in the morning, a Protestant at noon, and a Methodist in the evening; in fact, faith to you, my Lord, is a matter of taste rather than of principle. You change your religion with your dress; and hence you are a follower of John Knox, in your morning-gown, of John Calvin in your dress boots, and of John Wesley, in your night-slippers. You seem fond of namesakes in your various religions; and if Pope Pius IX. happened to be called John, ten to one, if the humor took your Lordship, but you would be found on next Christmas night, at Saint George's-in-the-fields at the midnight Mass of Cardinal Wiseman. St. Paul, uses the words "one Faith, one Baptism, one Lord;" by which he clearly teaches that unity of Faith is as essential as the unity of the Godhead; and, consequently, that two or more faiths are as absurd as two or more Gods.

Hence, my Lord, according to the clear logic of Saint Paul, your professing three faiths (as Mr. Bennett asserts,) is the same absurdity as if you worshipped three Gods; so that, after all, your Lordship is, unknown to yourself, a greater pagan, in point of fact, than all the heathen Irish, whom you have condescended to jibe in your late encyclical. The only thing in nature that bears any resemblance to this multitudinous faith and worship of yours is the sun-flower, alluded to in nice poetry in Moore's Melodies, as worshipping its God all day in different directions: or, as Mr. Bennett would say, turning its back in the evening on the point where it bowed its head in the morning; in fact, my Lord, there is a sort of diurnal rotation in your creed, which partakes rather of mathematics and natural philosophy than theology. Your Lordship appears to read the Athenasian Creed through a kaleidoscope, where every article appears under a variety of combinations, all equally beautiful. This idea enables me to comprehend why you pity so much the ecclesiastical system of the heathen Irish—poor wretches, they have, I admit, only one faith; and, therefore, they must appear extremely illiterate in revelation when compared with those elevated minds which have learned and profess three or four. You profession in this respect, reminds me of an anecdote of a man at an election for a Member of Parliament in Ireland, who carried the placard for the Tory member on his breast, and the placard for the Whig member on his back, and thus earned his hire shouting for the parties. This man was what might be called by your Lordship a liberal politician.

Your Lordship states, that the danger "within the gates is even greater," and causes to you greater indignation! than even the danger from the Pope. On this point I have the advantage entirely to agree with you; but the danger to be apprehended is, that all England will rush into wild infidelity, in consequence of your governing the Protestant Church, (of which I wish to speak with great respect) by the decisions of a Privy Council, and defining by your degree the doctrine, which is not necessary to be taught. All the world has heard of the Rev. Mr. Gorham, Vicar of Stampfordspeke, who believes in certain opinions relating to baptismal regeneration, the minutiæ of which are so well known to your Lordship. His Bishop refuses to present him to the vicarage—Mr. Gorham appeals, the Bishop persists; one says, that baptismal regeneration is not an essential doctrine of Christianity; the other says it is—Mr. Gorham says no: the Bishop of Exeter says yes: Sir Herbert Jenner Fust, of the Court of Arcees, says no: the Archbishop of Canterbury says, yes. The Chief Justice, Lord Campbell, says neither yes nor no: but in a letter to an English lady, says it is an "open question."

At length, my Lord, you who are learned in all creeds, take up the question, as chief in your Privy Council, and like the cat settling the dispute between the rabbit and the weazel, you make short work of it, and by a decision of the Privy Council! you decide what is not necessary to be taught in the Protestant church; and by way of proving the apostolicity of your mission, you would send down to Stamfordspeke a troop of dragoons, if necessary, to give a gentle hint of your infallibility. By the decision of your council, you have *bona fide* ignored the Protestant religion in England; and you would do well to record the event, by the following memorandum:

"The Protestant religion commenced in Germany, in the little town of Spires, about the end of the year 1517; flourished for 300 years and upwards in England, particularly in the neighborhood of cannon foundries and powder magazines; and ceased to be on the 16th July, 1850, when by an order of the Privy Council, Rev. Mr. Gorham was informed it was not necessary to teach any longer."

Now, my Lord, you are unknown to yourself, the Lay Pontiff of England, and your committee of three Judges are your infallible tribunal—and the decision which you and they assumed to Mr. Gorham, proves that you all belong to the respectable body of the "Society of Friends," since you all have decided against the doctrine of baptismal regeneration. Your Lordship, therefore, has by this act, shown that you have altogether four creeds! at present known to society. Now, my Lord, in sober sadness, can you imagine, that any thinking man will, or can remain in what you call "a church," where your Privy Council literally claims infallibility for the time being—that is, till the next variation of this thing called a church, will be made? In the time of Bossuet, there were 253 variations, and the remainder of changes since that period, are not necessary to be introduced in this letter.—But, can you seriously expect that men of learning and feeling can continue in an establishment where you set aside the ancient doctrines, once held to be essential—where you set aside the authority of a Bishop over his clergy, as you would the authority of a Custom-house Officer: where the Gospel is shuffled like a pack of cards; where the articles of faith, which were "trumps" to-day, may not answer "suit" to-morrow; where you settle the exact amount of the invisible grace of God, as a mineralogist would determine the per centage of iron ore; where you sell the cure of souls, as Rothschild would dispose of government stock to the highest bidder; and where you make essential doctrines, which were above par a year ago, now received at a discount, according to the whim of your Privy Council, and the demand for the gospel in the English market? St. Paul, in the quotation which I have already adduced, makes Baptism as essential a principle as "Faith, or as God;" but your Infallible Council thinks otherwise, and hence you decide the thing at once.

Bishops exclaim against you; but what do you care for bishops? The diocese of Limerick, in this heathen country, petition; but what does your Council care for the Protestant clergy of Limerick? Eighteen hundred Protestant clergy cry out against this interference with their doctrines and the authority of their bishops; but what care you for their clerical demonstration? All cry out for the right of private judgement in this grave discussion, the essential principle of their religion; but you cry out *nous avons changé tout celà*; that was heretofore the act of parliament, but since the seven hundredth variation! has been made, that principle now rests entirely in the Privy Council, and not at all in the bishops, or clergy, or people, *per Deum hominumque fidem!* Where this thing will end, no one living, not even your Lordship, so distinguished in theology, and in polytheism, can tell.

Your Lordship has been pleased to brand my church as a church of "mummery and of superstition;" but if ever mummery can be made palpable, it certainly can be seen and felt in three judges and a country gentleman, like your Lordship, changing the way to heaven as you would change a turnpike road; and if ever superstition stood naked before mankind, it is certainly to be seen in the act by which you expect that any man, in his plain senses, that any man except a born idiot, can make "an act of faith," in you who profess four creeds at once, as we know at present—in you, who, as Mr. Bennett asserts, are "bound by the laws and obligations of no church whatever"—in your Lordship, who make creeds, as a potter makes crocks, shaping them according to the public taste and the public demand—you even forgive sins.

The Bishop of Exter says it is a crying sin not to teach baptismal regeneration—you deny this assertion, coming from a common Bishop, and particularly not a member of the Privy Council; and, to show your spiritual power, you absolve Mr. Gorham from all guilt, and you give him your warrant of authority to present to God as a guarantee against his justice. 'Tis endless to recount the circumstances, the incongruities, the rank absurdities of your present Church establishment; and ten to one, unless it be managed by a skilful hand, it will bring a sad revolution on all the land. You seem to wonder at the danger arising from the crowds leaving your system, and joining the Dissenters or the Catholics—can you be so blind as not to see the just cause of this secession?

In order that any Christian shall conscientiously belong to this creed of your Council, it is necessary that he shall make "an act of faith" in its decisions; and what man under the sun can do that?—that is, "to make an act of faith" that you and your Council transmit the precise meaning of revelation from God—that what you decide is precisely the same as if Christ spoke—that your decision is beyond all doubt the unerring truth; that you and your Chancellor and Chief Justice, cannot deceive or be deceived. Now, without meaning any disrespect, you both are the two last men in England, on whose word in spirituals, a Christian would make an act of faith. You are clearly no theologian, or you would not profess four creeds at the same time, and the Chancellor has not read even Church history, as Mr. Bennett has already proved. Your decisions are, therefore, filled with doubt which is incompatible with belief; he who doubts clearly does not believe; and hence thousands of the unthinking masses of Englishmen are going into infidelity, as Rev. Mr. Jones has proved before a committee of the House of Commons; and all the reasoning portion, like the one hundred and forty-nine converts from Oxford and Cambridge, are coming to lay their weary heads beneath the roof of the Catholic Church, where God's testimony need not a warrant of the Privy Council as the foundation of their faith, and where they can with all their souls say, "I firmly believe."

I shall now conclude for the present, my Lord, and I

hope I have not uttered one word of disrespect towards you. I apologise if I have done so. I think I have read every printed speech and other works of yours which appeared these last twenty-five years; and having so long admired and followed you, I should be sorry to be wanting in courtesy towards you.

I have the honor to be, my Lord, your obedient servant,

D. W. CAHILL, D.D.

DR. CAHILL TO THE RIGHT HON. LORD JOHN RUSSELL.

My Lord—I shall take the liberty to trouble you with a second communication in reference to some additional passages in your late letter, which might create, if unexplained, considerable alarm in the minds of the Catholic Clergy and the people. The first passage is that where your Lordship writes:—

"Upon this subject, then, I will only say, that the present state of the law shall be carefully examined, and the propriety of *adopting any proceedings* with reference to the recent assumption of power carefully considered."

From these clear words, it appears evident that you are determined, if the present state of the law cannot meet the recent grievance, to *adopt* such measures as will effectually crush any further progress of the Papal power. This is a serious threat; and your Lordship being the Premier of England, you hold the precise office which can enable you to carry this threat into execution. You have, indeed, thus re-opened a burning question; and, from the history of your former life, you are the last man in England who, one could suppose, would so degrade your splendid name as to prop up your ministerial office with the old rotten "rack" and rusty "gibbet" of the sixteenth century. You have exhumed "More and Fisher," with tens of thousands of English and Irish martyrs to conscience; and you have called a coroner's inquest on the murdered dead, which will receive at present from all nations of the earth a verdict of "guilty" against all these sanguinary statesmen whose laws you are now about to "adopt."

You have brought to us the cruel remembrance of England's worst persecutors; you have stirred up from the forgotten depths of their crimson history a national agony which makes the Irish heart reel; and you have evoked an English spirit of intolerance which will not easily subside into its former composure. We, Catholics in Ireland, thought you incapable of entertaining even one intolerant feeling; but, my Lord, you have been educated, after all, in a prejudiced school, and, with your mother's milk, you have sucked in hostility to Catholicity. You took the bent in your infancy, which, now unknown to yourself, you evince against the Catholic Church:—

> "A pebble in the streamlet scant
> Has turned the course of many a river,
> A dew-drop on the baby plant
> May WARP the giant oak for ever."

Since, therefore, you are resolved to turn back on the path of legislation, and thus to rehearse the national tragedy of the penal code, will your Lordship be pleased to inform us, in which of the past reigns will you begin? which of the past Ministers will you take for your guide?

and which of the "legal proceedings" of these memorable days will you "adopt" in order to repel the Papal power?

These are important considerations for the "aggressors," as they will direct them to examine the conduct of the Catholics of the past days, and endeavor to imitate their example. Pray, then, Sir, will you begin in the reign of Henry the Eighth, and, with Thomas Cromwell for your model, will you "adopt the proceedings" of plundering the abbeys, demolishing the colleges, applying gunpowder to the priories, expelling the Priests, hanging the laity, and seizing the ancient legal property of the poor to the amount of forty millions of our money? If your Lordship will begin in this reign, and imitate your efficient ancestor of that memorable era, you will soon put an end to the present "sole and undivided sway of the Pope," and you will, at one blow, annihilate all the "mummeries of our superstition."

But perhaps you might rather choose to begin in the reign of Edward the Sixth, and follow "Somerset" as your example, when one Lord Russell hanged a Priest in Devonshire from the belfry of his own Church—when Bishoprics were seized to put down the bad example of the Bishops—when Churches were thrown down in honor of God's pure worship—when creeds were made and remade, in order, like a badly-made suit of clothes, that these creeds might have the newest cut, and fit tight to the conscience—when books of prayer were received or rejected by vote by ballot—when the office of St. Paul was set up to auction—and when the Apostles' Creed was won, or lost, or kept up by the distinguished players like a game of "spoiled five" or "blind hookey." There can be no doubt at all, this "reforming" reign will supply you with several facts which may serve as material for a second letter to the Bishop of Durham and the mob, and will enable you to "adopt legal proceedings" as "plenty as blackberries," for putting an immediate stop to Papal aggression.

I shall pass over the reign of Elizabeth, as I cannot suppose you would resolve to begin in this reign, and take either Cecil, or Walsingham, or Wentworth, as your models; and I feel rather confident that you would not "adopt the proceedings" of this Gospel reign, which entirely consisted of the constitutional laws of "hot-irons, racks, ropes, buckling-hoops, gibbets, and ripping-knives." These legal proceedings, if adopted, would save your Lordship the trouble of writing your late letter: "the Canon law on the doctrine of Grace, and on our enslaving mummeries," because these English decrees of the glorious Reformation, not only put an end to the abstract idea of Papal aggression, but they entirely silenced, removed out of England, and, indeed, out of this sublunary world altogether, the very aggressors themselves, together with their wives and children; and, alas! bearing on their mangled flesh and broken bones in the grave, the marks of "the proceedings" adopted by the Russell of these days to establish the Royal supremacy, and to crush the Papal power.

More blood has been spilled in England and Ireland on the subject of the Royal supremacy, than has ever been shed in any country on the earth, either from war, famine, or pestilence, or from all three taken together. Neither the Poles, under the Russian tyrant; or the Greeks, under the Turks, have lost so many of their children by the sword, the faggot, or banishment, as our country has lost by the axe, the rope, and by torture, in sustaining the question which your Lordship has introduced, by a gratuitous and wanton revival. Will you say, therefore, in what glorious reign; under what Christian chief, and under what legal statute, will you take your stand at the next Session of Parliament?

I wish to inform your Lordship, that I am not one of those who think your letter harmless, because it has, in *point of fact*, produced up to this period no very pernicious results. The same apology might be made for the assassin whose pistols hung fire, and missed his aim; the same excuse might be made for Guy Faux, who, in point of fact, did not blow up the whole Parliament. I do hold you guilty, and I do believe that you *intended* to produce a most violent attack on the Catholics in England and in Ireland; and, moreover, I believe, that if your letter were not ignored by the sense of the *English people*, and by the never-to-be-forgotten liberal feeling of the Irish Protestants, and by the Presbyterians in Ireland and Scotland, the Churches of England would in all probability have been torn down, and the Priests perhaps murdered in the streets.

There is one passage in your letter, in which any impartial man will clearly see you had intended the worst results. Your Lordship says:

"Even if it shall appear that the Ministers and servants of the Pope in this country have *not transgressed the law,* I feel persuaded we are *strong enough* to repel any outward "attack;" and again, "I rely with confidence on the *people* of England."

No language can be more clear than these words, to publish through England "that the Pope was not within the power of the *law*;" and that consequently, you relied on the people to exercise their *strength* (as mobs do) to trample down, kick, cut, and demolish the Papists, who were the enemies from without.

And hence, on the receipt of your command, scenes were commenced and acted, which the future historian of England will attribute to your name, with a censure from which that name can never escape. French Revolutionists, hear the conduct of the English mob, under the command of Lord John Russell! Yes, under your command—I repeat the words. Followers of Robespierre—you, who bowed down before the Goddess of Reason, hear, and reflect on the London mobs, under the command of the English Prime Minister! They burned the Pope in effigy—they burned Cardinal Wiseman in effigy; they burned Monks; they burned Friars; and, *proh pudor!* they burned the *Sisters of Charity!!!*

Lord John Russell, you have done this; and let me tell your Lordship, that the most ferocious bandit that ever lurked in the dark trackless Alps, whose dagger has not dried for years from the crimson stain of human blood—even from the black heart of that monster one generous feeling has been known to rise, and float above the tempest of his troubled conscience. That monster would not cross the path of a Sister of Charity, for fear his presence might alarm the consecrated virgin in her silent rounds to visit the abandoned sick, to bind the broken heart, to heal the wounded stranger.

And, *proh pudor! hinc lachrymæ!!* Alas! what next? Your mob burned in effigy; yes, they did—your mob, to the number of several thousands, burned in Putney, on the 5th Jan., 1850, the ever Blessed Virgin Mary! The daughter of David, the Virgin of Lebanon, and the mother of the God-man!—the descendant of Royalty, the genius of the Prophets, the Virgin "full of grace," the Mother of the Messiah, "blessed among women," could not escape your mob.

Yes, my Lord, you did this in free England; and the French Revolutionists never thought of such an act.—Even "Pilate" did not molest her, standing amongst the Jewish mob, while he condemned her adorable Son to the Cross; even the Deicide guards of thrilling Calvery did not insult her while she sat weeping at the foot of the Cross. No, no, my Lord, they did not; that act was reserved for the "Reformed" Minister of proud Albion, and for his Christian mob, "as by law established." No, no, she received protection from the Jews, but not from the Christians of Putney.

Sixty-two days elapsed from the date of your letter till this shameful occurrence at Putney; although you saw, and heard, and read the various insults offered to Nuns, Priests, &c., you never contradicted, by word or command, these proceedings; and hence, according to a well-know phrase, as "an accessory before the fact, during the fact, and after the fact:" you are decidedly guilty of this outrage against religion and common decency. Would you so treat the descendant of Alfred, merely because he revived Roman law, and drew the first draft of Magna Charta? Would you so treat the mother of "Nelson," merely because he widened the boundary of your Ocean Empire? I shall not dare the conclusion by making comparison between man and God. I shall only say on this point, that nothing further can be added to the insane extravagance of England's apostacy. And pray, my Lord, is the savage "Haynau" to be condemned for flogging women, who, after all, conspired against the State—who took part with their sons and husbands? And are your men to escape with impunity for burning inoffensive Nuns in effigy, and caricaturing the Mother of God? What ambition is there in taking the place of savage Haynau? He flogs—your men burn; he bleeds—your men scorch Nuns and the Blessed Virgin; and when next you honor us with a visit in Ireland, would it be surprising if the draymen of Cork or Dublin, would cry aloud, "Haynau, the burner of Nuns—Haynau, the caricaturist of the Blessed Virgin?

But the day may come, when Englishmen may have some heavier work to do than burning Nuns of pasteboard, and Cardinals of straw; and when Prime Ministers may have more important duties to mind besides encouraging infidelity, spreading national discord, burning swaddling preachers, manufacturing a splendid pinchbeck religion of the most modern pattern at present in use in England, and placing Christian Faith in the very apogee of Scripture, tradition, and theology.

My opinion, my Lord, of your penal threat is, that,

when you will have seen the general opposition to your proceedings, you must let the contemplated measure drop; and that, too, for many reasons—firstly, because the subject of the public panic is exceedingly frivolous, the whole thing being, the difference between the words "Bishop" and "Vicar-Apostolic;" and, again, between the words "District" and "Diocese." The dispute reminds me of the national horrors mentioned in Gulliver's Travels, where two nations went to war, and fought several sanguinary battles, to determine which end of an egg might be broken at breakfast! One nation contended that *the little end* should be broken, and hence they were called the "Little Endian," somewhat resembling the *diocese men* of the present controversy; others contended for the *big end*, and were called the "Big Endians," somewhat resembling the *district men* of the present controversy, and fairly representing your Lordship, the Bishops, the Clergy, and the London and Putney mobs. There can be no doubt, that there is no more difference in the *English* controversy than in the *Lilliputian* war; that Bishop and diocese, are convertible terms with Vicar-Apostolic and district; and that when men will seriously reflect on the matter, both your Lordship and the English people will be perfectly indifferent whether Cardinal Wiseman belong to "the Little or the Big Endians."

Secondly—The Catholics, Presbyterians, and Dissenters, are very numerous in our European part of the empire; (more numerous than Protestants,) and hence, it would be dangerous to make a law, which, in point of fact, would and should, and ought to be equally insulting to them, to the Catholics; and these are not times, my Lord, to be playing Parliamentary tricks with millions of people, and quarrelling with loyal subjects and devoted friends, in order to gratify the whims of a Church which cannot be in existence in one hundred years to come. Your Lordship's Cabinet will, of course, advise laws not only for the present generation, but for their successors; and I think it will appear evident (as Sir Fowell Burton used to say, talking of slavery in the West Indies,) that no Legislator ought to make laws, which he ought to forsee *must* end in revolution in half a century to come.

Thirdly, my Lord, I must take the liberty of telling you, that there is not the least use in your framing laws against the Catholic Church. She has triumphed over more powerful nations than England; defied even a greater man than the present Premier of Great Britain; and she has outlived tongues, and creeds, and dynasties, which had a stronger case against her than the Putney heroes.

Your countrymen are not more powerful than the followers of Ruric and Alaric the First; they never were so terrible as Attila or Genseric; your Bishops are not more learned than Gobaldus; nor any of your orators and philosophers at the late county meetings, to be compared with Julian. Your national creed, is not more extensive than Arianism; and yet, my Lord, these are all gone, departed, and forgotten, and their progeny extinct; while here we are, the young Catholic branches of the old stock, flourishing through the spring of ages, without sign or symptom of decay. As long as the old *roots* of the old parent stock are fixed in the soil, (which is true,) you may cut down as often as you can; we spring up again when the winter is past; and our motto is "*Recissa Resurge.*"

You threaten us with Acts of Parliament. Excuse me: we laugh at Acts of Parliament, because we know that the same hand that balances creation has raised our Altars, and will never disturb the foundation of His own Church; because we know that the power which can chain the whirlwind, and tame the swollen empires of the ocean, can, when he pleases, subdue your heart and the Putney mob; and, above all, we know that it is quite as foolish in you, to attempt to impede our onward progress against the will of God, by Acts of Parliament, and bonfires, and bags of chaff, and barrels of pitch! as it would be, if you sent the 12th Lancers to stop the tide, or called on your astronomer at Greenwich to put off till evening an eclipse of the English people.

And will you permit me to ask your Lordship, if we are the barbarian Priests of a heathen people, why are you afraid of us? How can such barbarian Priests, with their rude clubs of "mummery" stand a moment before the discipline of your Ecclesiastical "reformed" infantry of Oxford and Cambridge? What are you afraid of? Why do you meet our logic with the bayonet? Why guard off our theology with burning faggots, and stop our mouths with your favorite Scripture proofs (the rope) if we are the sadly educated wretches, the Pagan vulgarians, the heathen mummers whom you represent us?

Pray, Sir, why are you so much afraid of us? If our superstitions are so filthy; surely the merchants, the traders, the barristers, the solicitors, the physicians, the scholars of Great Britain, so remarkable for their talents, experience, tact, and knowledge, have only to see us, and hear our doctrine, to be horrified at our confining the intellect and enslaving the soul—why, then, are you afraid to let them hear us, and listen to our arguments? Is there no internal evidence in the prohibition to hear us, that you fear the force of our reasoning and the resistless strength of our traditionary title deeds? Say what you will—conceal it as you can—your fears show that we are your masters in learning, and that we alone possess the legitimate inheritance of being the lineal descendants of the Apostles.

We have met your best men in controversy foot to foot, and they were obliged to respect our learning, and pay deference to our talents. Your most polished men are becoming converts to our doctrine; and the erudition of 1800 years belongs confessedly to the Catholic name, long, long before your Lordship's many-colored Faith was known in the world. And yet, we, the modern Catholic Priests, fight only with the *small arms* of our ancestors in the Church. There is no man of the present day amongst us whom the armor of St. Augustine would fit: it is too large for modern men and too heavy for our strongest controversialists to bear up for a moment. No man of the present day could lift the club of Tertullian, with which, in his ancient battles, he conquered all the enemies of his creed; and the mouth of the "Amazon" can alone give you the best idea you can form of the golden flood of language, the resistless power of eloquence, which poured from the Catholic lips of St. Chrysostom.

My Lord, may I ask if you have read the history of these men, and the victories they won? Have you read the history of the brilliant exploits performed by their successors in all the Christian ages, and in all the countries? and if not, I shall only say, when you have read them, your Lordship will see at once how foolish it is to think of subduing conscience by faggots of burning straw; how insane it is to hope of teaching the Faith of the Gospel through the light of pitch-barrels and bonfires; and how ridiculous to fancy that "the children of the Saints could tremble before the sons of Voltaire," or how the descendants of "Fisher and Plunket" could blench before the successors of Cranmer.

Fourthly, your Lordship will not, I am sure, introduce the penal bill, simply because you have too much to do with other matters of greater moment to yourself personally. You have to compose all the elements which you have called into furious antagonism. Thus you have made an adversary of Lord Roden and his party some time past; and hence you have hoped to pacify him by giving the Catholic heathens (the Chippewa Indians,) the late knock on the head. You have irritated the Dissenters of England by your late education policy, and you wished to propitiate them by the late pitched-barrels, and the phantasmagoria of Guy Fawkes. You have offended the Protestant Bishops of England by your late liberal policy; and hence it was necessary to return back to the sixteenth century, and satisfy these Divines with recent lectures on penal enactments; and most strange (as a proof of your great talents,) you have so deeply offended the Catholics of the whole world by your letter; you now think, therefore, (in order to please us,) of uprooting the Protestant Church in Ireland!! That you will do this work, is as certain as that I am writing to you at the present moment; but on this subject I shall not say one word, for fear I should utter one syllable of disrespect towards any one member of that Church.

You have, therefore, a great deal to do. My Lord, during the next Session of Parliament, you have to pour oil on the waters which you have lashed into fury. In fact, there has never been a Minister of Great Britain who has been playing such tricks with the nation, as your Lordship has been playing with all parties during the past year; you have been encouraging the nation to carry on the children's play of "weighdee bucketdee;" you have yourself presided over the machinery—lifted all parties up and down at your pleasure, like a magician, and all this, in order to throw dust in the eyes of all England and Ireland, while you yourself keep the secure post of Prime Minister.

But if the Protestants and Catholics of Ireland could only see this lessening performance of yours in its true colors of knocking our heads together for the amusement of the English, we would unite in one compact body of Irishmen, (making it a crime even to introduce the demon discord of religious rancor into their Assemblies,) and if this body would enter on their duties, not in giving opposition to Government, or in doing any such foolish thing, but attending to their own national interests, they would soon compel your Lordship, or any of your official successors, to treat us with more respect, and more seriousness than setting us to fight with each other, and carrying on a shameful State-hoax upon the entire country.

In conclusion, my Lord, there is no more reason to show that you will not unfrock the English Bishops just now. There is a Royal personage who will not permit you. Her most gracious, and most beloved, and most excellent Majesty will not give you leave to put your thumbscrew upon our Church. No person can ever forget the silent, dignified censure which her Majesty passed upon you, during the reading of five most important addresses. I need only mention the address alone from the Corporation of London, her own chief city; yet she never alluded in her answer to this address from her own city, by even one word, to any one word in your letter. This Royal silence on this important occasion, was, without any exception at all, the most withering, the most degrading rebuke to a Prime Minister recorded in English history; and there you stood in a pillory, swallowing your own words, and, (to use a term from the clubs,) "snubbed" to your face.

I say, that the Pope can never return sufficient thanks to the Queen of England for this most brave and generous conduct. I question much, if any Catholic Sovereign in Europe would have the heart or the courage, under similar circumstances, so to treat her Prime Minister. She did not endorse any one of your Lordship's sentiments. You are, therefore, clearly, my Lord, no longer the exponent of the Royal mind, and not to be the exponent of the Royal mind, is the very definition of your dismissal. Yet, your Lordship holds your place. For this and all her other acts of kindness, may she long live to rule over her boundless empire—may she triumph over all her enemies, and confound their politics; may God add still more to her domestic happiness; may her court continue to be a model of virtue to every Palace in Europe; and may the stability of her throne be transmitted to her children's children, is the prayer of every Catholic Priest in her invincible empire.

I shall, my Lord, watch the progress of the next Session of Parliament; and if you will persevere in fulfilling your promise of enacting any penal law against my Church, I shall, most humbly, trouble you with a third letter, in continuation of the same subject.

I have the honor to be, my Lord, your Lordship's obedient servant,

D. W. CAHILL, D.D.

DR. CAHILL TO THE RIGHT HON. LORD JOHN RUSSELL.

AIRDRIE, SCOTLAND, *November* 4, 1851.

MY LORD—This day brings before the minds of the Catholics of the whole world the painful recollection of your letter to the Bishop of Durham. Twelve months have now elapsed since the publication of that inflammatory and persecuting document; and time and experience, which are the best tests of political wisdom, have proved that your views have been incorrect and your speeches exaggerated. The Bishops have assumed their titles, and they exercise their diocesan jurisdiction without infringing on the principles of the Constitution, or trenching on the prerogatives of the Crown. Your statesmanship, therefore, is a palpable failure—your penal law is a political lie; and Lord John Russell stands before the gaze of mankind, a false leader, and a naked bigot.

As your Lordship is about to enter on this day into the second year of your ministerial Hegira, it may not be amiss to present to your Lordship, a historical review of the conduct of your Cabinet during the last few years—and to inform the people of Ireland and Great Britain, of the disastrous position to which you have reduced the British Empire, both as regards its internal interests and its external relations. I have already laid before my most persecuted fellow-countrymen the intrigues of Lord Palmerston and his corps of diplomatique, in aiding the revolutionists of five different countries in Europe; and I have proved, that he attempted at the same time to overthrow the authority of the Pope, and to uproot the discipline and the Faith of the Catholic Church. You were, of course the abettor and the prime mover of these two-fold intrigues; and thus, we clearly convict you of *appearing* during five years, as the advocate of our national and religious liberties, while, in fact, you were secretly undermining our inherent rights, and treacherously sapping the foundations of our creed.

Your letter of November, 1850, disclosed your real character, developed your long concerted plans, and will be distinguished in our future history, as the Russell conspiracy; and it will take its place in enormity, and precedence in the paragraph, next to the atrocious memory of the Gunpowder Plot. Guy Fawkes and Lord John Russell, will, therefore, fill two correlative pages, alike in their aim, treachery, and their failure.

I informed my poor faithful countrymen, in last March (that is such of them as you had not starved, and *pitted* at that time,) that your intrigues were well known in every Court in Europe; that you were digging a pit for England, which very soon would engulph the whole Empire; and that a European combination against the machinations of the English Cabinet, would be the inevitable result of your unexampled political and religious deceit. And I informed my bleeding country not to despair, that the sword of God's justice would be soon drawn against our oppressors—that the hour of their deliverance was nearer than they imagined; and to stand fearlessly and firm together in a national confederacy. I am now in a position to prove these points, and to lay before the Queen and the country, the undisguised expression of universal hostility, which your unprecedented cabinet schemes have lashed into fury in almost every Court in Europe. May I, therefore, my Lord, beg your calm perusal of the following extracts; they will point out the unmistakable combination of foreign Courts, and the gulf which you are preparing for England:—

"A private letter from Frankfort, dated the 6th, and received in Paris on Monday, states that Lord Palmerston has directed a note to be presented through Lord Cowley to the President of the Diet, Count Thun, in which he requests the Assembly to take steps with respect to the Neapolitan government, in order to induce it to abandon the political system it has hitherto followed. The note was accompanied by several copies of Mr. Gladstone's pamphlet. The affair was discussed in the sitting of the Diet, held on the 20th September. The President, in an address at once clear and precise, showed how unusual and unbecoming such a demand was. He dwelt particularly on the extraordinary proceeding of a government claiming on the authority of any individual statement to interfere in matters purely domestic of another nation, and with the administration of justice of an independent government, and he concluded by calling on the Assembly to reject the demand made upon it. The Minister of Prussia to the Diet, declared it as his opinion that the demand of Lord Palmerston was neither more nor less than *defiance to all continental policy,* and should be met by a very decided answer. It was, therefore, resolved that the President of the Diet should be authorised to reply to Lord Palmerston to the effect that the German Diet, having made itself acquainted with the note of the British government, and the contents of which appeared to it as unusual, as they were little in harmony with the ordinary usages of international relations practised by all Governments, felt all the less disposed to interfere with the domestic affairs of a foreign Government as independent of itself, as it *would not permit any one,* whoever he may be, to meddle with those of the Confederation; and it was for that reason, it disapproved and rejected the line of conduct proposed by Lord Palmerston in the name of his cabinet. An answer to that effect has been made to Lord Cowley."

The Frankfort journals state, that Russia has replied to Lord Palmerston's note, inclosing Mr. Gladstone's letter, in *a strain exactly similar* to that put forth by the Germanic Diet against interference with the concerns of foreign countries.

In the foregoing communication, Lord Palmerston, with his usual duplicity, endeavors to concoct a conspiracy against Naples, and he sends one of his characteristic despatches to one of his characteristic companions (your nominees and servants,) to intrigue with the German Diet—and Prussia to intrigue with Russia, and when this snaking and most cowardly conspiracy should be finally formed, then to menace Italy and Naples with a combined attack, in order to *redeem* your pledge to the unfortunate dupes and victims whom your diplomacy excited to revolution, and drove to exile and death. But Germany, and Prussia, and Russia, have clearly "snubbed" your colleague, and have read to you and to him a lesson of defiance, which places your Cabinet in the most humiliating posture. But the contempt offered to you, does not end here; Lord Palmerston grounded this your conspiracy, on the private communication of Mr. Gladstone, which has been disproved, word for word, by Mr. M'Farlane and Monsieur Condon. And here I shall take leave to present to the Queen, "snub the second," which your honorable colleague has received from Prince Castelcicala, Minister of the King of Naples; let England read this second contumely cast on this country:—

PRINCE CASTELCICALA TO VISCOUNT PALMERSTON.
15, Prince's-street, Cavendish-square, August 9th.

MY LORD—In a report which appeared in the *Times* paper of yesterday, of the sitting of the House of Commons, I have read that your Excellency, in answer to a question put by Sir De Lacy Evans, relative to some publications of Mr. Gladstone against the Government of the King my August Master, said you considered it your duty to send copies of the same to the British Ministers at the various Courts of Europe; and since a reply to the said publication, grounded upon substantial documents has recently made its appearance, I have the honor to send fifteen copies to your Excellency, and therefore request your Excellency will take precisely the same means for distribution, as you have done for those of Mr. Gladstone.

The known maxim *Audi alteram partem*; the courtesy of your Excellency, and, in the present conjuncture, what is better, your justice; all lead me to hope that your Excellency will not find my request indiscreet.

CASTELCICALA.

It is impossible not to see the sneer of contemptuous derision with which the foreign Prince demands reparation for the national slander, backed as he is by all Europe, and the painful position of Lord Palmerston in his shifting reply, excites pity for the man, and shame for the

Minister. Your Minister of War stammered, hesitated, shuffled, before this honorable, and firm, and decided request of Naples; and finally, with a doggedness so peculiarly his own, refused to make the reparation of a gentleman, for the most palpable misstatement, and the most obvious perversion of facts.

My next extract shall be taken from one of the highest ministerial and commercial journals of Austria—an extract which places your Cabinet in a position degrading to the whole empire, tending to tarnish the high reputation of British honor, and which ought to be a sufficient reason to remove you from a station which you fill with discredit to the State, and with injury to the Crown. No British subject can read the following extract without shame, and horror, and indignation:—

(*From the Austrian Lloyds.*)

"The ovations, which are now under preparation in England, in honor of an Austrian subject guilty of treason to his Sovereign, and of having ignited the flame of revolution in his native country, do not arouse our indignation to any great extent. We feel a pity, mixed with uncommon contempt, for the stupid, well-fattened (*stupiden wahlgemastatem*) aldermen of Southampton and London. In 1848 the English Foreign Office gave *itself every possible pains to dismember the Austrian Empire.* The noble Lord at the head of the government tried all that *intrigue, duplicity, treachery* and *deceit* could do, to obtain his ignoble ends. Whilst a Minister of the highest diplomatic rank, represented his Queen at the Austrian Court, and ostensibly in public, spoke of the friendly relations existing between Great Britain and Austria, secret agents in the *pay of the English Cabinet*, and its public servants—men like Lords Minto and Abercrombie—were laying intrigues which were soon to acquire an historical importance. The mines were dug, the powder laid, and on a signal *transmitted from Downing street*, the explosion followed. A portion of South and Central Europe was in flames. Lord Ponsonby remained in Vienna, a guarantee of England's Punic faith to her old ally. Meantime, that unhappy King, whose tragic fate shields him from too severe a judgement being passed upon him, was driven to distraction and *to death* by British intrigue; and as Kossuth can boast of *Lord Palmerston's friendship*, with equal right may it be claimed by all the rebel leaders in the different parts of Europe

That many of them were discarded by their *quondam* friend in their hour of distress, is no refutation of the fact. Even English Journals have declaimed against Lord Palmerston for having *unmercifully* abandoned the men *he had mislaid,* as soon as their plans proved unsuccessful.

"Every victory of the Austrian arms in Italy and Hungary—the close alliance between Austria and Russia–the successful suppression of the revolution wherever it broke forth —the failure of the Prussian scheme to drive Austria out of Germany — finally, the consolidation of the power of the Empire — were so many severe and keenly felt blows to English policy. Never was a Cabinet compelled to make so *many miserable retractions,* never did a Cabinet suffer so many painful defeats, or *lose* so much *influence, honor and respect,* as the English Cabinet at this period. Its influence in the Mediterranean, to which England attached so much importance, vanished. The Cabinets of Madrid, Naples, Athens, justly regarded England as their *enemy.* The infamous proceedings against Greece, aroused the slumbering sense of honor and justice even of the British Parliament, and threatened the ministry with a disgraceful termination of the office.

"Rage at foiled plans, vexation at the defeats sustained by Sardinia, shame at being *convicted of dishonesty,* had been gnawing for some time at the hearts of leading men in England. Their impotency to harm Austria makes them give vent to their feeling, by making grimaces at it. A man convicted in Austria of high treason, is therefore to be received as an honored guest. This is not done so much in his honor as to offend loyal Austrians. We scarcely think this demonstration will attain its object. The loyal Austrian has reason to rejoice, that the mightiest and most hostile endeavors, that the most deeply laid and deceitful plans of one of the most powerful Cabinets of Europe; have not succeeded in preventing the regeneration of his country; and that England has no other means left to resort to, to express its rage at its failure, but to render honors to a man who had been banished from his country for political offences."

Verily, my Lord, your diplomacy on the European Continent, is likely very soon to inflict a heavy blow on our common country. There can be no doubt that all Europe is beginning to combine, and, in fact, to arm itself against England. You have roused (and the world will say, justly,) the anger of Switzerland, and Naples, and Germany, and Prussia, and Russia, and Austria. Lord Palmerston is, in fact, the Captain Rock of Europe, and under the pretext of preserving European peace, you are fomenting a European war. Take care, lest the mines you are digging under other nations, may be imitated in return under England; and beware, lest the explosion you have prepared for them, may not involve your own country in irretrievable ruin. Verily, Lord John Russell is rather unfortunate in his foreign relations, and as Lord Stanley has already prophesied of your Cabinet, "unless you are checked in this unrestrained career, you will inevitably bring on a European war."

There can be no greater enemy to England over the civilized world, which sooner or later will check her dominant power, lower her high national name, and vitally damage her commercial interests. The clear statements of all reform associations show that the taxes, direct and indirect, on every twenty shillings worth of consumption and manufacture in England, amount to thirteen shillings and two pence; that the people of England, therefore, can claim as their own, (for their capital and skill,) only six shillings and ten pence in every pound, which they give the State. And hence, Sir, if through your unbridled ministerial dictation and domination through Europe, you *compel* foreign nations to quarrel with us, to dread our connexion, to establish their own factories, and to annihilate or diminish our trade, you will cause a revolution in England, such as history has never recorded, and your name will be transmitted to posterity, as the greatest enemy that England ever saw. For the first time in English history, we behold a decided and universal attitude of defiance, assumed by Europe against England; your Ambassadors are insulted, your votes of diplomacy scoffed, and one loud voice of contempt and indignation is raised against your diplomatic conduct and your country, from the Baltic to the Mediterranean.

This is a fact beyond all dispute, and it establishes by a clear demonstration, that England is regarded at this moment by universal Europe, as the disturber of international peace, the fomentor of revolution, the secret enemy of foreign thrones, and the insidious persecutor of the Catholic Church. If I were actuated by the revenge to which your unexampled perfidy has reduced your country; but I am neither a revolutionist or a rebel, but I am an Irish Priest. These two words contain the record of national honor and of national loyalty. And when you and your colleagues would behead the sovereign, as you did Charles, and join a plebeian usurper, as you did Cromwell, and expel your monarch, as you did James, and receive a foreigner, out of a poor house, as you did William I., and every one of the ancient order to which I belong, would bleed at the foot of the throne, as we have done, through every age and country. And when you and the class to which you are associated, would change your creed from Presbyterianism to Protestantism, and *vice versa;* and from somethingism to anythingism or nothingism; and while you prove before scorning men, weeping angels, and laughing devils, that your official cravat, or the cut of your official coat; we, the glorious Catholic people, and we, the heroic Priests, stand through all time, and place, and circumstances, faithful to God, and loyal to the throne; and we stand forth, a contrast to your officiality, like truth to falsehood, light to darkness, and national honor to national perfidy.

Such, my Lord, being your official work on the European Continent, I shall proceed to enquire how matters stand at home, in persecuted Ireland. But before I shall commence this melancholy view of your disastrous legislation, I must beg leave to tell you, that, although Ireland is bent to the earth by the heartlessness, the calumnies, and the cruel oppression of your rule, we are still firm and fearless, and we are undismayed, either by the threats of unjust power, or the scandalous jibes of a lying and bribed press. You may cut down, but you cannot eradicate—you may strike us prostrate for a time of ferocious triumph, but we shall rise again—you may expel us from the soil of our fathers, but we shall appear again, renovated in number and power, on the glorious American Continent. You may make cruel laws for the year 1851, but take warning of the results of these laws before the year 1951. You cannot keep us always in slavery and degradation, the history of the world is against this position. Where you least expect a reaction, you may receive a fatal national blow; and your name as an English gentleman, and your character as a statesman, will live longer in the future applause of the historian, for being the advocate of honor and justice, rather than the supporter of perfidy and persecution. Powerful as you are, we shall never learn a lesson difficult to the instructions which our fathers have taught us; we have never yet yielded to your injustice through three centuries of cruelty, and we shall not now begin to take you, for our political and national master.

We believe, besides, that between the Kaffirs, and the

Australians, and the Canadians, and the peoples of all Europe, you have rather too much on your hands just now, to appear in the second act of the late dramatic State Trials, and we think (that is, as many of us as are alive,) that in the present state of France, (with which your Captain Rock appears on such good terms,) you will rather defer, for the present, the ancient custom of erecting your gibbets and your old racks, on the red cross-roads, which bear your name. Indeed, I may as well tell you, my Lord, that, without meaning the least disrespect, of course, to the Queen's Minister, we fearlessly set you at defiance; and we are thoroughly convinced (a position which I could prove, if I wished,) that you have not the most remote notion of persecuting us at present; and we know, that you know, that we know that you are very near a crisis, when you will be compelled to cultivate our friendship rather than provoke our further anger at your unprecedented conduct.

Alas! alas! where shall I begin to tell your political career, as regards poor trodden-down, faithful, persecuted Ireland? Nor is it with ink and paper, I would attempt the description of the woes of your rule. No, no, my Lord; the deserted village, the waste-land, the unfrequented chapel, the silent glen, the pale face, and the mournful national voice, stamp the history of Ireland with the deep, deep impression of your administration; while the ferocity of the unbridled landlord, and the terrors of the uprooted and mouldering cabins, and the cries of the houseless orphan, and the tears of the broken-hearted widow, and the emigrant ship, and the putrid workhouse, and the red oozing pit of the coffinless and shroudless dead—these, these, oh! all these, are all the thrilling and eloquent witnesses, to publish to coming generations, and to unborn Irishmen, the character and the laws of the Russell Cabinet! Ah, Sir, when you had read the terrific facts of the mother living on the putrid remains of her own child; and when you saw the awful account of several cases, of the dead bodies of the poor Irish being exposed for days in unburied putridity, and devoured by dogs in this unheard of state; and when you had heard the cries that were wafted across the channel for help, and those that rose to heaven for mercy, from Skibbereen, from Ballinasloe, from Kilrush, and from Ballinrobe—has your heart, Sir, ever smote you with remorse, that you heard these cries of Ireland with a pittiless composure, and sent to starving and dying millions, a heartless pittance from your overflowing treasury?

I distinguish your Cabinet from the English people—they stretched forth their hands with the characteristic generosity of their nation; the Society of Friends well fulfilled too, the expectations of their own philanthropy in our regard—but you, Sir, from an exchequer filled with eighteen millions of bullion; you doled out in withering insult, (as to the beggars of a foreign country,) a miserable and totally inadequate relief: and you called by the name of charity an act, which should be designated the first demand on the realm, and the highest duty of the Crown. Lord Stanley paid twenty millions sterling, to give *liberty* to a few descendants of African slaves in your petty West Indian colonies; to men who never manned your fleets, or swelled your armies, or fought for your name. But you, Sir, grudgingly *lent* in part, and bestowed in part, the paltry sum of eight millions, to aid the last struggle for *life* of the faithful people, whose misfortune in all our past history, was imperishable loyalty to the throne, and undying devotion to our unfortunate kings—men who belong to an ancient, unbroken race of forty generations; lion hearts, which crimsoned with their blood every ocean where your navy fought and conquered—which stood before the bristled steel of England's foes in all your struggles; which shared the perils of a thousand fields of blood by the side of your countrymen, and won your victories—these are the men, and this is the nation to whom you have given your paltry usurious charity to preserve their lives. But the history of all nations will yet tell that you permitted *five in ten* to perish of hunger, while your exchequer was *filled with gold*. You, therefore, Sir, have made my country a desert—you have banished and starved the people—you have made a grave for the Irish—and you have buried our race and name. May God forgive you this cruel treatment of our fine people—this ministerial atrocity. We charge you before a revenging Heaven, with the exile and the death of our people; both crimes lie at your door. And you have added ingratitude to cruelty. We honored you, we followed you. You did not so much surprise us by the introduction of your Penal Bill, as by the historical falsehood, and the insulting bigotry of your speeches; they were unworthy the historian, below the dignity of the statesman, and dishonorable to the man. A third-rate orator amongst your own party, and a fifth-rate speaker in the whole house—you never could lay claim to distinction, except from the supposed honesty and liberality of your political opinions; but now your inconsistency and your bigotry, having torn from your face the mask which concealed your mediocrity; it is agreed, that the foremost leader of the Whigs, has now been befittingly transformed into the last hack of the Tories. Oh, for the ancient truth and honor of the old English statesman!—oh, for the sterling word, the generous foe, the brilliant genius of the days that are gone; or as Pope would sing it:—

"How can I Pultney, Chesterfield forget
While Roman spirit charms and Attic wit?
Argyle, the State's whole thunder born to wield,
And shake alike the Senate and the field,
And if yet higher the proud list should end,
Still all will say—*no follower but a friend.*"

Now, the origin of all these misfortunes at home and abroad, arises from a two-fold cause; firstly, to organize an English party in every country, as you have done in Spain and Portugal; to keep a perfect internal system of disorder in every nation, in order to keep the power of each country engaged in quelling this Confederacy, and thus leaving England free to pursue her views of conquest and commerce, without fear of resistance from the surrounding nations: and secondly, the object is to uproot Catholicity. This latter point, is in fact, your chief and sole aim: and so wide-spread are your present stratagems to speech-down, preach-down, write-down, drink-down, eat-down, dress-down, sail-down, and shoot-down Catholicity, that all orders of the State are actually gone mad, with what may be called a furious fanaticism to get rid of Catholicity. All the lawyers are infected, from the well-known Chancellor to the parish beadle; all the clergy are bitten, from Canterbury (the cubical head of your present creed,) down all along to the thin curate; who being the living definition of a mathematical straight line, may be considered as the clerical element of the Archbishop. All your ambassadors, are actually become swaddlers in every Court in Europe, as I have already proved---so that yours should be called the Swaddling Cabinet. And the omnipresent navy, and the invincible army of Great Britain have raised their swaddling colors nearly as high as the Union-Jack all over the earth. All your modern writers are innoculated with swaddleomania, down from the historical lies and rhetorical foppery of Macauley, to the half-penny sheet; there are even swaddling commercial travellers, swaddling hotels, and swaddling boarding-houses; and such is the vast ramification of this most absurd, but terrific movement against Catholicity, that "Moore's Melodies," are banished from the society of all anti-papal pianos, because they relate to Ireland, and were composed by the native fancy, that drank its poetic inspiration at the fountain of Irish genius!

But amongst the various incongruities of this mania which you have originated, there is not one which strikes the observer with such preposterous associations, as to see an admiral of a fleet dressed in the garb of Joanna Southcote! or to see a general of an army converted into a Praise-God Barebones. Nothing can be so extremely ludicrous as to see Neptune kneeling and praying on a three-legged stool, dressed in a white cravat and a coat of shabby black! or to behold Mars habited in lawn sleeves and a powdered wig, reading and singing psalms on a tar-barrel! There is scarcely a paper which does not contain, with the cognizance of the Duke of Wellington, religious collisions in chapels, in barracks, and in churchyards, between the faithful, fearless Priest, and some Jumper in epaulettes, at the different military stations. Take my advice, my Lord, humble though it be, and put an end to this monstrous state of things. The individual who checks this incongruity, is the best friend of the throne and the Catholic Church; stamp on the earth, and stop its motion; command the tide, and arrest its progress; prove your commission, and preach down the Cross, and we shall believe you; but until you will have demonstrated that your words are more credible than "the language of an angel from heaven," we shall laugh at your folly and despise your impotency.

In conclusion, my Lord, I must tell you, with the greatest respect of your exalted position, that this letter is not so much intended for you as for the Courts of Russia, Prussia, Austria, France, Naples, Spain, Portugal, and the glorious Republic of America. I do not mention this fact from any puerile allusion to myself; I cannot so far forget the rules of public courtesy, as to be wanting (while in your presence,) to the serious respect and becoming reverence which so humble an individual as I am, owes to your exalted station; but I repeat that, men equal to you in station, and your superiors in aristocratic associations, have made official arrangements to publish my letters to your Cabinet all over the civilized world. My only merit consists in publishing the woes of my country, and the unparalleled cruelties of your administration to the whole people of Ireland, and to our ancient Church, and I shall undertake to say, that the *united voice of Europe is already expressed against you* in the various cabinets, (which I shall furnish to you in a succeeding letter,) and that your treatment of Ireland, and your persecution of the Catholic Faith, will raise such a combination against you, during the *next three months*, that your Sovereign will be necessarily and justly compelled to remove you from an office which you hold at present with such injury to the English name, and so much indignity to the British Crown. I am not influenced in the course I am taking, by any revengeful feeling towards you. I am grateful to England for whatever favors she has conferred upon Ireland, and I am most ready to acknewledge it; and I pray to God that he may change the hearts of our rulers to govern us by the justice of law, and not by the bigotry of persecution; but I shall never flinch from the post I have taken in defence of my country and my creed, though that defence were visited with punishment or death.

I am, my Lord, your obedient humble servant,

D. W. CAHILL, D.D.

LETTER OF THE REV. DR. CAHILL

TO HIS GRACE FIELD MARSHAL

THE DUKE OF WELLINGTON.

"The French *could detach* a force from their army, which, if it were transported across the Channel, could reach and *occupy London*. The passage across the Channel *could not be with any certainty prevented* by an ENGLISH FLEET. As to smaller expeditions, an army, exceeding in numbers the entire military forces of Great Britain, *could in all human probability* be lodged in a fortified camp on our shores *within a week* after the declaration of war. Not to mention the purely military considerations, it is obvious that in the very names of *peace and humanity* such *measures would be* PREFERRED as would terminate the war at the earliest moment by forcing the enemy to TERMS."

(London Times, Friday Jan. 23, 1852.*)*

NEWCASTLE-ON-TYNE, ENGLAND,
Saturday, Jan. 24, 1852.

MY LORD DUKE—The announcement just quoted, and published on yesterday by your own journal, cannot fail to fill with surprise and delight all those who, throughout the world have been accustomed, up to this period, to hear no language uttered by England except the voice of triumph, defiançe, domination and tyranny. There can be no mistake in the official *succumbing* of the *Times*. For the first time in the history of the last six hundred years, England acknowledges the superiority of her old rival, the facility of the occupation of her shores, the successful storm of London, and the total weakness of your fleet to meet the emergency. Alas! is it come to this, in the craven article of your own organ; that England sues for "peace" before war is declared—already offers "terms to the enemy; and, more strange still, talks of "humanity" in arms? Proud Albion at last cries for mercy; and the world has lived to see the joyful hour, when the fleets of Marlborough and Nelson lower their meteor flag before the old Eagle of Napoleon.

The hour of her degradation is therefore come; her name is fallen; her prestige is at this moment a mere historical remembrance; and I think I speak the universal sentiment of mankind, when I say, that the voice of justice, liberty, and religion, will be heard all over the earth, proclaiming the news that Babylon is fallen; and the armament which rode over all the oceans in undisputed sway; which swept the waters as with a brush; which dictated laws to the world from Trafalgar and the Nile, is the same armament which now craves "terms" in the very Channel which flows by their best fortified gates, and where the chiselled coast was once declared impregnable under the cover of their bristling guns. But there is a Providence which, sooner or later, will inflict just punishment on human wrongs, will listen to the cries of the persecuted, and will humble the oppressor; and the history of Babylon, and the drunken sacrilege of the cruel rulers of that infamous city and Government, stand as a warning to all future tyrannies, to prove that the most powerful nations and the most impregnable cities, surrounded by armed fortresses and by gates of massive brass, are no defence against the almighty vengeance of heaven and against the retributive justice of God.

My Lord, there is no concealing the fact, that England has provoked all the nations of the earth by her insidious policy. She has created sanguinary revolution in all the Catholic countries, and she has employed all the machinery which bribery and infidelity could place at her disposal, in order to overturn Catholicity in Europe. Your Grace knows much better than I can presume to inform you, that the unprincipled agents of Lord John Russell have fomented rebellion, and published infidelity in not less than five kingdoms of Catholic Europe, and the excesses of unbridled mobs, the pillage of Monasteries, the plunder of Convents, and the crimes of mutilation, rape, banishment, the flogging of women, the exile of men, pillage, fire, and murder, and then all the consequent and just retaliation of the offended laws of those countries in the infliction of confinement, exile, and death, have been the clear and the culpable results of the mad and fanatical career of a Cabinet, which has trampled on all the legal institutions of man, and which has set at defiance the very ordinances of God. I should not dare to make any assertions in the grave presence of your Grace, which I am not prepared to substantiate by unexceptionable documentary evidence; and, I can, therefore, produce for your perusal, letters, and despatches, and testimonies, which demonstrate, beyond all dispute, that the present Whig Cabinet did begin, conduct, and bring to maturity, political and religious rebellions in Rome, Naples, Lombardy, Switzerland, Austria, Hungary, Germany, and Prussia. All the rebels, and revolutionists, and infidels, in these various countries, claim acquaintance, and even friendship, with Lord Palmerston and his colleagues; and, whether the object on hand was to overthrow a foreign king, or a Catholic Bishop, an English Envoy; or Ambassador was recognised in the van of the foreign insurgents; and a printed English libel on the foreign Government, or an English printed tract of religious slander on the Catholic religion, were always found scattered round the quarters of the well-known English agents.

No record of infamy, of either ancient or modern history, bears any comparison with the profligate and insane fanaticism of this English bigotry; and at every scaffold in Europe, where the victims of this English demoniacal scheme were executed for their crimes, the names of Russell and Palmerston are heard in the piercing cries of the living, and may be read in the atoning blood of the dead.

At this moment, there is but one opinion amongst the crowned heads of Europe—namely, that England planned the ruin of their thrones; and amongst the classes of order and of religion, there is a universal shout of horror and execration raised against the Cabinet which could employ the resources of an empire, and degrade the majesty of our Queen, in the execution of a system subversive of justice, abhorrent to humanity, and accursed by God. And what renders the national disasters inflicted on these countries so unendurable, is the incongruous and perfidious tone of the English despatches. These curious, vile productions, publish panegyrics on *justice,* while they advocate national *spoliation;* and they put forward the words "righteousness" and "sacredness" in almost all these documents of holy dissimulation, while at the same moment, the writers of them were slandering religion, burning the effigy of the ever-blessed Virgin, and spitting on the Cross.

But this conduct, my Lord, as you are aware, is the

usual, plausible, sanctified show of holy insulting cant, which England has ever practised during all her national wickedness, since the beginning of the sixteenth century. Henry issued a holy commission under the sanctified Tom Cromwell, to inquire into the morality (!) of the Religious Orders in England, while he was debauching his own daughter, taking off the heads of his wives, and committing perjury and murder before God and man. He piously complained of the injustice of all rich, wealthy Monasteries, while he was plundering, by fraud and force, the entire Church property of this country; and he piously inveighed, in holy indignation, against the intolerance of the Pope, while he was preparing knives, and the gibbet, and the rack, to rip up men's bellies, to stake them through with steel, and to break their bones, if they dared refuse subscribing to his new formulary of faith. Elizabeth reddened the soil of Ireland with the blood of the Irish, at the time when she was set up in England as the Apostle of "the Reformation," the head of Christ's Church, and the fountain of divine perfection. And Cromwell and his soldiers, sang psalms to God, while amusing themselves in the holy recreation of tossing grown children into the air, and in their descent catching them in scientific zeal on their holy bayonets! or these ancient Whig zealots in epaulettes, changed the holy fun, by holding a Papist infant by the legs, turning round twice or three times, and then dashing out its Papist brains against the wall.

You know, Sir, I am stating facts, strictly historical facts, which time, and your scanty toleration, had covered up in our aching hearts, and sealed up in our burning souls; and which, in our sickening hopes, we never suspected should be revived into malignant vitality, till the iniquities, the cruelties, the oppressions, and the slanders of the Russell Cabinet had worn away the superstratum of charitable oblivion, and revealed the bleeding wounds of the ancient persecution and tyranny which robbed us of our national rights, proscribed our faith, murdered our fathers in cruel torture, and consigned their mangled flesh to a martyred grave. In a word, the history of England, during the three last centuries of her godliness, furnishes but one unbroken narrative of calumny, slander, lies, spoliation, perfidy, perjury, persecution, exile, chains, and death.

And the spirit of the English Cabinet towards Ireland, possesses, at the present moment, the same malignant character which it had during the most sanguinary period of Elizabeth's reign. The power, not the will, is wanted to renew the list of proscription, and to repeat the scene of Mullaghmast. What part of the tragical history of the last three hundred years has been omitted in the Russell Administration towards Ireland? With a treasury overflowing with nineteen millions of bullion, he permitted the death by starvation of upwards of half a million of poor faithful loyal Irishmen. I am speaking facts—he is the guilty man. A jury of respectable men, on their oaths, at a Coroner's Inquest on the starved death of a poor Irishman, brought in a verdict of "*willful murder* against Lord John Russell, in the year 1848." The Coroner refused to admit the verdict; but still, that rejected verdict is registered in Heaven, and will form part of the future judicial history of Ireland; and it is true, to say, that if such sworn verdicts would be received by the Irish Coroners, Lord John Russell would stand charged by the united oath of a nation before God with more cases of Irish murder than all the Irish culprits, taken together, of your entire Penal Colonies. He therefore, folded his arms on the Treasury benches, and he did aid culpably in the starvation and death of our fine people. His Cabinet encouraged (and justly,) the fitting up various naval expeditions in search of one man in the North Seas; but, alas! you would not send one ship or one surgeon to convey the poor Irish exiles to a foreign land while living, or give one shilling extra to buy a shroud for them when dead in putrid, national neglect.

The English Cabinet makes laws to protect the Irish wild fox and the game, while they look carelessly on, seeing the cruel landlord uproot whole villages, exterminate the poor, and kill them like vermin, as they make their escape from the falling walls of their ancient home, and the burning roof of their birth. Mazzini is lauded, Garibaldi caressed, Ciceroacchio modelled in plaister and marble, and Kossuth embraced; all the rebels of foreign nations are entertained; all the revolutionists feted, or pensioned, and all the infidels of the whole earth panegyrized in the periodicals of the day, by this anti-Irish, anti-Catholic English Cabinet, while any one who dares to raise his voice in defence of Irish liberty, or the Irish Faith, is seized as an assassin, tried for his life, condemned to be "hanged, drawn, and quartered;" sent in chains to the English terrestrial hell, and even there, amongst the living damned, his mouth is gagged by his English keeper, lest he utter a word of reproach against the persecuting laws that murder the living and dishonor the dead. Algiers has offered a home to the Irish exile; Spain has allotted part of one of her richest provinces to shelter our afflicted race, while England, that has grown great by our labors, powerful by our numbers, and triumphant by our courage, banishes us in tens and hundreds of thousands of naked victims to America, where the hospitable forest gives us a free home, and where the sheltered, untrodden valley, affords us a friendly and honored grave. We carry nothing to America but our ancient Faith, and we bring nothing from Ireland that belongs by right to England, but our undying, inappeasable vengeance. And when every poor exiled, persecuted Irishman, (stript of everything,) sets his foot in the ship which is to convey him to a distant shore, he looks to the avenging skies, as the swelling canvas urges his breaking heart from the home of his fathers, and in the language of the English merchantman, once mutilated by a Spanish crew, "he cries to Heaven for mercy and to his country for revenge." And be convinced, my Lord, that this universal cry shall yet be reverberated from America on cruel England, in the ferocious shout of national triumph, and in the just retaliation of accumulated revenge.

Oh, Sir, no pen can describe, no language can paint, the heartless cruelties of the Whig Cabinet towards Ireland during the last four years; and that cruelty has, if possible, been increased, by the shameless bigotry and the slanderous malignity with which our national charac ter and historical race; our political principles, and our religious convictions have been assailed by the bribed press, and the venal literature of every department of the English administration. Having robbed us of our trade, we are described as incapable of commercial enterprise; having banished to America all our best tradesmen and artisans, we are put down as men incapable of progress in artistic talent; having filled all places of trust and eminence with men of English kidney, they ask where are our men of distinction? and having centralized all emolument, and all gain, and all wealth in England, they jibe our poverty, and proclaim the national beggary produced by their elaborate injustice, as the result of Celtic blood and hereditary recklessness! Having made at different times what is called "plantations" of Scotchmen and Englishmen, in all the rich parts of Ireland; having banished the proprietors to "hell or Connaught;" having allowed only half an acre of bog and an acre of arable land to the persecuted Irishman, with fetters on his feet, manacles on his hands, and a halter round his neck, with rackrents, and middlemen, they then employ such fabulous writers as the black Calvinist, Macaulay, to publish, under the name of history, the hereditary English lie—that *Popish* agriculture has never flourished in Ireland or anywhere else like Reformation tillage!!

This rhetorical fop is about to favor us with a continuation of the fabulous production; and it would be only doing justice to his system, if he would furnish a botanical diagnosis, explaining why the "Reformation" potatoes have failed in Ireland during the last four years, placed as they were in such favorable circumstances of Lutheran cultivation. What a pity, my Lord, that Lord Minto did not succeed in scattering more Bibles in France and Italy! If Macaulay be correct in his calculations, the grape and the maccaroni of these countries must be prodigiously improved by the holy presence of the English Bible there. If mangel wurtzel, my Lord, grow to such perfection under Lutheran culture, to what celestial improvement could not the Popish French champagne be brought, if your Bible could be only read under the idolatrous branches of the vine of these countries. Such an infamous system of perfidious lying, and atrocious humbug never has been carried on in any part of the world, for the degradation, the oppression, and the burning injustice of a people, as is shamefully practised towards Ireland in every department, by every villainous conspirator employed by a persecuting and a fanatical Government, to set our nation mad, and to drive a whole people to distraction and despair. But, above all, and beyond all, having uprooted our altars, demolished our churches, plundered our monastries, robbed us of all our legal ecclesiastical revenues of ages, and still, withall, saddled the nation with the yearly revenue of eight millions and a half! for the support of this apostolical establishment.

Lord John Russell has, in addition to this scalding tyranny and consuming insult, encouraged the agents of this living congregation of impostors to calumniate our creed, during the last five years in every city, town, village, hamlet, and cabin in Ireland—to slander us by sermons, speeches, tracts, ballads, and placards—to call the priests by the names of idolaters, perjurers, murderers, and assassins—to post them on all the pillars, walls, gates, and corners of streets, as the priests of Antichrist—the emissaries of the devil—the corruptors of God's gospel, and the preachers of perdition. Can the nations of Europe believe, that England can encourage such disorder, such injustice, such blasphemous antichristian antagonism as forms the daily record of present Irish history ?—or how can you calculate on the allegiance and dutiful loyalty of a people, whom England thus excites to disaffection by every art which the most refined perfidy could produce in the hearts of an excitable people ?

And can you again wonder, my Lord, when you hear of an agrarian murder in Ireland ? If Government set the example of perjury, and persecution, and death, why should you not expect to see the example followed by the victims of your tyranny ? If you form a conspiracy against them, can you wonder at Ribbonism against you ? On the contrary, one is rather astonished that there are not more scenes of blood, under a system of such monstrous national provocation, insult, and oppression. And before God, I hold the Government of England more guilty of the Irish murders, than the scarlet assassin who reddens his accursed hands in the blood of his marked victim. The Government are absolutely guilty of the murdered blood that cries to heaven for vengeance, from their maddening career in Ireland. What can we Irish priests do to arrest the murderer, while such extended materials of provocation to slaughter, lie all round us on every side ? For my part, my Lord, I would willingly, most willingly, most ardently, take the duties, if I could, of a policeman, and follow the assassin of Mr. Bateson, and arrest him, at the risk of my life. I would, with pleasure, if it were necessary, stand sentinel before the door of Mr. Fortescue, and watch and protect his life, or the life of any other man, be his creed or his politics what they may; and every priest in Ireland would do the same to prevent the curse on the soil, imprinted there by the shedding of innocent blood. But what can we do, calumniated, abused, distrusted, as we are on one side, while on the other side, there exists a fearful amount of provocation, which the cruel Government seem rather disposed to increase than to diminish? And as if to render the entire nation frantic, and incapable of entertaining one solitary ray of hope, from the kind, altered feeling of our rulers, the journals in pay of the Government, suggest the *withdrawal* of all former Catholic privileges—the removal from office of all Papists, and the total *extermination* of Irishmen from the soil of Ireland.

There is, my Lord, no resting place now left for hope for our country. All is persecution. A war is made even upon our intellect; and we are called on neither to read, or write except through a Parliamentary tutor. Knowledge of the most refined manufacture at Bamfordspeke, is offered to our longing Irish minds; but we must drink it from a scientific distillation, through a Lutheran alembic. The mediæval and imperfect education of Bossuet, Liguori, and Doctor Doyle, is to be removed, and replaced by the modern and improved system of Carlisle, Tom Payne, and Straus. The ancient vulgarity of introducing the name of God in science, shall in this modern polite programme of studies, be entirely omitted; and the imbecile meanness of mixing up the old fables of religion with the fashionable development of the modern human mind, will be avoided through the new collegiate curriculum, as an exploded thing, and only suited to such undeveloped minds as those of St. Thomas and La Place.

Why, my Lord, one would think, to hear these "raw-head and bloody-bone" scholars speak, that the studies of a modern apothecary and the doctrine of potash constituted the very extreme point of literary, scientific and Cristian education; and if a beardless tyro happened to have A.B. attached to his ragged classics and shabby science, he is put forward in collegiate reports as a man capable of teaching the Twelve Apostles, and making laws for Charlemagne. The world is disgusted with this loathsome and nauseous cant on education; and it is quite certain that if the illustrious Sir Robert Peel lived now this fanatical and schoolboy ribaldry would not have been tolerated. From the absurd notions of this inane class one might suppose it impossible that Shakspeare could compose *Hamlet* as he had not read "the Binomial theorem" under a Bible-man; and it is even wonderful how your Grace gained the battle of Waterloo, since the metallurgic difference between potasium and sodium was not discovered till after the year 1815.

And besides this intellectual war these is also another war made upon our conscience. We are compelled to believe that the Queen has received a commission to teach the scriptures, so very superior to the commission of the

Apostles, that any one named and appointed by them to teach (contrary to her wishes) is to be silenced, deposed, and deported beyond the evangelical boundaries of this eucumenical empire; and we are called on to deny an office which we have sworn to profess, to commit perjury as a duty to the Queen; to deny God as a proof of our loyalty, to tell a lie, as a mark of our integrity; and, we are gravely told by Parliament, that in order to make us good and trustworthy subjects, we must be first perjurers, blasphemers, and consecrated hypocrites. My Lord, I have always, since 1829, presumed to entertain the loftiest notions of your naked candor, and your transparent integrity. And will your Grace, therefore, permit so humble an individual as I am, to ask you, could your Grace depend in the field of battle on the fidelity of the soldier who would forswear God to please the Queen; and who, at the bidding of a minister, would sell his faith for gold?

And there can be no doubt, my Lord, that you will want perhaps, even sooner than your Grace imagines, the whole energetic and loyal support of *every man in Ireland* to maintain the very existence of your Empire. Being rather successful in my predictions during the last twelve months; do not, I pray your Grace, make light of these warnings of mine. The lightest and smallest cloud that floats on the breath of the morning, is the first to announce by its flight, the approach of the storm. England is certainly in danger—and war once proclaimed by France, her fate is sealed. Russia takes India—Canada revolts; and how can we, the priests, or your Grace's name, keep in fixed loyalty the Irish discontent, inflamed by wrong and insult? Should the French, (which is not improbable) make a successful descent on our Irish shores, I would most delicately suggest to your Grace not to enlist the Irish, till at least you strike off our chains—till you withdraw entirely the burning insult of Lord John Russell—till you confine the Protestant calumniators within their own mock churches—till you promise tenant-right; that is to say, a bed to lie on, and a house to live in, for the wives and children of the soldiers—till you induce the English journals to cease telling lies of Ireland, and till the Queen can return to revisit us, and hear from our devoted hearts (*when all these conditions shall have been fulfilled,*) the loud, long, and ringing huzza, declaring that we forgive and forget—and that she can command our life's-bloood in the service of her throne, and the maintenance of her authority. I am no rebel, my Lord, and I *abhor national agitation,* as a most unhealthy state of society; but I would rather die than flinch from the post of duty, when my Irish country, and my Irish creed demand my services.

But while such is the character of my determination, I am prepared also to live in peace and amity with the Government of the country; *to thank them for their favors;* to aid them in their efforts; and to *identify my heart* with their duties. But I will never consent to execute these dutiful conditions till my hands are *unchained,* my country *emancipated,* and my creed set at liberty—*perfectly free.*

With distinguished admiration for your Grace's unrivalled military fame, and craving your pardon for this long letter, I have the honor to be, with profound respect, my Lord Duke, your Grace's most obedient servant,

D. W. CAHILL, D.D.

LETTER OF THE REV. DR. CAHILL TO THE RIGHT HON. THE EARL OF DERBY.

"In the first place, then, I can sincerely assure you of my earnest desire and determination to promote, to the utmost of my power, the cause of Protestant truth, in opposition to Popish error; and upon the particular question of the grant to Maynooth.......... my inclination and my opinion are, and have always been, opposed to the grant...... I am strongly in favor of an inquiry, and shall support Mr. Spooner's motion for a committee on the whole subject of the grant; and shall cordially and strenuously concur with Lord Derby's Government........ for the entire repeal of the act of '45. More than this, I cannot think you will require from one, who aspires to be a Member of the Administration to which alone you can look with confidence for the sincere and effective support of Protestantism against the spirit and inroads of the Papacy."—*Fitzroy Kelly.*

PAROCHIAL-HOUSE, NAVAN, *April* 17*th*, 1852.

MY LORD EARL—The extract just quoted, is taken from a letter recently written by your Solicitor-General; and as he mentions your Lordship's name, the sentiments expressed in his communication must, of course, be adopted by you. So, then, your Law Officer for England and Ireland sends forth a preliminary missive, in imitation of the far-famed "Durham letter;" and the Parliamentary eloquence of '52, is about to rehearse the same foul-mouthed bigotry as the disgraceful Session of '51; and the words "Popish error," and "the Papacy," are again to form the filthly vocabulary of legislative rancor; and the new Tory Cabinet are ranging themselves under the old faded colors of the "mummeries of superstition;" and the Catholics of Europe, and the Catholic victorious army of England, are again to hear the language of burning insult uttered from the seat of justice, and stamped by the authority of the Crown. If, my Lord, the lowest law-officer of the lowest court of (what is called) justice in this Empire, uttered the words of the extract quoted above, he would be pronounced, by universal condemnation, as unfitted for the impartial discharge of his duties; and he would be distrusted in his decisions by every client of his Court.

And can it be, that what would be disgraceful at the Old Bailey, is honorable at St. Stephen's? or, that the language and the conduct which would be contemptible and criminal in the lowest officer of police, is professional and suitable in your Lordship's colleague? Europe has not as yet had time to take repose since the revolutionary convulsion which was planned and executed by your Whig predecessors in office. The name of English bigotry is associated with the plundered Convents of Switzerland, with the assassination of the Priesthood, with the floggings and hangings of the monster Haynau, and with the sanguinary scenes of Hungary, Germany, Prussia, Lombardy, and Naples.

Since the expulsion of the perfidious Russell, and since the humiliation of his colleague, Captain Rock, we, the Catholics of this country, seemed to have a gleam of hope that the official descendants of Pitt and Fox, of Grenville, the Duke of Wellington, and Sir Robert Peel, would not have the mean cowardice to kick us on the ground, as we lay prostrate beneath the ravages of famine, the cruelties of extermination, and the insatiable vengeance of religious penalties. We fancied that the Earl of Derby, would not condescend to walk in the footsteps of Lord Stanley—that the narrow prejudices of the green lordling would be lost sight of on the elevated ground of the matured Earl; we fancied that the unripe, petulent acrimony of the beardless Secretary of Ireland would be dissipated before the meridian greatness of the imperial Premier of England; but we have been deceived, and the letter of your subordinate, proves that the giant-oak will take the warp of the baby-plant, and that the ministerial successors of Somerset are ready to-day, in the nineteenth century, to malign, to insult, to persecute, and to exterminate our race and our name, as their ancestors were, in the very worst days of our ill-fated country, and in the reddest scenes of our disastrous persecution.

The history of the whole world presents no parallel to the ceaseless and the unmittigated ferocious bigotry with which England has assailed our creed since '46. The records of the Catholic Courts of Europe, furnish no modern instance where public official insult has been offered to the Protestant creed of their subjects; but in Great Britain and Ireland, the Priest is not allowed to touch the ermine of a judge, although he has sworn to maintain the supremacy of the laws; and his name or his profession cannot be pronounced in the presence of royalty, although he is prepared to fight for the honor of the Queen, and to spill his blood in defence of tho throne.

This gratuitous insult, this governmental persecution, the scalding bigotry, the flagrant injustice, this anti-Catholic, this anti-Irish conspiracy, may be clearly defined, the perfect exponent of English tyranny; and if we, the Catholics of Great Britain and Ireland, will tamely submit to this incomprehensible insult, our base cowardice is the admitted definition of national slavery. The insane bigotry may, for a time, by its cumbrous weight, smother our crying revenge; but the day may not be far distant when Europe and America may adopt the insult offered to Ireland, and prove to your Lordship's Tory successors that there is more loss than gain in exciting religious sanguinary animosities, in alienating the unbroken allegiance of seven hundred years, and in dividing the devoted strength and proverbial courage of the one-third of your Empire.

As your Lordship is pledged through your colleague, to support, in reference to the grant to Maynooth, Mr. Spooner's motion for the entire repeal of the act of '45; I can, therefore, have no hope of arresting your Lordship's decision, in what I shall call "this mad career of legislation on this question;" but, like the humble historian, who can, perhaps, describe the battle much better than the general who commands, your Lordship will not, I trust, consider it presumption in me, to lay before you what I consider the clear case of "the act" referred to, and to warn you against the trick, and the deceit, and the injustice of "the repeal," to which your subordinate seems to pledge both your Lordship and the Cabinet.

For several years before 1782, your country attempted

to trample on America, in something of the same fashion as your Cabinet now attempts to overawe unfortunate Ireland; you inflicted "tonnage and poundage" on the insulted Americans, just as you now inflict your spurious Bible and your piebald creed on the maddened Irish Catholic. And, as there is nothing new under the sun, be convinced, that in the same manner as your beardless senators, and your Biblical Cabinet lost heretofore glorious America, the time is fast approaching when your scalding tyranny all over the world, may yet rehearse the tragical history of Bunker's Hill and New Orleans.

The revolution of France followed in 1789, and England, therefore, gave the Catholics a vote in the election of a Member of Parliament in 1793. England was threatened by French Republicanism in 1794, and therefore England determined to educate the Irish Priests at home, in 1795; and Napoleon conquered Italy and Austria before the end of 1796, and therefore Maynooth received the grant of £8,700 a year. I am not ungrateful for this act of English political generosity; on the contrary, I am actuated by deep feelings of acknowledgment, although I am forced to believe (from the avowal of the government of that day,) that State policy, and not friendship towards Catholics, urged the Parliament to decide on the paltry, unwilling endowment. Sir R. Peel completed in 1845, the common decency of English justice, in raising the yearly grant to £30,000; and, although the Protestant Church, of only half a million of souls, has £1,300,000 annually, and although the Presbyterian conventicle, of a mere section of the population, has £38,000 a year, the

Catholics, who numbered seven millions, were grateful for this additional, kind, and unsolicited grant of Sir Robert Peel.

And although the Catholic Monasteries have been thrown down, the Colleges dismantled, the Churches plundered, the Abbey lands seized, and the consecrated legal property of the poor and the stranger confiscated by Henry and Elizabeth, and then settled by what are called "Acts of Parliament," on our slanderers and calumniators: and although this plundered State of the poor of Ireland and England amounts, at the present day, to the astounding sum of eight and a half millions sterling, (annually,) we, the Catholics, had nearly forgotten this robbery of our Church, and of the patrimony of the poor: and we were beginning to entertain feelings of charitable intercourse with the descendants of the greatest villains, assassins, and murderers, that ever the world saw in any age or country, till Lord John Russell raised the fury of the Empire against us, by an insult and a slander, without a parallel in modern history. And as if it is intended to tread out every feeling that could bind us to the throne, your colleague, (which means your Lordship,) has commenced the Session of 1852, by a gratuitous insult on our creed, and has threatened, in a rare combination of slander and bigotry, to support Mr. Spooner's motion for the entire repeal of the grant to Maynooth.

And now, my Lord, will you be kind enough to tell us, Catholics, how we have forfeited the confidence of the English Government, and what fault have we committed which merits the penalty of reversing the act of 1845.—

This is a case in which the laity are not implicated, it is a charge which solely concerns the Priestshood : I am a very humble individual, indeed, but I demand from your Lordship the precise criminality which justifies you in making this grave charge through your subordinate, and to pronounce the verdict of guilt, by visiting us with the penalty of £30,000 a year. Your Lordship has, no doubt, your Parliament at your back, to defend you ; but we, too, have our Parliament to support us. You have bigotted England, rancorous Scotland, and Orange Ireland on your side; but we have all Catholic Europe, and all-glorious America on ours. You shall have your verdict at home, and we shall have ours abroad. And great as is th eEarl of Derby in Downing-street, it may happen that the Irish Priesthood may be more respected at Washington, and that the shouts of your triumphant, base, bigoted majority in your venal House, may be drowned in the loud, angry cry of shame and scorn, which we shall rise against you all over the civilized world. As your Lordship is about to put us on our trial, we shall demand your evidence ; and if you are determined to pack your jury, we shall publish to all mankind the lies and perjury of your witnesses, and then your verdict will be national dishonor, and your victory will be royal disgrace.

Pray, then, Sir, what crime have we committed to justify your judicial "Praise-God-Barebones," in insulting one-third of the Empire by the words "Popish error," and "the inroads of the Papacy?" And will your Lordship condescend to inform us, in what manner Maynooth, forfeited the confidence of your Cabinet, to deserve to be ejected on the "crowbar" principle? We, the Priests of Ireland, have never, within my recollection, even in one instance, opposed the administration of the laws. We have never, in any one instance, encouraged insubordination to the constituted authorities. There is not a stain on our conscientious allegiance. We are the avowed abettors of order, and the public advocates of peace. Our fault, if we have any, is our slavish submission to the most grinding tyranny that ever the world saw—a tyranny that has ejected the aged, banished the youthful, starved the survivors, and dishonored the dead. If your Lordship, therefore, persevere in your determination of repealing the Act of 1845, you will be guilty of a palpable injustice, which has no parallel even in English Legislation, save the perjury of Limerick, and the murder of Mullaghmast. If you succeed in this injustice and insult, we shall publish your Lordship throughout Europe, as descending to a mean trick, practising a low deceit, and guilty of a dishonorable injustice.

When your official ancestors (for the ends of State policy,) first endowed Maynooth, the Irish Clergy had forty-six friendly colleges on the Continent of Europe, having funds appropriated for the education of the regular and secular Clergy of Ireland. Portugal, Spain, France, Italy, Austria, Holland, Belgium, and Germany, opened their seminaries to the Irish student, when the racks and the gibbets, and the ropes, and the scaffolds of your Evangelical Government were reeking with human Irish blood, in honor of God. And if you had left the Irish Priesthood to continue their educational course on the Continent ever since, these forty-six colleges would now be supplied with superabundant additional funds from the charity and the zeal of Catholic Europe, in favor of persecuted Ireland; and we should be now spared the galling insult of your Tory fanatical Solicitor, and of your Lordship's known bigotry.

Why did you take us on board your State ship against our will in 1795, and then heave us into the ocean in 1852? Why did you encourage us to build our houses over your political magazine, in order to blow us up at a given moment? Why did you dry up the charity of Europe in our favor, in order that after upwards of half a century of suspended charity, you might cast us abandoned and friendless on the world? Why did you flatter us, in order to throw us off our guard for our ruin? But above all, why do you slander and malign us, eject us, banish us, starve us, put us to death?

But in the name of the honor of your nation, do not belie us—do not forge calumnies on our coffins, or print perjury on our tombs—break our bones, as your ancestor Wentworth did—banish us, as did your predecessor Somerset; let your Solicitor hang us without a jury, as his countryman Jefferies has formerly practised his profession at the bar of the ancient Lord Truro: but, Sir, leave us our name, our zeal, our honor, our patriotism. Earl Derby! let not your hatred of Ireland, or your insatiable rancor against the Catholic creed, make you forget the dictates of conscience, the principles of honor, and the laws of justice. Do not, in imitation of some infamous landlords of Ireland, eject the Priesthood with their rent paid. Do not brand the honor of the Queen, by associating Royalty with the Crowbar Brigade. Give us due notice to quit, till we can have time to secure a Collegiate home on the Continents of Europe and America: and if your Lordship is the person selected to act the part of Tom Cromwell, in Ireland; you may, like your predecessor, be approaching a near abyss of personal humiliation. At all events, our case is clear; namely, that without a shadow of a fault against the laws of our country, against our allegiance to the throne, and against the honor due to the Queen, you have, in the face of God and man, opened your ministerial career with a threat of persecution, which, if carried into execution against us, has never been surpassed, even in our country, for trick, insult, falsehood, treachery, deceit, and injustice. But, believe me, the time is fast approaching when the Methodists, the Presbyterians, and the Chartists, will force you or your successor to repeat the same experiment towards the Protestant Church, which you now practice to Maynooth; and a breach once made in the old walls of the establishment, not all the artillery of your Lordship's eloquence can repel the assailants, or defend the rotten, tottering citadel.

What your Cabinet will do next, no one can tell; one mistake, often leads to another more fatal error; and that it may happen that "the errors of Popery," with which your Solicitor seems so well acquainted, may bear no comparison in point of number and magnitude with the errors of the Derby Administration. But while we are partly ignorant of the precise line of your persecuting policy, our course is clear and decided; namely, to combine together legally and constitutionally, as one man, throughout your Empire; and if it appear that your instructions are decided on new penalties, and on increased injustice, we must be equally determined to raise a shout of contempt at your policy, and boldly set you at defiance.

When Lord Stanley purchased liberty, in 1833, for a handful of slaves in Jamaica, he gave seven years' notice to their masters, for fear of injuring the feelings of two hundred and forty slave-drivers; surely, then, when the Earl of Derby (related somehow to that Lord Stanley,) inflicts slavery on the millions of Catholic Ireland, and on the spotless Priesthood of their nation, he should give a proportionate notice to the Ministers of God. But the rage against Popery and the Papacy is the present cry of bigotry; and from the Premier to the village Sexton, all are inoculated with the virus of this insane distemper, and all look delirious, when the name of the benevolent, inoffensive Pope, is uttered. And one should think, your Lordship has had a salutary warning against this shameful trick in the downfall of Lord Palmerston, and in the defeat of Lord John Russell. Europe is now perfectly aware of their machinations, and alive to the danger of trusting English fanatical diplomacy. An Englishman is now watched all over the Continent, as if his presence were the signal of treachery, and his correspondence deceit. Your Biblical Societies have been expelled from all the Catholic and Protestant countries of Europe, at fifteen days' notice, and the letters of the English correspondents to the London journals, are stopped or opened in all the post-offices, with the same terror as if they contained treason against the Monarchs of those countries. And I think, I speak the exact feeling of those nations, when I assert, that while they hold the name of English Whig in contemptuous detestation, they view the name of English Tory in irreconcileable abhorence.

The universal voice of mankind, at this moment, brands England as standing alone in the civilized world, the perfidious advocate of religious persecution; and the conduct of the Sultan, standing uncovered, while a Catholic Bishop in last August, married at Constantinople the daughter of a Greek functionary of the Court to an Italian Roman Catholic, (Signor Fetaldi,) stands in reproaching contrast to the audacious bigotry of the Queen's Chamberlain in the late case of Monsignore Searle; and it proves that we can expect more courtesy and higher consideration from a royal Mahomedan and a royal Turk abroad, than we can hope for at home from the Christian Monarch, for whose honor, name, and throne, our fathers in arms have died, and for whom we ourselves are prepared, from conscience and duty, to spill our heart's blood.

There is no one department of your Empire, social, naval, military, forensic, religious, political, in which we Catholics are not now met by studied insult and ribald slander. The word "Popery," (as you insultingly call our Faith,) is the universal watchword of reproach—the combining signal of persecution; and if the Catholics who fight your battles on the banks of the Sutlej, and win your victories, are subject to your degrading insult, even while leaning on their bleeding arms, the trophies of their cou rage and your dominion, how can we expect your truth, or your sympathy, or your friendship at home? Although my poor Catholic countrymen pour out their life's blood for you on the burning sands of India, you refuse them the happiness of a Chaplain of their own creed, in all the internal stations of the country; and when the poor Italian Priest, Father Francis, followed the 50th Regiment to the battle of Moodkee, and was killed, while in the heat of the fight, among the dying, your Christian Government refused to give him a mule to carry himself and his slender baggage, you refused him the common necessaries of life, you would not give him one penny to console the dying Catholic brave soldier.

And hear it, Robespierre; hear it, elder Napoleon in your grave; hear it, French Guards of Marengo; hear it thou, Irish Commander of our Forces at the Horse-Guards: when poor Father Francis lay dead on the field, with two sabre cuts on his neck, no British hand bore him to a foreign grave, no British honor saluted the fallen Priest over an honored tomb, two poor Catholic privates laid him in a rude coffin, made from the remains of two tea-chests, and the abandoned fate, and the cruel neglect, of poor Father Francis, at Moodkee, is the whole history of England to Catholic Ireland, from the first moment, when their red gibbet was erected in 1543, to the late epistolary insult of your Lordship's Solicitor.

I shall take the liberty of occasionally coming into your presence, and publishing my humble views of your policy to Ireland; and I wish to inform you, that, these letters of mine, will be read in every city in Europe, and in every village and hamlet of America. I have the honor to be, my Lord Earl, with profound respect, your Lordship's obedient servant,

D. W. CAHILL, D.D.

LETTER OF THE REV. DR. CAHILL TO THE RIGHT HON. THE EARL OF DERBY.

HOUSE OF LORDS, MAY 21st.

"Earl Derby said: 'What I have stated before is, that her Majesty's Government have no present intention of making any alteration in, or proposing any repeal of, the existing act, by which an endowment was granted to the College of Maynooth.' " (Hear, hear)

HOUSE OF COMMONS, MAY 21st.

"Mr. Spooner, in answer to the appeal made to him as to whether he believed in the present Session that an inquiry could be carried to a satisfactory conclusion, would at once say that he did not think it could. (Hear, hear, from the opposition.)

"The Chancellor of the Exchequer said—'The vote meant that the House of Commons should express an opinion whether there should or should not be an inquiry in respect to the system which was carried on at Maynooth, and when he heard the words 'a mockery and a delusion, used with respect to this debate, and the manner in which it had been conducted, he must say, that with regard to the people out of doors, it would indeed be a farce and a mockery, if, after all that had been said, and all the feeling that had been expressed, the house did not come to some conclusion on the subject of Maynooth.' (Hear, hear.)

" The Attorney General for Ireland said—'The Hon. Member for Middlesex, referring to the Established Church, renewed the old exaggeration with respect to the value of its property, and the Right Hon. Member for the University of Oxford, as well as the noble Lord the Member for London, warned the friends of inquiry to be careful what they were about, lest they should bring about the reconstruction of religious establishments in Ireland generally. As a Representative of the Church, however, he (Mr. Napier) would not acept that statement. If it were thought a desirable thing, on its own merits, to interfere with the Established Church of Ireland, let such a proposition be brought forward, and he would give it a fair consideration. He did not forget that in earlier days that church had neglected its duty; that Ireland condemned it, that the Almighty condemned it, but let it be borne in mind that Eng'and did not condemn it. Now, however, that it had become an active and living interpreter of God's word; speaking in the native language, and had acquired spiritual power, an inquiry into the establishment was menaced, with a view to its reconstruction.' "

CAERNARVON, *Wales, June* 2, 1852.

MY LORD EARL—The history of our Imperial Legislature, affords no parallel to the hypocrisy, the meanness, and the trick, by which the Government of England is now systematically executed. I presume to express towards your Lordship, personally, the most profound respect; but what politician of any age of England's history, has ever seen such contradiction, such swaddling, such shuffling, or, as it is now-a-days termed, such "dodging," as are all contained in the extracts quoted above? The Mover, (Mr. Spooner,) for the Maynooth inquiry, who, but some few days ago, spewed such filthiness on the confessional, now gives up that inquiry as not likely to lead to a "satisfactory conclusion;" next comes your Chancellor, who contradicts the mover, and thinks an inquiry necessary to "satisfy people out of doors," and to escape being branded with the charge of "mockery and delusion;" your Lordship next comes forward in the order of the political dodging, and takes a course peculiar to yourself, stating, that you have no intention of making "any alterations in the act of the endowment of Maynooth;" from whence it must be concluded, that all the past debates on Maynooth have been a mere Parliamentary farce; and lastly, your Attorney-General for Ireland, concludes the official melo-drama with a kind of ministerial doxology, in which he declares, as *ex-officio* theologian to your Lordship, that the Irish (Protestant) Church has "neglected its duty," (oh, strange fact!) that it had been "condemned by Ireland, and the Almighty," (what a happy coincidence of opinion, between Lord Roden and the Almighty,) that at present the same condemned Church has learned to speak and pray in Irish, (oh! liturgy of Elizabeth!) that consequently (the Lord be praised,) it has again recovered the good opinion of Ireland and the Almighty! and is, at the present moment, (oh, ghost of Oliver Cromwell!) the "active and living interpreter of God's word."

I declare, I have never read, in the same number of words, coming from the members of any responsible society so much trifling inconsistency, reckless insult, and swaddling puerility, as may be collected from these specimens of Cabinet wisdom. I assure you, my Lord, nothing but my deep personal respect for your Lordship, prevents me at present from laughing in your face, seeing the ridicule and the contempt with which your administration must be covered, all over the world, before every man of common sense and common honor. Who can avoid smiling in melancholy scorn, at seeing the reins of Government in this great, and powerful, and enlightened country, entrusted to men who plainly avow that they are humbugging the nation, and that, in order to please the unjust cry of ferocious bigotry, they are keeping alive the feelings of religious rancor; and, without necessity or a useful aim, ranging two hostile parties of our common country in a perilous and a sanguinary struggle?

And is there never to be an end of this furious malignity against the Catholic name? Is the British Parliament to assemble, year after year, uttering the grossest falsehoods, publishing the basest lies, and encouraging the most relentless persecution against the creed of Catholic Ireland? From Dioclesian to Elizabeth, from Julian the Apostate to Lord John Russell, there never has been displayed, in any part of the world, a more debased, unceasing system of shameless misrepresentations, ribald insult, and debauched lies, than has been promulgated from your Senate House, against the Faith of two hundred and fifty millions of the present population of the world, against the creed of your English ancestors, and against the venerable and imperishable records of all that has been great, learned, and virtuous, of the past eighteen centuries, in every nation of the earth.

This frantic warfare did not begin in drunken clubs, or in infuriated fanatical enthusiasm; it did not commence in Tyburn or Smithfield. No, it burst forth in the British Senate: it was first announced from the Treasury Benches: it originated with the Premier of England: it was the offspring of the English Cabinet: it was planned in silent deliberation, urged in ministerial eloquence, and executed under the sanction of Parliamentary wisdom. It employed Lord Minto to deceive the Pope; sent Peel to light the fires of Switzerland; licensed Canning to endorse the pillage of the Monasteries; gave a military medal to Garibaldi; feted Kossuth; aided Haynau to erect scaffolds to hang men and to flog women; encouraged Bem; and transported Smith O'Brien; and, while standing in Lombardy, in the sight of Europe, flinging the red hissing balls of sanguinary revolution over all nations; it was seen, at the same time, turning with the other hand the leaves of the Bible, polluting God's gospel with reeking hypocrisy, and provoking the indignation of man, and the vengeance of God.

Yes, my Lord, the Legislators of England, during the last three hundred years, have practised the Reformation Act of presenting the appearance of sanctity in language, while perpetrating, in fact, the blackest enormities of crime. From Dean Fletcher, who had the shocking indecency to preach incongruous godliness to the Queen of Scots, while the perjured executioner uncovered his murderous axe, down to the Jumpers of Connemara, it is all the same system of lies, hypocrisy, and guilt. And, as a matter of course, from the 4th November, 1850, (the date of the Durham letter,) up to the present sittings of your "crime and outrage committee," there could be no possible phase of calumny and insult put forth in sanctimonious baseness against the discipline, the doctrine, the practices, and the Ministers of the Catholic Church, which has not been shamelessly exhibited with a perseverance, a malignity, an indecency, and a fury, which have no parallel in the history of modern times. Depend on it, my Lord, that all this base slander and national injustice, will end in the disgrace of your name, and in the weakness of national power.

Vespasian and Caligula, tried this policy before the administration of Lord John Russell, and they failed: Attilla attempted in his day to uproot the Gospel and letters, before the time of Lord Palmerston; and while the furious Hun is forgotten, they both survive: and Tom Cromwell was appointed the head of a commission, similar to the plan by which you now assail Maynooth; and Catholic Colleges still remain in spite of Cromwell and his profligate master. All the enemies of Catholicity through the past ages, have had the malignant triumphs of their short space of life against our Church; and they are all now dead, and she lives. Their lives were counted on the narrow scale of years, months, and days, but her age is reckoned on the endless revolving circle of ages; she enjoys a perpetual spring of youth, they are sealed in the frozen winter of death. Their forgotten ashes are now inorganic clay, the grave-worm sleeps in their black hearts, and brings forth her young in their disastrous brain, while her lofty spires, and million altars, and myriad congregations, spread all along the nations, from the golden gates of the East, to her sombre turrets in the Western twilight, proclaim her activity, and her life, and her jurisdiction, wide as the National horizon, and comprehensive as the human family.

Depend upon it, my Lord, you are placing yourself in a wrong position, by employing the prestige of your great name (for great it is,) in the cause of bigotry—persecuting a people whose loyalty is without a stain; and inflicting an unmerited insult in gratuitous vengeance against a Seminary, which, during the venerable period of upwards of half a century, has sent forth a Priesthood, the teachers of morality, the abettors of the public order, the promoters of peace, and the too faithful and zealous defenders of the stability of the English Throne. Your Lordship has acquired great practical power; you have a just political illustrious reputation amongst your followers, and hence, you can, with prudence, calm the storm of party strife, subdue the rage of religious prejudice, and be the father of your country, not the demagogue of a ferocious faction.— Those who presume to know best your Lordship's sentiments, assert, with confidence, (what I am anxious to believe,) that you are personally and sincerely opposed to the religious persecution of Catholic Ireland; but that the tide of popular opinion running against you, you are forced to yield to the public clamor. But it must not be forgotten, that, it was your official predecessor, who has excited this popular fanaticism; and hence, your Lordship, who now holds the helm of the State ship, has only to reverse the machinery, go back to the liberal, just course of Sir Robert Peel, silence insane devilry, unite the conflicting energies of the Empire, give liberty to conscience, correct past errors, and surround the throne with the civilized courage and the invincible fidelity of the universal people.

The entire aim of the present English Legislation, in reference to Ireland, is based on insult, misrepresentation, and injustice; the minds of men in office are so infected with a hatred towards everything Irish and Catholic, that it is painful to hear, in every society where the traveller mixes, one unbroken tale of the grossest lies and the foulest bigotry. The slanders uttered in the Houses of Parliament, have passed for legalized facts through all the walks of life in these countries; and although one listens at every turn to the most monstrous calumnies, it is perfectly useless, in the present diseased state of the public temper, to attempt to correct their absurd statements, or to allay their ferocious rancor. Time alone, and the good sense of the generous English people, will remove this wicked scheme of the English Government; and as sure as the swollen tide will recede in due time to the opposite shore, the excited feelings of the Nation will yet recoil in accumulated anger against the base Ministry, which could from motives of vengeance, or mischievious power, gain majorities by perjury, make laws by political prostitution, and stamp on the doors of the Senate House, a notorious national lie, on the religion and the people of Ireland.

Perhaps, the most fatal error your Lordship has committed since the commencement of your administration, is the foolish malice of your spiteful Attorney in his Orange interrogatories at "the crime and outrage committee."—The attempt to connect the priest with the murders of Louth, is a clumsy device, and shows what the heart of your subordinate could execute if he had the power. But the priest stood considerably beyond the range of the Orange rifle, and the lead fell harmless at the feet of the unsuspecting victim. I consider the assassin of character and the assassin of life, to stand in nearly the same category of guilt; and the priests of Louth, must in future begin to learn, that they have foes in power, with hearts as deadly scarlet as the murderers of Bateson.

I could wish it lay within the rules of Parliamentary usage, that my oppressed poor countrymen could appoint me as an occasional chairman of that committee, and I think, I should be able to prove to the satisfaction of the whole world, that the English Government are the real assassins of Ireland—that the English Church is the great Biblical mill, where all the lies against religion and morality all over the world, are manufactured ; that Lord Palmerston, is the Captain Rock of Europe ; and, that Lord John Russell, is the "Ryan Puck" of Ireland. If I were permitted to examine the Archbishop of Canterbury, and Lord John Russell, and Lord Truro, for *three hours,* I should hope to elicit to a perfect mathematical demonstration, that all the lies, and all the uncharitableness, all the religious rancor, and all their smothered hatred, that, like the tide, rises and threatens to roll in flooded devastation over the barriers of Irish society—all the disorders, and the heartburnings, and most of the riots of Ireland, are solely to be ascribed to the irritating, unceasing provocation and insults of the Established Church. I should be able to prove, that each successive Government of England have robbed Ireland, (by successive enactments of oppression) of her commerce, her protecting laws—have transferred to England every removable place of honor or emolument—have purchased her Constitution by bribery; have debased her leaders by corruption; have drained her resources, weakened her strength, gutted the national fabric of her ancient rights, and left her a helpless victim, a whining beggar, and a chained slave at the gates of England. I could prove, that the laws are made to protect the Irish trees and the Irish fences ; that the fishes and the foxes are taken within the care of our cruel masters, but that the poor Irish Catholic ; the poor faithful, grateful, enduring Irishman, is placed at the mercy of a capricious or cruel landlord; that he may be ejected, exterminated, and banished without appeal; that he is deprived of the right to live in the country of his birth; that the laws leave him friendless, unprotected, deserted; that the cruelty of his Legislators fills him with revenge; the ill-treatment of his landlord teaches him retaliation; that the combination of his superiors against him, produces a corresponding confederacy of his class; thousands perish by his side from extermination, disease, and hunger; that the laws make him savage, and their administration provokes him to revenge, and in his madness and fury he stains his hands with murder; and while he erroneously yet naturally, thinks you kill his class in tens of thousands, he cannot be restrained in his wild anger from taking your lives in dozens.

More lives have been lost in Ireland since 1847, under the vile accursed administration of the Whigs, by extermination, starvation, and exile, than have fallen in *all the countries of Europe* during the late revolutionary wars of Napoleon; and while my unhappy country is starved, banished, murdered, and shovelled, and pitted, by the cruellest and most heartless Government that ever degraded the name of law; and while their tyranny still rolls over the soil, like a spring-tide, forsooth, a committee of crime is called together to try, (by jibing and insult,) and trace to a few assassins in Louth, the heartburnings, and the disorganization, and the wild phrenzy, by which the Whigs have torn asunder the very frame of society. My Lord, I am not drawing a picture to my own taste. I am copying from your original, which I abhor. I am sketching the strict historical truths of Ireland; and sc help me God, I look upon the frame-work and the administration of your laws, together, with the monstrous grievance and the provoking insult and lies of your Church Establishment, to be the cause of all the disasters of Ireland; the source of our social disorders; the root of all illegal combinations; and, the sole maddening draught which arms the hands of the assassin, and stains our country with the red mark of murdered blood.

Lord Derby, I hereby accuse you and your subordinate, with a shameful and an insulting perversion of our oppression and your conduct, to attempt to shift the murders of Louth, which your laws have notoriously excited, from your own guilty heads, to the shoulders of the zealous, pure, unoffending priest. That is to say, while Ireland lies at your feet a bleeding corpse, assassinated by your treachery, you, forsooth, summon a jury, and, in ferocious mockery, you examine into the cause of her death; while you yourself are stained with her blood, and the reeking knife is seen in your hand. This insulting hypocrisy and conspiracy is a crime which no time can efface; it is a sin against the Holy Ghost, since it ascribes the wicked results of your own unjust laws to the agency of the holy priest of God. Ah! my Lord, we have received already superabundant insult from Russell and his despised cabinet; but surely, while the rotting masses of human flesh still are scented on the putrid air of Skibbereen—Russell's work—while the oozing blood still reddens the clammy pit in Lord Sligo's field at Westport, (where fathers, mothers, and children died under a melting sun without covering in the wild agonies of scarlet fever and desertion,) you should not have permitted your Attorney to add the last drop of shameless provocation to our former trials. While the history of the workhouses of Ballinasloe and Ballinarobe is recollected; while the name of Gross Island is remembered; while the smoking roofs of demolished villages are still seen; while the emigrant ship is still laboring under its load of your ragged, starved, and exiled victims, your man should have the decency not to outrage every feeling of common sense, by abscribing the clear, palpable, ferocious results of your own vile legislation to the humble minister of God, who would arrest the murderer if he could, who counsels obedience to the laws, honors the Queen, and prays for his enemies. And he is only one of a class. Every Priest in Ireland is the same, it is our duty to respect even your bad laws, to maintain obedience even to your cruel authority, to support even a wicked Administration, to aid you in the suppression of all illegal societies, and to die, if necessary, in defence of the throne.

Lord Derby, you have behaved very badly to insult us, by the shameful insinuations of your Orange official. We are not able to resent this cruel injury, this crying injustice: but we have the gift of speech left in spite of your "committee of outrage," and we shall make all nations re-echo the meanness, the indecency, the venom, and the sneaking, cowardly insinuations of your swaddling Attorney; and we shall inform all mankind, that while religious intolerance and fanatical persecution are certainly given up in every country in the civilized world as obsolete and disgusting, England alone keeps up her heavenly hatred–England alone has sickly mottoes from the canticles carved on her Protestant mouse-traps, electrotypes her reformation-crockery-ware with orthodox prayer and lovely hymns, and pours the abhorrent cant of her saintly hypocrisy round every word of Godly slander which she utters on Ireland.

Your Irish Attorney, my Lord, has thought proper to enter the field of Theology in the extracts quoted above, and in his swaddling divinity, has made some gross misstatements, or rather blunders, in reference to my creed. He is very candid, in saying, that the Irish Church had neglected its duties, and was condemned by the voice of Ireland and heaven; but that having recovered from her church frolic, she is now rather a sober, well-conducted church, and is going on very respectable indeed in her line, having had the advantage of learning Irish, within the last twenty years, and thus is enabled by vernacular flippancy to be an active servant, and very lively in the interpretation of God's word. Really, my Lord, your Theologian is no great witch in logic, or he could never have uttered such a facetious admixture of the forcible-comical, and the feeble-religious, as is contained in the official extract of his notable speech.

I think, my Lord, I understand him, when he stated that Ireland condemned the Irish Law Church. Your Theological Lawyer must have alluded to the tithe-system, when the Widow Ryan's son was shot in Munster; when the murder of Carrickshock was perpetrated for your church in open day; when Father Burke, of Meath, refused to take the census of his butchered flock, and when the cross-roads of Ireland were red with the blood of the Irish Catholic, slain in the name of God, in order to feed the profligate luxury of the huge Moloch of your sanguinary creed. I think I understand your subordinate, when he asserts, that your crimson church once stood "condemned before Ireland and before God." I think, too, I can well explain the true meaning of that passage of your Law Officer, where he states, that his recovered church is now "an active interpreter of God's word." And I assure your Lordship, that in following the absurd position of Mr. Napier, it is very hard to abstain from expressing the ridicule which his speech deserves, and to maintain at the same time the solemn respect, the distant veneration, and the becoming reserve which suits my position while addressing your Lordship. No doubt your church has been a most active interpreter of God's word, since it has put seven hundred and seventy-six different interpretations on that word since the time of your great reformer, Luther; for the truth of which statement, in part, I beg to refer your Lordship to Bossuet's Protestant Variations.

By the first active interpretation, Luther threw off the authority of the Pope.

Secondly—He modified, re-interpreted, re-modified, re-believed the doctrine of Transubstantiation and the Holy Eucharist.

Thirdly—He and his followers, interpreted the Sixth chapter of St. John, as "conpanation, impanation, perpanation, hyperpanation," and ultimately, this active church has settled down into a *Judaical type* on this Christian doctrine.

Fourthly—The old Mass, and the Invocation of Saints, and Purgatory, and the Sacrament of Penance, Confirmation, and Extreme Unction, and the Sacrament of Marriage, have been successively abandoned by this holy "activity" of your church: and the Archbishop of Canterbury and Lord John Russell, have respectively given up the Sacraments of Holy Orders and Baptism within the last two years. The "activity" of the ministers, has given up the divinity of Christ: and the activity of the "Greek Protestants, has denied the personality of the Holy Ghost;" and thus your Christian church has reduced her faith to the simple idea and doctrine of merely belief in the existence of God. This is pure Paganism—and when we add to this fact, that Luther sanctioned plurality of wives, with the Landgrave of Hesse, (that is Mahomedanism,) we are forced to conclude, from clear premises, that your church, in its "active interpretation of God's word," has unchristianized, has Mahomedanized, has unscripturalized, has infidelized, has paganized, and has demoralized the whole world.

There can be no doubt that, by the active interpretation referred to, the Protestant Church (as its very name implies,) has protested against the entire ancient record of Christianity, has thrown down the whole fabric of the new law, and has raised on its ruins a system of human theory, wild speculation, philosophical compromise between reason and faith—all of which, clearly subject religion to the *laws of progress*, inconsistent with the *im-*

mutable decrees of God, and with the *mysteries* of Revelation. The Church of your Attorney-General possesses at this moment an imperfect (scripture) of the New Law—the mere words of the Law, without the inherent rights of that Law; and as well might a Laplander, who chanced to find and possess the *parchment* of the English Magna Charta, insist he was an Englishman, and entitled to the rights of British subjects, as for your Church to call herself Christian and Catholic, from the mere possession of a printer's copy of the Law, without acknowledging the legitimate authority, without possessing practical allegiance to the recognized head of the Christian Constitution, without her name being enrolled amongst the accepted subjects; and without fulfilling the practical duties required, as the *essential legal conditions* to enjoy the rights and the privileges of the new Royal Heavenly Dispensation. Your Lordship must blame your Attorney, and not me, for this brief theological reply to his unnecessary and unexpected strictures. Believe me, my Lord, that no Attorney can be a proficient in theology; and hence, the sooner you keep your man in his own department of ex-officio informations, the better for the reputation and the honor of your Administration.

Penetrated with the greatest respect for your great name and lofty position, I wish I could presume to tell you how much good you can effect for the Empire, by a course of truth, honor, and justice to Ireland. The disastrous divisions which your Government has excited at home; the unmeasured contempt, with which your name is assailed abroad; the perilous state of your commerce;

the conflicting interests of the various factions of your country; but, above all, the keen watchfulness with which a hostile neighboring power observes all your panics, should induce you to heal the public acerbity, to forget past rancor, to begin a new era of legislation, and combine all your strength, to govern with impartial justice, to leave conscience between God and man, to soothe the flagrant oppression of Ireland, to soften the tyranny of ages, to be the father of the poor, the advocate of the oppressed, the emancipators of the slave, to have your name graven on our hearts in national love, and to combine, unite, concentrate, and bind in indissoluble amity the energies, the courage, and the loyalty of this great Empire, in one great invincible bond of national fidelity. This is a work worthy of you, and a work which you can execute; and a victory over bigotry and falsehood, which will transmit your name to posterity as the benefactor of my country, and not the persecutor of my name and race.

I have the honor to be, my Lord and Earl, with profound respect, your Lordship's obedient servant,

D. W. CAHILL, D.D.

DR. CAHILL TO THE RIGHT HON. THE EARL OF DERBY.

BILSTON, ENGLAND, *August* 24, 1852.

MY LORD EARL—As your Lordship has thought proper to dictate new laws for reforming Popish cravats; and as you have condescended to apply the English evangelical standard to the length and the cut of our Catholic beard; and as you have surprised the world by becoming Constitutional tailor and barber to the present Pope; and, finally, as your co-reformers in the Old Clothes Department of our glorious Constitution, are actuated with such zeal to advance your Protestant views throughout this Empire, as on several occasions to seize anti-Derbyite scarfs, to knock off anti-Derbyite hats, to spit in the faces of anti-Derbyite Priests, and to do several other Cabinet celebrities, you cannot be surprised, if I, too, influenced by your Lordship's example, change my former official position, and assume the novel character of satirist on Privy Councils, and of impartial chronicler of the incomprehensible follies of Ministers, and the incredible meanness of Cabinets—when grave Judges turn buffoons on the bench, when they discharge the tripple office of witness, judge, and jury; and when Prime Ministers turn Jack Ketch, I fancy I am not much out of the present fashion in my new vocation.

My silence since your Lordship's late proclamation, (which I am flattered to think you have observed,) has arisen from the fact, that I have been occupied in searching the pages of ancient and modern history to find some Pagan or Christian parallel to the official careers of Lord John Russell and yourself. Being aware, that there is nothing new under the sun, I concluded there must have been some persons somewhere like you both, in the former records of our race. You must not be surprised or angry, if I tell you, that I have discovered the exact resemblance of you both in the History of Gulliver's Travels.

Lord John Russell's tour in Greece, in 1849, in order to settle the *vast claims* of the loss of some furniture and a kitchen-garden belonging to Messrs. Finlay and Pacifico, is most perfectly identical with Gulliver's career in Lilliput; and your Lordship's late expedition to the Bay of Fundy, is precisely the history of Gulliver in Brobdignag. The poor Grecians (a diminutive race, only two inches high in stature,) retired beyond the pass of Thermopylæ, when they beheld the *great* Whigman from England; they procured ladders to scale the heights of his breast, as he lay asleep at the foot of Mount Helicon. The entire Grecian fleet weighed anchor, and sailed out under full canvas, with the yards manned, between his colossal limbs, as the giant British Minister bestrode the Gulf of Lepanto. The flags of their men-of-war at their mastheads, did not reach higher on that thrilling occasion than the large circle which surrounds the immeasurable circumference of his unponderable mighty Whig legs. According to the despatches received from our Admiral in the Mediterranean, he stood on Parnassus in the sight of the Muses; and the enormous creature (according to the Greek historians,) extinguished a raging conflagration in the palace of King Otho, with the same kind of an effort, and with nearly the same description of mechanical appliances, and with the same sort of *éclat*, as Gulliver, (after a night's hearty wine,) put out the fire which threatened destruction to the palace of the Empress of Laputa. And so wonderful and tremendous in Greece, is the terrestrial glory of the GREAT WHIG, (as he is called there,) that King Otho, *as you are well aware*, has ordered him to be styled henceforward, " The Whig Man-Mountain."

The remaining part of the history is perfectly illustrated in your Lordship's late voyage to America. The scene, however, is strangely changed. Your Lordship, when compared with the monstrous Websters of that country, appears only about four inches high—placed side by side with the great Leviathans of the fishing grounds, you don't seem much larger than a scorpion; you would be considered a mere dwarf at Bunker's Hill; your Lordship would not be a match for a tom-cat at New Orleans; your Lordship and Lord Malmesbury, and the Right Hon. Mr. Walpole, and your entire Right Honorable Cabinet, placed over each other, pillar-like, on each others Right Honorable shoulders, could not raise the uppermost Right Hon. Minister high enough to enable him to look into an *ordinary sized teapot* at Philadelphia! You could hide your whole Cabinet in a lady's muff at Washington! and if the reports be true, which the American giants have circulated at the fishing-grounds against English greatness, your Lordship was nearly drowned in a Yankee cream-jug (others say, a small fish-kettle,) at the Bay of Fundy, in your endeavor to escape from an American rat, in order to hide your Lordship's head in the breeches' pocket of Mr. President Fillmore. Your Lordship can scarcely believe the indignation of all Europe, to see England so contemptuously treated; our noble country! the mistress of arts and science! the scourge of France! the arbitress of Europe! the seat of virtue, piety, sanctity, honor, and truth!!! the pride and the envy of the whole world!!! the patron of the oppressed! the emancipator of the slave! the country of the free, and the beloved sister of Ireland!!!

Ah, Lord Derby, your Government can bully, and persecute, and spoliate, and infidelize, when your victims are changing, and unable to offer resistance to your tyranny and your accursed oppression; but, Heaven be forever praised, the scene is at length beginning to change; the sun of GREAT Britain is fast descending from its culminating point; your day of *unrivalled* sway is certainly drawing to a close; your national character and prestige, are beyond all doubt gone; your nation is now universally branded as deceitful and degraded; you have decidedly forfeited the confidence of Europe, and you are hated, despised, and abhorred, by the whole world: your two successive Governments have exposed England to the contempt of mankind; you have made her a jester at St. Petersburgh; a revolutionist and a base cringer at Vienna; a time-server at Paris, and an infidel at Rome; a traitor at Naples; a burglar at Madrid; a perjurer at Lisbon; a persecutor at Berne; a tyrant at Athens; a coward at Washington; a hypocrite at Rome; and the devil in Ireland!

Oh, shame on you, Lord John Russell! and oh fie, fie on you, Lord Derby, to employ the time of two successive Parliaments in degrading your country, and to engage the official services of bishops, judges, barristers, surgeons, lords, and ladies; in endeavoring to dethrone the Pope; searching out for the private scandals of ecclesiastics; mending and dressing up for inspection at Exeter Hall, old tattered calumnies on our creed; peeping into the bedrooms of Convents; listening behind our confessionals; dogging our school-girls to the Church; watching our orphans at their meals; jibing Priests at their prayers; mobbing Nuns in the public streets; counting the charities they receive for their humble support; and stealing through lanes and alleys, looking for a case of slander against the Faith of two hundred and forty millions of the human population, and against the creed of the most ancient families in England and the most devoted subjects of the Queen. Oh, fie on you, Lord Derby! to join in this most disgraceful and insane ribaldry, and, instead of walking in the footsteps of Canning or Peel—instead of standing before the world as the sublime exponent of British honor, truth, and justice, to ally your great name and proud position with such gross bigotry, and to seek renown from rolling in the mire with canting hypocrisy, indecent impiety, and blasphemous falsehood.

Is there never to be an end of this Parliamentary absurdity?—is there no business to be done by the Cabinet but maligning the Catholic faith?—will Government never cease the degraded and shameful practice of uttering the grossest indecencies, and the most filthy abominations and palpable lies against the Catholics of the whole world? Why do you appear in a farce?—why seek applause from the gallery?—why do you become a harlequin when *you can succeed* in the deepest characters of Moliere and Shakespeare?—why do you take Russell for your model, when you *can imitate* the meteor genius of the master-spirits whose place you fill? You are a man of talent, we own it; and why employ your great mind in the scullery of St. Stephens? If you are called to be the centre of a microcosm, why are you not the sun of the creation?—why do you choose to be the satelite of the world of which you ought to be the light and the ruler? Believe me, you are fallen; your occupation is gone; your jaded audience will not hear you much longer. Rely on it, if you persevere in your present career, you shall feel the disgrace of being universally hissed off the stage.—Your own countryman, Mr. Pope, will read your Lordship a lesson on this point:—

"Fortune in men has some small difference made,
One flaunts in rags, one flutters in brocade:
The cobler proned and the parson gowned,
The friar hooded and the monarch crowned;
'What differ more,' you cry, 'than crown and cowl'?
I'll tell you, friend—*a wise man and a fool.*"

There can be no doubt at all, that Lord John Russell and his vile Cabinet, endeavored to create throughout Catholic Europe a revolution in religion and government; and although your Lordship and Lord John, hold opposite opinions on general politics, you are the conjugate foci of each other on Catholicity, and you reflect each other's hostile feeling on my creed, as faithfully as the unerring science of your positions. You are certainly agreed with him in his policy of weakening all Catholic sovereignty, and of overturning the Catholic Faith. But you both have signally failed, and in your discomfiture, you have added a new proof of the strength of my church, and you have at the same time, ruined your name and your country. You have unconsciously done a lasting service to Catholicity, and you have permanently awakened all Europe to the perfidy and the deceit of your Governments, whether Whig or Tory.

While you were laying the plans of your traitorous views on the surrounding nations, the Irish Church seemed cherished with your perfidious care; your gifts had nearly worked her ruin; but since your schemes have been detected here, and in the neighboring States, we are made the appalling victims of your disappointed rage.—Our defenceless institutions, and the unprotected monuments of Irish piety, are now assailed by all the malignant power of your hostile Empire—your Senate, your Courts of Law, your army, your navy, your universities, your literature, your church, your historians, your pamphleteers, your novelists, your caricaturists, your aristocracy, your merchants, your artizans, your mobs, are all united into one powerful force of infuriated assailants against our creed; and by misrepresentation, falsehood, calumny, slander, lies, persecution, extermination, banishment, starvation, and death, you and your associates have attempted, through solicitation, seduction, place, pension, bribery, intimidation, and stratagem, to thin our ranks, to shake our faith, and to break a passage through our ancient camp, and seize our fortresses; and although you have uprooted the cabins of the poor, thrown down our villages, wasted our fields, starved our tradesmen, expatriated the living, murdered the dead, and filled the poorhouses and the red grave with the martyred Irish; praise be to God for ever, and honor to the ever blessed Virgin Mary, you have not taken one stout heart from the faithful ranks, or disturbed one stone in our ancient and time-honored turrets. Eternal praise to the faithful Irish, who preferred exile to an alliance with you—who died of starvation sooner than taste the bread of apostacy, and who preferred the coffinless grave, rather than live in the dress of perjury and perdition. Your perfidious predecessor and yourself, are avowedly beaten; the worst is passed, and we now set you at defiance. We have the voice of Europe and the world in our favor: and our honor, our courage, and our national fidelity, will damn you and your cruel confederates to eternal fame. You are certainly defeated; and when you now calumniate us, we have an answer ready from the sympathy of Europe.

When you malign the Jesuits, we point to Hungary, where the Emperor is now employed in placing these pious, exemplary, and learned men, over all the schools of his subjects. When you speak of the success of your Bible Societies, we send you the judicial decision of Austria and Naples, where an English Protestant missionary is ordered from these countries within fifteen days under penalty of public and forcible expulsion. When you talk of your Protestant liberality, we call your attention to Naples, also, where no Protestant teacher would be permitted to superintend any public class, in consequence of the interminable calumnies which these creatures are ever introducing against the Catholic faith. English travellers, English tourists, are now stopped, questioned, and examined throughout Europe, as if they were intriguing villains, disseminating rebellion and infidelity wherever they go. The correspondents of the English journals are hunted like felons from every city in Europe, their letters examined, and themselves ordered to quit in forty-eight hours, when their occupation of slander and infidelity is known.

Yes, our answers to your base calumnies are now published in our favor, by the universal cry of shame from all foreign nations.

Hear it my Lord—while you were slandering us in the Lords, and while Russell was spewing his Woburn apostacy on Bishops in the Commons, the French army, the invincible sons of the glorious Franks, were kneeling before the mitred Archbishop of Paris; and as he raised the adorable Host beneath the blue unfathomable vault, the loud clang of the French steel, at "the Elevation," as the army drew their swords, and presented arms to the God of battles, amid the thunders of one hundred pieces of ordnance, was the significant and appropriate answer which glorious Catholic France sent on the morning breeze to bigoted England, in reply to your Parliamentary vituperation. And when you issued your proclamation against the processions which took place at Jacob's Ladder! and at Solomon's Temple! and in all Christian places all over the world, from Constantine to Prince Louis Napoleon, and when you spread the awful majesty of your laws (with such a master stroke of statesmanship) over the evangelical town of Ballinasloe, formerly called by the Popish name of Kylenaspithogue; in order to protect these holy places from the danger of wax-candles and white rosin: did your Lordship remark the cutting reply which the Prince immediately sent to you in the studied bow, which on his return from the passage of the Rhine, he made to the surpliced Archbishop and Clergy of Paris; and did your Lordship read that passage in his processional progress along the Boulevards, where seeing the cross raised "he rose in his carriage, took off his hat, and bowed long and reverently to the cross."

There, Sir, is the glorious answer of France to your far-famed poclamation; there Sir, is the triumphant, scathing, crushing reply to your "anti-long-beard—anti-candle—anti-cross—Derbyite—anti-shortbreeches-proclamation." I have never read anything on any subject which has filled me with more sincere pleasure than that Christian conduct of the Prince. In that bow, Sir, read your own shame; and in his bare head before the cross, learn to spare your Catholic fellow-subjects; and learn to respect the emblem of your salvation, the cross of Christ.—For that glorious act of the Prince, I hereby offer him my heartfelt gratitude and my sincere homege; and I also present him with the ardent love of one million of my countrymen, proceeding from breasts as faithful and as brave as the world ever saw. I must also inform your Lordship that the Prince will read this letter on next Thursday morning before his breakfast; and moreover I must tell you that he will send to me a vote of thanks by the very next post—a piece of good breeding and courtesy which I have seldom received from my correspondents in the English Cabinet.

You have decidedly put yourself at the head of a vast mob in these countries by issuing your late proclamation; and it is quite true that we are indebted to the good sense and generous feeling of the English people for having escaped the most degrading ill-treatment in all places of public resort. But we have our satisfaction in the universal contempt with which your name and your laws are received in every country in the world. Three members of the American Cabinet (Protestants) have already spoken on the subject with unmeasured ridicule; and one of them joined in a Catholic procession, as the best testimony he could offer against English bigotry. I beg, therefore, to offer to President Fillmore, and to these three members, my warmest acknowledgments, and to assure them that they command the liveliest gratitude of the Irish and the English Catholics in these countries, and that we all long for some occasion to testify to them that we love them as much as we abhor the English Government.

The case between you and Catholicity, stands thus: the schemes which your Government have been devising against our Faith, our discipline, and our system of education, have been palpably detected, and as clearly defeated. Your name is detested in all the neighboring countries, and your accomplices have been expelled with a summary command, and, indeed, with an insult, which you have not, or dare not resent. Beyond all doubt, you and your rebel and infidel accomplices have been removed from Austria, Hungary, Prussia, (Protestant,) from Rome, Naples, and Lombardy. Your Bible Societies, which are reported as your emissaries of insurrection, have been watched as public enemies; and it is an historical fact, admitting of no doubt whatever, that neither in public, nor in private, will these countries tolerate English influence to be exercised in their religious, social, or political concerns. The Continental education, which you had nearly corrupted by your money and your emissaries, has now undergone a total change. The Catholic Clergy are now placed in all these countries as the sole directors and guardians of the education and literary and religious training of the rising generation; and Prince Louis Napoleon, now so much abused by your journals, has introduced changes in all the educational schools of France, and will soon restore the ancient discipline of the Catholic Church, which placed education in the hands of the ministers of religion. The "College de France," which, according to the testimony of the Count Montalambert, sent out nine infidels to one Christian pupil, (un sur dix,) has been remodelled, and the infidel element extracted under his vigilant care. You are, therefore, defeated in every part of the world in your schemes against the Catholic religion and education.

Your last effort is carried on against Ireland, where as sure as the sun will rise to-morrow, you will be surely defeated: and if the Board of Education in Ireland, will permit you to interfere in their arrangements, Ireland will lose her life's blood sooner than have Voltaire her class-book, and Carlisle her master. Depend upon it, if there be a God ruling His Church, you cannot change His laws, no more than you can arrest the tide, or stop the earth's motion by a proclamation from Downing-street. Our Faith, and our discipline, and our mode of education, existed before you were born, and will, in all likelihood, survive your Lordship's name many years, and even outlive the English rule and German blood.

"Shall burning Etna, if a sage requires,
"Forget to thunder and recall her fires,
"On air or sea, new motions be impressed,
"Oh, blameless Albion! to relieve thy breast;
"When the loose mountain trembles from on high,
"Shall gravitation cease when you go by"

Under these circumstances, our duty will be, to obey all the laws, as we have ever done, but to keep clear from all contact with you. During the late revolutions of Europe, there is not one instance recorded against the Catholic Clergy, of disloyalty to the throne. Under all the provocation and insult which you and your coadjutors have heaped upon us, we stand blameless before God and the laws of our country. We appeal to universal mankind for a verdict of our innocence and blamelessness under the most grinding tyranny, calumnies, and lies, that perhaps ever the world saw. We have been ever, we are at present, and we shall continue to be in the right.

Let you proceed then against us in your usual course, and advance in the wrong—go on in your career of insult, and injustice before mankind, and we boldly set you at defiance. We do not court your hostility, or challenge your persecution; no, but take your own course, proceed in your national perfidy, and we despise your last effort of vengeance. We have been grateful to former statesmen and former friends, for the small measure of justice which they offered to our plundered Church, and to our wounded and bleeding country. I own it, we have been grateful; but if you, Sir, retrace their steps and blot out their generous acts in the consuming fire of your well-known bigotry, we boldly hold your threats in utter contempt; we believe it better to have our Church surrounded with a crown of thorns than purchase a diadem for it made of apostate gold; and we are convinced it is better, far better, to have our rising generation bred and educated Irishmen and Catholics, as our fathers, at the foot of the mountain, (if necessary,) sooner than drink from your poisoned fountain of knowledge the coward draught of education, which must be swallowed at the expense of national honor, and by an insult on our ancient Faith.

Pray, Sir, how have you returned from America? How did you effect your escape from Mr. President Fillmore's breeches pocket? Ten thousand blessings upon his giant heart, if he had kept you and the "great Whig," and all your tiny Cabinets, a sport for his cats at Fundy. But, indeed, he has exhibited you before the world in your fallen greatness. England has been literally horse-whipped, and she sneaks away a grumbling coward, degraded by Whiggery and sunk by Toryism. You had no idea, my Lord, of going to war. What! With the Kaffirs decimating you; the Burmese occupying your time; the old Sikhs beyond the Sutlej; the Chinese keeping you engaged; the Canadians waiting their time; a national debt of nine hundred and fifty-four millions; with a Protestant establishment of nine millions and a half yearly; with two millions of Chartists, with their staves ready for an onslaught on your purses, the day you sell a dear loaf; with one million of armed hostile Frenchman at your gates; and with one million of Irishmen, goaded, and wounded, and bleeding with the chains of your wanton cruelty; and you pretend to go to war with America, (or as Lord Palmerston calls them,) your cousins, with all these trifles on your hands!! Pshaw—the world knows you are water-logged, and that an additional ton would sink you. No, Sir, but the Americans could even come into the Bay of Galway to fish, and you could not resist them, you dare not; and more than this, if they laid claim to Ireland, in right of all the Irish whom you have unlawfully and unjustly expelled from their country, you would surrender Ireland to America, nearly as readily as have given up your claim to the Lobos Islands. You, Sir, are openly, and avowedly snubbed, and cuffed, and kicked, all over the world at this moment; and the only *glorious* achievement in which you stand unrivalled above all mankind, just now, is your conquest over poor, helpless Nuns, and unoffending Priests.

If you could be influenced by the magnanimity which belongs to your exalted place, you should be struck with admiration at the incredible fidelity of the Irish people, who present to the impartial historian a spectacle of national virtue and national greatness not surpassed, or equalled by any generation in the story of Grecian and Roman patriotism and virtue. You behold a people ground to the very dust, with the most merciless administration of law which ever cursed society—you see them beset on all sides, with the persecutions of land grievances and surrounded with all the torturing machinations which the furious zeal of a bigoted hostile Church would employ against their Faith; you observe them crowd the putrid poor-houses, fill the emigrant ships, and die in naked starvation sooner than surrender what they believe their truth and national honor, and with such faithful instances of the endurance of a whole people, could any, except a soul pierced through with the incurable cancer of bigotry, fail to give credit to the feeling which could stand with such invincible firmness in defence of creed and of country? Why would you not court the confidence and secure the love of such a race? Why would you not endeavor to connect them with the throne by a tie which Ireland never broke—namely, the tie of gratitude? Why would you not open our metallic mines to keep them alive, rather than open the grave for their death? Why would you not purchase implements of trade and husbandry for the wealth of the nation, rather than buy coffins for the extermination of the people? Why do you not give us bread instead of your apocryphal Bible? Why not justice instead of calumny? Why not treat us as subjects, and not as slaves? Why meet us as enemies in all the walks of the Empire? Why not try the rule of equality with us? Why do you weave Protestantism into all your dealings with Catholicism? Will you never permit us to address God unless through an act of Parliament? Why do you insist on putting a chain of Swedish iron on our consciences? Protestantism has deceived you; bigotry has set you mad; and in placing your laws above God you have insulted mankind, misinterpreted religion, and ruined your country.

In my next letter, I shall place before your Lordship some few important facts, with which I do believe you are unacquainted; and till then, I have the honor to be your Lordship's obedient servant,

D. W. CAHILL, D.D.

DR. CAHILL TO THE RIGHT HON. THE EARL OF DERBY.

New-Brighton, *Saturday, October* 21, 1852.

My Lord Earl—Some few months ago our gracious Queen, in a speech from the throne, very emphatically announced her royal determination to uphold the principles of the Protestant church, and she called on her servants there assembled, in her presence, to assist her in maintaining the liberties of the Protestant Constitution. There must be, my Lord, in the royal mind some hidden fear of this church being in danger, in order to account for the large space which this idea has taken up in the royal oration. If this declaration had been made by your Lordship, or by any one of the present Ministry, it would still command an important attention; but when it proceeds from the head of your church—from the ecuminical source of all Protestant truth, it comes before the world, invested with all the realities of parliamentary gravity, and English history. For the first time in my life, I do agree with the sentiments deduced from a royal speech; and I do, therefore, believe that your church is in imminent danger at the present moment; and I believe, moreover, that neither her most gracious Majesty, with all her royal power, nor Lord John Russell, with the base Whigs, nor your Lordship, with the most judicious combination of Whig and Tory, which your skill in parliamentary chemistry can produce, will be able to stay much longer the downfall of an institution, which is a libel on God's

Gospel, a fortress for public injustice, and the scandalous disturber of our national peace. The danger to be apprehended, however, will not proceed, in the first instance, from an external enemy; it will come from her long internal rottenness; and the public shame, and the public common sense, and the public indignation will soon be seen struggling for the mastery in levelling with the earth, and eradicating from the soil this anti-Christian monster, which has been reared on the plundered food of the widow and the orphan, and which now makes its enormous daily meals and annual feasts on the life-blood of the entire nation.

The long silence of the Catholics under your shameful and shameless calumnies, and our superhuman endurance under savage parliamentary insults and lies, such as are actually unknown in any other country in the whole world, have had the effect of encouraging our insatiable enemies, in place of mitigating their fanatical ferocity.—The oblivion which our writers have cast in charity over the first flagrant iniquities of your church, has been misunderstood by your professional bigots, who, like a swarm of locusts, crowd every thoroughfare in the Empire, enabling the passengers of all nations to read, in the malignant domination of their brows, that the hatred of Catholicity, the fury of unappeasable malignity, and not the mild spirit of Christianity, is the predominant feeling of their hearts, and the very mainspring of their entire conduct. The Catholic public, too, have forgotten the early pedigree of the Reformation; and have, therefore, considerably relaxed in their watchfulness against their deadly foes; and hence the public mind must be again roused to a universal resistance against a congregation of calumniators, who, not content with living on the plunder of our ancestors, are engaged, year after year, in maligning their victims, spreading abroad uncharitableness, disturbing the public peace; and positively, and without any doubt, disturbing the name and maternal interests of England, throughout the entire world.

As Lord John Russell and your Lordship, have been the principal promoters of this strange evangelism, I have decided on addressing to you twelve letters on the subject just referred to. They shall be divided into distinctions, in which I shall prove beyond all doubt—Firstly, the unscriptural enormities and the theological incongruities of these Protestant principles which you say are now endangered—Secondly, I shall demonstrate beyond all contradiction, that this Protestant Constitution has committed the largest crime of plundering the poor, ever recorded in history, and—Thirdly, I shall enumerate, to the satisfaction of every impartial man, the historical records by which this church is charged with spilling more blood of innocent, and defenceless, and unoffending Catholics, than has ever been shed by the most ruthless tyrant that ever crimsoned the page of human woe. In the treatment of this subject, I wish to inform you, that I mean no offence to the present generation of generous-hearted, honest Englishmen; my charges are not against individuals, but against the anti-Christian system, of which they are made the wretched dupes. Nor shall I found my observations upon exclusively Catholic authority, or on hearsay, however respectable the testimony, or on loose historical assertion. I shall quote all my proofs from your own great historians, from the Protestant Synods of Germany, Switzerland, Holland, and France; and I shall complete my demonstrations from the acts of the English Parliament. I shall not confine my views on the horrors of your evangelical system to Great Britain and unfortunate Ireland. I shall trace them through northern and central Europe; and I shall place before the Christian world the clear fact, viz., that in whatever country Protestantism has been introdued in the room of Catholicity, there may be traced all the maddening disorders which have almost ever accompanied and followed it; namely, ferocious bigotry, relentless persecution, sanguinary atrocities, social disunion, and universal wasting, public brand of beggary and national distress, graven by the ruthless bigot on the heart, and the bones, and the narrow of the wretched, subdued Catholic.

And if I shall fullfil faithfully these my preliminary promises, there is no honorable English or Irish Protestant, (who will take the trouble to read my proofs,) who can, as a scholar, a gentleman, and a Christian, be reasonably angry with me for exposing to the public indignation, a system calling itself the Gospel of Christ, and which, on examination, will be found an iniquitous aggregate of hypocrisy, lies, rebellion, spoliation, murder, and blasphemy. I own it requires much deliberate reflection before these grave charges should be made against your national Church, and addressed to so exalted a person as the Earl of Derby. I feel this responsibility, and I fully conceive my position; but I again repeat my charges, and I shall forfeit all claim to truth, if I do not perfectly substantiate every point I have adduced. It is with feelings of tremulous confusion that the historian of the present day, will even attempt to write the details of the crimes of this infamous band of anti-Christian monsters; and hence, who can describe what must have been the bewildering, the shocking, the racking woes, of the persecuted past generation which witnessed, and bled under their terrific realities.

The first unparalleled imposture which "the Reformation" invented, and which it has practised to this day, was the self-appointment, and self-consecration of Henry VIII., to assume the title of "Head of the Church." One might suppose that the man who robbed the Convents of Englishmen to the amount of millions of money, built and secured by the ancient laws of the realm, would be ashamed to appear before his countrymen stained, as his character was, with this public profanation; one might believe that a monster who had divorced three wives and beheaded two, (one of them probably his own daughter,) would be afraid to let the eye of mortal see his hands reeking with the blood of his innocent victims. Through all the past history of mankind, if such a demon succeeded in escaping the arm of public justice, or the hand of the avenging assassin, he fled from human intercourse to bury his guilty head and racking conscience in the lonely cell of perpetual penance, in order to expiate the thrilling enormity of his black crimes.

But your apostle, the first head of your Church, seemed rather to rise, than sink by his iniquities; they appear rather to qualify than incapacitate your gospel-founder for his exalted spiritual post; and hence, he stands before your tabernacle with his red hands lifted in prayer to God! Yes, in prayer to God, your accredited proto-apostle, your appointed Bishop and your consecrated Pope! the guardian of innocence, the model of virtue, the terror of vice, the teacher of Gospel truth, the ornament of religion, the standard of evangelical perfection, the infallible guide to heaven, the successor of the Apostles, and the Vicegerent of Christ himself on earth! He appointed and consecrated himself (Act Par., 1538,) Pope and Head of the Church; and he appointed Tom Cromwell (Act 1533,) his "Vicegerent in *spirituals;*" and he gave him, as his Vicar-General, a commission with nineteen sub-commissioners, named by his "English Holiness," to report on the discipline and moral conduct and Faith of all the Religious Orders of England! The only parallel that could be devised to equal this incomprehensible farce on Christianity, would be to see the Devil ascend the Mount where our Lord delivered his first sermon, and to hear him address the multitude on the Eight Beatitudes, in mimicry of our Saviour, without any attempt during his discourse to conceal either "his cloven foot or tail" from the congregation.

Do you wonder, Sir, why we Catholics laugh and shudder at this, your first hierarchy? Can you be surprised why a learned Catholic trembles at this blasphemy of the Holy Ghost, this mockery of Christianity, this jesting with God, this sporting with the Gospel, this jibing with damnation? There is nothing like this scene of palpable mimicry of Christ and the Apostles to be found in the entire record of the most insane infidelity. It surpasses in atrocious and tragic infamy, anything that has ever happened in the whole world; and it stands before all mankind as the first page in the charter of your religion, the inauguration of your hierarchy, and the undoubted source of "the Reformation." There were many faithful, courageous Englishmen, who resisted this monstrous iniquity, and if you wish to learn their names, go to the prisons of your Apostle, where thousands of your countrymen died in confinement; go to glorious France, where hundreds of your relatives fled for safety; and, Sir, go to the reeking block, where you can read in the martyred blood of the illustrious More, the venerable Fisher, and in the shameful murder of the noble Countess of Salisbury. Read there the origin of your creed, the law of your Gospel, the decalogue of your ethics.

If these astounding scenes were enacted under the excitement of mere popular, or mere political fury, they should not find a place in this letter to your Lordship, which is intended for the discussion of the religious foundation of your Church; but they were the Acts of Henry, as your ecclesiastical superior, [see Act,] they were executed in the name, and under the sanction of this new Church; as such they were agreed to by the Drummonds, and the Russells, and the Derbys of that day of English infamy; and in the preambles of the Acts of Parliament, the Assembly sat in deliberation "in the Spirit of the Holy Ghost," and hence, these Acts of Henry, form, without contradiction, a record of your ecclesiastical jurisdiction, and not of your political history. There is no generous, candid English Protestant, at the present day, who, I believe, does not blush at the recital of these atrocities, and yet he lives contentedly and unconsciously under the very same hierarchal law; is governed by the reigning monarch as the head of the Church; pays religious obedience in faith and morals to the persons called, appointed, and commissioned to lead men's souls to heaven; and all this by virtue of the royal prerogative, as the supreme spiritual authority of the realm. Take away the crimes of your first founder, and your present system is perfectly the same—namely, human commission, human jurisdiction in the kingdom of Christ! You might as well apply the laws of gravitation to the soul, as to adopt a temporal rule to produce the spiritual results of grace. You might as well tell the world, that original sin is remitted in baptism according to the laws of hydrostatics, as to assert that the queen or king of any country can give, *ex-officio*, a commission to save the souls of their subjects.

It is the Monarch alone of that Spiritual Kingdom who can frame its laws, appoint his officers, give them authority, define their duties, and decide rewards and punishments; and this leads me to examine this principle of supremacy in the reign of Edward the Sixth. Mr. Cobbet has already glanced at this subject; but Mr. Cobbet was no theologian—I am; and he confined his views to England; I shall extend mine to every country in Europe where your Gospel has been preached; and I hereby humbly request of the Ambassadors of the Catholic

Courts now resident in London, (to each of whom I shall send a copy of this letter,) that they will so far have mercy on Ireland as to publish my proofs in each of their capitals, in order to inform their Nations of the insatiable injustice exercised towards us, by the cruelty of the English Government, and to warn their countrymen of the danger of permitting English missionaries and English spies to reside amongst them, calumniating their creed and revolutionizing their laws.

One can scarcely avoid bursting out into a commingled torrent of indignation, contempt, and horror, against a band of plunderers, infidels, and assassins, who, in the face of civilized Europe, could set up a *child* of ten years of age as Pope the Second, thus placing the nation in a position of spiritual ruin, and perpetuating the mad apostacy of the last reign. This, my Lord, is a new practical-spiritual phase of your Church. In the late reign, the King proclaimed himself Pope; but here we have a born Pope, a born Bishop, an Apostle in swaddling clothes, coming into the world with a mitre on his head, the inspiration of the Holy Ghost transmitted to him from his father Henry, like freehold property, the grace of God running in the child's pure blood by virtue of the character and ecumenical position of his father; a born saint, like his father, and, like a child born with a wooden-leg, holding the crozier in his new-born hand, and wearing the mitre on his apostolic-hereditary head! Lord Derby, are you serious in belonging to a system of such disgusting, incomprehensible folly? You might as well assert that a hawk could beget a whale, as that a Bishop could be naturally elaborated from the blood of Henry VIII. But this is not all; this child-Pope made the "Book of Common Prayer," and almost entirely drew up the Thirty-nine Articles of what is called your creed.

And what renders the thing so utterly shameful, is, that this weak, sickly boy, never perhaps, saw the book, or read one of the Articles referred to; so that this principle of the headship of the Church, which, in itself, is so ludicrous, is, besides all this, a most monstrous, notorious, palpable lie, as the baby-Pope, who is said to be head, has actually, and in point of fact, no more part in this Reformation-jugglery, than the Grand Turk. The idea of a child making Articles of Faith, and composing prayers, through an Act of Parliament as *head of Christ's Church*, is so palpably ridiculous, that the Catholics at once ask you: "What insanity has come over you, to leave a learned old Pope and a Council of Bishops, in order to follow a child in a cradle and a Senate of shopkeepers?" You decide religion, as you decide the duty on your manufactures; you settle the way to Heaven, as you fix the direction of a turnpike road—namely, by a majority of votes; and in the face of mankind you set up a baby in a cradle as the expounder of the Gospel, although it cannot read; as the teacher of the Gospel, although it cannot speak; and as the head of your Church in all its duties, although it has not got one idea in its head of any one thing in this world!!

But the principle has to be examined, in a new, astounding, third phase, viz:—After the death of Edward, it is to be seen, residing in a young woman of six-and-twenty years of age! of course, she too, is the sanctified descendant of the first head, Pope Henry. She, too, it seems, inherits her father's sanctity; but the inspiration of the Holy Ghost, does not fall upon her, till the mature apostolic age of twenty-six. Blessed family! to have men, women, and children, all born apostles—angels of grace. This lay Pope, this royal Nun, this consecrated virgin, was the person who completed the inspiration of the far-famed Thirty-nine Articles of your Faith, not more than ten of which, any educated respectable Protestant can conscientiously believe. Some of them are contradictory, others absurd, and two or three of them impossible. You, my Lord, who are so deeply read in canon-law, as to see heresy in our cravats, and to read the violation of your constitutional laws in our shoes and hosiery, will you say how many of these articles do you believe? I never knew any Protestant who had such a capacious draught of sanctity. Lord John Russell, although a Presbyterian, a Puseyite, a Methodist, a Protestant, and a Pagan, (as he has expunged baptism,) does not, perhaps, believe from these five creeds of his, so many as these Thirty-nine Articles of Godliness. I believe it to be true, my Lord, that; like razors made to sell, but not to shave; these Articles are made more for show than devotion. Excuse me, my Lord, if I, at the present moment, smile in your face, at seeing your name enrolled in such an incongruous, insane system of absurdity, imposture, and infidelity.

But, my Lord, I am not quite done with this young lady-Pope. There is a new feature in her apostolic reign, which we learn from *Act of Parliament,* passed in the year 1571, and in the thirteenth year of her reign, to which I refer you. In this Act, passed by her Parliament of Englishmen, (manufacturers of faith,) and subscribed of course, by her holy hand, as head of your church, it was enacted (Christ protect us!) that the crown of England should descend, if she had no lawful heirs, to her "natural issue." Do you blush, Lord Derby, to see the crown of Alfred and Edward given by your evangelical Senate to such "an issue," by Act of Parliament! Do you blush to see the head of your church subscribe a public law of her own public shame! signing her hand manual, to an act that would degrade the most infamous inmate of the lowest of your London brothels—haunts of pollution! I fancy it was this Act of Parliament which Mr. Drummond read, on the night when he spewed the filth of his Reformation creed on the spotless consecrated Catholic virgins of Europe. He mistook them for the virgin head of your church; he did—the wretched old Reformer—he did mistake them; and in his filthy language he was *protected* by the Speaker, and thus *applauded* by the whole Senate of England. I say, Sir, he was, and Catholic Europe should never forget the insult offered to their honor, their morality, and to their creed. My Lord, what do you now say, so far as I have gone as yet, to the early foundation of your "Reformed Church?"

Amidst the records of the human race, there is a sense of shame in the most abandoned, which prompts them to conceal their personal crimes—wretches who have lost every virtue, and are immersed in every vice, have still left in their black hearts one small remnant of untainted nature; namely, the inward feeling of condemnation of their own guilt. It is so in the most degraded wretch that expiates on the scaffold the enormities of a long obdurate life; it is particularly so in woman, whose fine nature can never be utterly trampled out by vice, but with her life; and hence, when we find a Queen of a most powerful Empire, the head of a church calling itself Christian, in the face of mankind, at the age of forty-nine, summon a Parliament to make her prospective shame legal by English law! and when we behold herself in person sign the record of her own crime—she stands before the world the vilest miscreant, the most abandoned wretch, the most shameless monster, in woman form, that has ever stained the profligate records of either ancient or modern infamy. We have borne your calumnies too long in charitable forbearance—we have abstained these many past years from repeating the anti-Christian, the scandalous, incongruous tenets of your abhorrent creed—we have carefully kept from the hands of the rising generation of Ireland the records of your Church infamies—we have actually robbed our Irish children of the history of their fathers, in order to maintain peace with you; but you have outraged our endurance; you and *your* church party, both Whig and Tory, have aided in calumniating us, with an indecency of falsehood, that makes even bigotry blush; and you forced us to come forward against our inclination, to recommence the exposure of your blood-stained creed, which will end, as sure as I am penning these lines, in the overthrow of this iniquitous establishment, and perhaps in the degradation of your country. We shall no longer be silent on a system of religion, where your piety is vice—where your Gospel is imposture—and the charter of your creed is hypocrisy, shame, and sin. In order to meet the objection, "that these Acts of Parliament had reference to the political, the religious, not prerogative of Elizabeth," I subjoin the words of the Synod of London:

"The *sovereign government* of all her subjects, "lay and *clerical, belongs to her in all matters* without being subjected to *any foreign power.*"

Having thus glanced at the principle of the supremacy of your Monarch, the next point in the regular order of your hierarchy, is the ludicrous variety of your confessions of faith. From the year 1530 to the year 1557, Protestantism has issued not less than eighteen confessions of faith—all different, and varying not only in general principles, but contradictory in most of the Articles of Faith, and contrary on the same points of belief in not less than four essential dogmas of Christianity. Your Confessions of Faith, are as follows:—Augsburg, 1530; Genoa, 1531; France, 1534; Melancthon's Apology, 1535; Scotch Confession, 1536; Smlacald, 1537; Dort, 1541; Szenger, 1543; Sendomar, 1546; Saxonic, 1551; Wurtemberg, 1552; Book of Concord, 1556; Explications repeated, 1557.

Now, my Lord, if any one of our theories in chemistry, in reference to the analysis, or the products of any chemical agents, underwent eighteen different, contradictory and contrary demonstrations, is there any scientific scholar in the whole world, who would take his oath that all these contrary theories were right: and, moreover, who would hang, behead, and quarter any one who should refuse to take his oath in the same contrarities? And if this doctrine in science would make all mankind shudder, will you say in what language shall I attempt to explain your faith, which ascribes to the inspiration of the Holy Ghost, eighteen different systems of the grossest lies, the most palpable contradictions, and absurd contrarities? If the meanest man in Great Britain, were charged with wilful prevarication on his oath, in his statement in eighteen different assertions, he would be branded as a debased wretch, a public perjurer; and hence to ascribe this conduct to the Holy Ghost, in your eighteen sworn Confessions of Faith, is a depth of blasphemy, a hardihood of insane iniquity beyond the comprehension of the impartial observer; but, like an old Juggler swallowing a dozen of razors at a time; a feat which would kill twelve ordinary men, your long habit of unpunished infidelity, has accustomed you to stand before the gates of heaven, and call God a liar to his face. Saint Paul, endeavoring to express to us unity of faith, could find no other image by which he could convey his belief, except by likening it to the unity of God, in that remarkable passage of Holy Writ, where he writes to the Ephesians—"one Lord, one faith, one baptism." As this language is so clear, it follows that there cannot exist in true faith any change, contradiction, or contrariety, any more than in the very being of God; and it follows, moreover, from the clear logic of the text, that two or more faiths, are just as absurd as two or more Gods.

But what signifies the testimony of St. Paul in comparison with that of Elizabeth, and what value can be attached to any scriptural record, when placed in juxta position with an English Act of Parliament! When a church has arrived so far in the mysteries of faith, as to place at the head of all spiritual power a monster, who has discarded three wives and murdered two; when it can propose for the salvation of the soul, a creed said to be made by a child in a cradle; when a public sin against the sixth commandment, by the head of a church is made legal by an Act of the English Parliament; when the Holy Ghost is publicly declared on oath, to have published for the guidance of the soul in sanctity, eighteen avowed systems of palpable lies, in the short space of twenty-six years—I fearlessly say, if these records cannot be disputed, there is no candid Protestant who can complain if such a system of perjury, pollution, and blasphemy, be vigorously denounced before the indignation and the horror of the entire Christian world.

Notwithstanding these synodical contrarieties, we learn the strange doctrine from "the Synod of Charteron," that the entire varying Protestant communities of Europe are still "the one society" of true Christian believers; that eighteen different "distinct things" are the self-same "one thing," is a proposition so utterly incomprehensible, as even to surpass the phenomenon of your supremacy. The only thing I ever read, which can at all approach this article of your faith in point of absurdity is the Dutch tragedy representing Adam, *about to be created:* at a certain part of the tragedy, when all eyes are turned to the deep, solemn tragedian, who is about to perform the act of creation. Adam himself, the first man, (though not yet created,) comes out on the stage, with a new doeskin breeches, boots, and spurs, to be created! With these palpable absurdities, you call your Church the spouse of of Christ—a lie which makes the skin creep, and the blood run cold, to hear you connect with the name of the Saviour, such an aggregate of obsceneness and impiety. From the first year of your foundation, through the three hundred years of your existence, no three individuals of your co-religionists could agree in doctrine; and at this moment you present to the laughing world, a congregation divided in all points, except the stereotype doctrine of "hatred of Catholicity."

Lord John Russell, who can agree to almost any form of Faith, cannot admit baptism; the Archbishop of Canterbury, who is paid £24,000 a year for the gigantic amount of his Faith, will not admit Holy Orders as necessary: even in time of general English cholera, our Doctor Wheatley, in Dublin, the pre-anti-Catholic Archbishop of Ireland, exempts unmarried clergymen from their attendance in blue Asiatic cholera. In their Lordships' theological opinions, the attendance of clergy is only necessary in fine weather, when new kid gloves can be worn, when the tainted air does not blow from the east, when the patient can receive these apostles on Turkey carpets, and when there is no fear of the stench of the dying Christian coming "between the wind and their holy nobility." And more strange than all, is the new change of the Bishop of Exeter, approving the practice of "hearing confessions;" what an edifying Church you have! What a venerated Senate!

You abuse, malign, and insult us, for the practice your good Exeter now exclaims is the sure road to heaven. And this is what you call the "enviable wisdom of the English Parliament, and the evangelical unity of the Reformation." And these are the laws which you call on us to respect and obey; this is the religion to which you hope to convert the Irish people; and this is the creed you offer to poor old Erin, in the fourteenth-hundredth year of her Christian age. The venerable old lady, I assure you, is not accustomed to see her apostles dressed in diamond rings and London boots. After her long tuition under Saint Patrick, she is quite surprised to receive religious instruction from your Voltaires and Paynes; she cannot understand why the education of Faith in Christ, *must* be preceded by the knowledge of potash and pyrites; and she is utterly astounded, to hear men assert that the temple of the science of the saints *must* be approached through fields of Swedish turnips and nicely-drilled mangel wurtzel. After her long intercourse with Columkill and Saint Bridget, she has learnt so completely the Irish accent, that she can with difficulty comprehend your Lordship's Saxon tongue; and although she has often heard of the dialects of Greek, and the vocalic varieties of the Eastern languages, she has never understood, till she read your Eighteen Confessions of Faith, how there could be such a thing possible, as varieties and dialects in the unchangeable professions of God's Gospel.

If you give me fair play, my Lord; if you do not set your *Times*, and your *Globe*, and your *Standard*, and your *Punch*, to ridicule and to abuse me; if you call on them to reply to me by argument, and not by abuse, I undertake to rid this Nation of your Church Establishment, and thus to save for the Empire the eight and a half millions annually, which it devours from the just revenues of the naked widow and the starving orphan. Depend upon it, my Lord, that I shall lay bare the appalling foundation of your Church, before I shall have concluded my next three letters on that subject. And believe me, I shall convince you, that it is far wiser to make Catholic Ireland your friend, than to make all Europe your enemy; it is cheaper to secure the arms and the hearts of one million of Catholic Irishmen by the words of truth, honor, and justice, than to pay half a million a year to an inefficient militia, by a useless, a pernicious, an angry taxation. Rely upon it, that your diplomacy will be more respected and feared by foreign nations at seeing peace than divisions in your own country; and take the advice of an humble individual, when I presume to tell you, to commence the next Parliament, (where you will keep office precisely till the Christmas recess,) by retracing your steps towards Ireland, and legislating for your country, not in the burning records of persecution and insult, but in the imperishable laws of eternal truth and public justice. And never forget the remarkable words of the illustrious Lous Napoleon the Third, "Woe be to him (that is to you,) who gives the first signal of collision, the consequences of which will be incalculable."

I have the honor to be, my Lord Earl, your Lordship's obedient servant,

D. W. CAHILL, D.D.

DR. CAHILL TO THE RIGHT HON. LORD VISCOUNT PALMERSTON.

CAMBRIDGE, *February 23d*, 1853.

MY LORD VISCOUNT—I feel much difficulty either in renewing my correspondence with you, or reviving the controversy in the case of Madiai—that controversy is now at rest. Proofs incontrovertible have been brought before the public notice, to show that palpable misstatements have been made by English correspondents, and by the universal press; and an additional case has thus been placed on the records of English bigotry, to confirm the public impression that the British Government will grasp at any vague stories, and pervert every dubious occurrence, in order to malign Catholic political legislation, and to belie the Catholic Church.

But, my Lord, I have, in the present instance, a graver charge than all this to settle with your Lordship in the case before us. I am come to accuse you and Lord John Russell with a guilty suppression of the truth, on the point at issue, in your ministerial capacity; and consequently arraign you both before this Nation and the Catholic world, of having encouraged, during the last eight months, in this country public vituperation of the Catholic Church, and the Catholic community; while at the same time you both held in your hands the despatches from your own ambassadors, which contradicted in toto this unceasing and groundless insult to two-thirds of the citizens of this country, and the millions of the population of those kingdoms, with which you state you hold international and friendly relations. I owe it to the Catholics of this country, to expose your unpardonable conduct in this case, and I owe it to myself as a public writer, to prove the accuracy of my statements, and to demonstrate the indubitable sources from which I have, in my late letters to the Earl of Carlisle, derived my political information.

I shall divide this letter into seven heads; and I beg to assure you, that in the treatment of the subject, I mean no personal offence either to your Lordship or Lord John Russell. I am solely actuated by the desire of doing public justice to injured truth, placing the subject before the impartial judgment of an honest British public, and warning them in future (an advice scarcely necessary,) against giving implicit credence to any assertion of yours involving any statement where the Catholic Church, Catholic Faith, Catholic practices, or the political laws of Catholic States, are the subjects under your official examination.

Firstly, then, every one who has read the furious articles of the daily London press, must have been struck this some time past, with the painful description given, of "the appalling prison in which the Madiais were confined; the damp floors on which they lived, the unendurable penal dress in which they were clothed, the cruel treatment they received, the barbarous tyranny of excluding all intercourse with their friends, and the murderous results of this Papal persecution, which must very soon end in the death of these most unoffending, most resigned victims of Popish intolerance." Even Lord John Russell, writing on the subject to Sir Henry Bulwer, the pink of toleration and truth, has said, "It is the same thing in effect," said his Lordship, "to condemn a man to die by fire like Savornarola, or to put him to death by the slow tortures of an unhealthy prison."

Here is the Foreign Secretary himself joining in the cry of the furious bigots, charging the Duke of Tuscany with the indirect murder of the Madiai, and, as will presently appear, clearly *prejudging* the case. This point will, I fancy, be sufficiently proved by the following letter of Mr. Erskine, in reply to Lord John Russell, and received by him on the 4th of the present month:—

"I am informed by Mr Chapman," writes Mr Erskine, "an English gentleman, who has interested himself most warmly in favor of the Madiai, and who is permitted to visit them occasionally in prison, that he has no fault to find with their treatment. The prison is in a healthy situation at the top of a hill: and the infirmary in which the husband is lodged, is in every respect as comfortable as any well regulated hospital for persons at large. Mr. Chapman is equally satisfied with the attention bestowed on the physical wants of those Madiai at Lucca."

Again, we have an additional testimony in the Hon. Mr. Scarlett, directed to your Lordship, December 19th, 1851, as follows:—

"In consequence of the great interest felt in the state of the Madiai, I conversed with Rosa Madiai for some time in prison, and I am happy to inform your Lordship, that the place of her confinement, though small, is exceedingly clean, well ventilated, and warm. She possesses, by her own admission, all the accommodation she requires under the circumstances. She makes no complaint of want of good food and clothing; she has books to read, and she speaks in high terms of the superintendent of prisons, Mr. Peri: and she has not suffered in health."

Upwards of a year has elapsed since your Lordship has received the letter referred to, and nearly a month has expired, since Lord John Russell has heard the facts issue from Mr. Erskine, and hence, the public will learn with surprise, that in place of the one retracting his misconceptions, or the other checking the misrepresentations of the press, you both, on the contrary, have repeated, on last Thursday night, in the House of Commons, (as is reported,) nearly the same words, in the face of the public cognizance of the facts, and in the teeth of the official letter of your public servants. These brief remarks of mine on this point, spoken in pity for you both, rather than in anger, will, I fancy, settle lie the first.

Secondly, the entire press, Exeter Hall, and the inoculated conversion of private society, have all promulgated, during the past eight months, "that there was no liberty of conscience tolerated in Tuscany for any dissenting creed." This statement being perfectly understood, what must be the astonishment of the thinking portion of our community, when I inform them that in Leghorn, there are, at the present moment, a Mahomedan Mosque, a Jewish Synagogue, and a Protestant Episcopalian Church; that there are at least five thousand Jews residing there, and possessing (as I am instructed to say,) about two-thirds of the landed property of that district; and that there is not even one instance on record where any Protestant, Methodist, Presbyterian, Jew, or any member of any religion whatever, has ever been prevented from worshipping God as they may think proper in their own houses of worship, and in their own families! But, my Lord, I have the authority of the Hon. Mr. Scarlett, your official servant at Florence, in a letter written to yourself on the same subject, nearly two years ago—viz., on the 22nd Aug., 1851—as follows:—

"I have been made aware by the Duke of Casigliano that *all foreigners professing a different religion from that of the Roman Catholic, were always permitted in Tuscany, as much freedom of conscience as they pleased in regard to themselves.*"

Here, my Lord, we have a clear statement made to yourself nearly two years ago, giving an authentic account of the point at issue; and yet you have in the midst of the public misrepresentation of this country, kept the above correspondence from the public eye—suppressed the clear known truth at the very source of official information; and thus, Sir, I impeach you before the whole world, of the greatest crime a public officer can commit—namely, cushioning a public document, and thereby encouraging, and being a principal party to the slander, the censure, and the calumny, which, during eight months of unprecedented bigotry in public meetings and acrimonious journalism, has been flung (through your culpable connivance) on the temporal laws of an unoffending State, and on the tenets of a Church, which even your own official organ has been compelled to vindicate in the letter just quoted; and this statement will, I trust, fully prove my second point—or lie the second.

Thirdly, the public report has everywhere declared in this country, that the Madiai have been condemned for "reading the Bible." To this statement is opposed the fact, that Rosa Madiai had been a Protestant since 1847; that she attended the worship of that church, and had never been disturbed in reading the Bible, no more than all those other religions—Jews, Mahomedans, Methodists, Presbyterians, and all other foreigners referred to in the foregoing letter of the Hon. Mr. Scarlett; and this short statement, my Lord, settles the proof of lie the third.

Fourthly, it has been industriously circulated, that at

least no Tuscan Catholic dare change his religion and become a Protestant, under the heaviest penalties of the Papal law. To this statement of the English press, and to this mistake of the universal English people, it will be sufficient to quote an extract of a letter from Mr. Erskine to Lord John Russell, on this particular point:—

"The Madiai, says he, are not, as is alleged, convicted of having apostatised from the established (Catholic) religion, but of having sought to seduce from that religion."

I shall not, my Lord, add one word to this appropriate extract, which palpably demonstrates "lie the fourth."

Fifthly, the statement which through your connivance produced the bitterest feeling in England, was that part of the impeachment which declared "that all this tyranny was to be ascribed to the authority of the Pope in Tuscany; and that all the consequences of this murderous case, were to be traced to the doctrines of the Catholic Church."

To this part of the question, it will be sufficient to say, that the case at issue, is entirely one of the civil authority of Tuscany, and has no more connection with what is called Papal authority (as such) than the submarine Telegraph between Dublin and Holyhead has to do with the oath of allegiance to the Queen of England. The Duke of Tuscany could relax these laws, change them, modify them, or abolish them altogether, without interfering in the slightest degree with the principles of the Christian ceremony, which belongs to the province of what is known and obeyed as the Papal authority; and these observations will make the public perfectly understand "lie the fifth."

Sixthly, the most malignant part, perhaps, of the entire

English mania, is that view of the question, where, the Catholic Clergy are represented as the sole instigators of these laws and these penal enactments. Your Lordship has even given utterance to these sentiments in the reply which you thought proper to make to the deputation, which, having waited on you some few days previous, solicited your kind interference on behalf of the martyred Madiai. Your Lordship is reported to have said :—

"An Italian when he hears of the complaints made concerning the restrictions imposed on reading the Scriptures, maintains that such restrictions are necessary, because, if *the people are allowed to read the Bible,* they would become Protestants either from conviction, *or to escape the tyranny of Priests,* and thus the Priests would be deprived of power and support."

Without daring to contradict you, that no Italian can be supposed to utter one word of what your Lordship states, I am still very much puzzled, indeed, to comprehend the statement you make, as it is founded upon a notorious falsehood—namely, that the Italians are not allowed to read the Bible. There are, in the first place, (as far as I have learned,) upwards of forty editions of the Bible published within the last three hundred years on the Italian Peninsula; and how, and why all this trouble, care, and expense could be incurred by the crafty Italian booksellers; and why all these books, which "are to take all the power away from the Priests," are tolerated by these all-powerful priests; or why they would print in such abundance books which no one is allowed to read, are really such startling historical difficulties bound up with your assertion, that I hope your Lordship will excuse me if I shall take some considerable time before I believe what you say.

But pray, my Lord, in what part of Italy has your Lordship heard this strange statement, or amongst what description of persons has it been uttered? As the fact to which you allude, is at variance with the doctrine of the Catholic Church, which permits and encourages the reading of the Bible, it must, I am convinced, clearly turn out that this statement must have been made to you by the companions of Lord Minto in Italy—viz.: Mazzini, Garribaldi, and Ciceruacchio, &c. His being your family correspondent there, during the last five years of your administration, it is more than probable he is your authority on the Bible-reading question; and, here, again, your Lordship must excuse me, if for a moment I pause before I receive his statements, even made through you, when placed in contradiction to my own positive knowledge of the subject confirmed by the world-wide doctrine of the Catholic Church. Go on, my Lord, and continue your correspondence, your statements, and your English bigotry; go on, and have and enjoy your momentary triumph; but it is more than probable, you will yet adopt the language of the victorious Roman general—"Another such victory will ruin me."

But, my Lord, there is a meaning rather significant in this late speech to the Madiai deputation. Perhaps you were speaking figuratively, as you did when you wept over the destruction of the Convents and of the Colleges of Switzerland—as you did when you *interfered one week too late* in saving the lives of hundreds of persecuted Catholics from the murderous fire, and the inhuman butchery of the free corps of the sanguinary Calvinists; or perhaps you intended to throw out some sage hint to your brother Whigs (previous to Mr. Spooner's motion,) that the Irish Priests have too much power in Ireland, and consequently that the clear plan of depriving them of their power and their support, would be still more to join the Protestant Alliance; to turn all Ireland into a universal Clifden, or a Connemara, or a Kells; to expend as much money in repelling Catholicity, as you are now squandering to guard against your maligned victims, the French. Perhaps, my Lord, this was your intention, (for what man living is able to fathom you, except Lord Clarendon ?)—and if so, the Catholics of Ireland have gained one advantage from this calumnious, or figurative speech; namely, they must be more than ever on their guard against your machination; and these lengthened animadversions conclude all I have to say in reference to "lie the sixth."

Seventhly, the last most remarkable, and most embittering misstatement in this ministerial connivance, is that part where the punishment of the Madiai "is represented purely a spiritual tyranny, solely directed against the Word of God, and intended by the Priests and the Tuscan laws, to crush spiritual freedom of opinion, and the indefeasable rights of conscience."

These opinions have been circulated during the last twelve months in every English journal, and the whole mind of the British public, has been thus maddened by the baneful prejudices of frenzy, arising from the continued refuted publication of this anti-christian doctrine. And what will Englishmen say now, when I shall lay before them a letter which you received nearly two years ago from the Hon. Mr. Scarlett, in which the very statement at issue is denied; and the language of the most emphatic denial communicated to you. Yet you have suppressed that document, and by that suppression you have banded the Protestants of this Empire in a course of falsehood and furious insult against their Catholic countrymen; you have looked on quietly, while you saw the Catholics urged into unjust provocation, by an unusual outcry against us, while at the same time, you retained for eighteen months the very document which would cure the public rancor, and restore peace to your injured and insulted Catholic subjects. The document referred to, is a letter you received August 29th, 1851, an extract of which is as follows:—

"The Policy of the Tuscan government could not permit foreigners to temper with the religion of the native subjects of Tuscany, more especially at this time, as it is notorious that the *pretended conversions* to Protestantism were a MASK for carrying out political views, which *were intended to sap the foundations of governments in Italy.*"

I shall not take away from the force of this extract by adding any remark of my own. This is my last point in this unpleasant subject, and I now fearlessly assert, that, in all your political career, during the last six years, there is no one phase in your official capacity, which places you before your country in so discreditable a position, as the clear proofs of your having witnessed the grossest lies published against Catholic States and people, while you held in your hands the very official documents, the bare inspection of which, would in one day, have spared this country such scenes of degrading bigotry, as has no parallel in any country on the face of the civilized world; and these demonstrations leave no doubt whatever as to "lie the seventh."

What a suitable time it was to open a mission of Godliness, just when the Pope was driven from the Vatican! when Naples was enveloped in the flames of revolution! when your friend and your correspondent, Kossuth, had nigh overturned Austria! and when your victim, Charles Albert, was on his deathbed, broken-hearted! No language can sufficiently condemn the palpable scheme of revolution, devised by a set of British officers, under the appearance of prayer and the Word of God. What a Godly, appropriate time, to commence the work of the Reformation of Tom Cromwell and Somerset! But, above all, my Lord, what an appropriate set of apostles began the work; namely, Captain Walker, Captain Wilson, and a full military staff of evangelizers! how like the work of God in such hands, and at such a time. I am surprised that the French never conceived such a holy design as this, during the rebellion of 1798 in Ireland, and send a batch of French officers to Munster, like Ledru Rollin, General Cavaignac, and others, to evangelize the Irish, just at the moment when Hoche was approaching Bantry Bay, with ten thousand men. Why, my Lord, the heart sickens at contemplating the palpable audacity of the English spies, in their cool attempt to persuade the world that they mean to preach the Gospel, while the swords and the muskets of their perjured apostles appear beneath their crimsoned surplices.

My Lord, I am not influenced by any desire to give the smallest offence or discourtesy to any one of her Majesty's Ministers; I am, in my inmost soul, solely governed by a conviction that you and your Whig associates have been running, during the last few years, a most disastrous course; that you have laid a fatal plan of overturning Catholicity by falsehood, by misrepresentation, and by stratagem; that you have, perhaps unconsciously, been the advocate of the most notorious revolutionists of Europe; that you have made fierce and lasting enemies of some of the most powerful kingdoms on the Continent; that you have, beyond all doubt, been laying the foundation of the ruin of your own country; that you are, at this moment, squandering the public money in building harbors, equipping armaments, constructing fortifications, preparing fleets to resist an aggression, which your own palpable bigotry has excited against you; and that in the midst of all these warlike preparations you neglect the chief defence, the only defence—namely, cultivating the universal love, the undoubted allegiance, of the whole people to the throne, and giving vigor to the blood, and nerve to the arms which are to feed the cannon, and man the ships, and lead the assault on the enemy.

Lord Palmerston, do not reject an advice coming from the humble individual who has the honor of now addressing you; high as is your ministerial flight, higher points can be reached than you have yet attained, and you may fall from the perilous eminence when you least expect it; you are not beyond the reach of other men: the lowly twig on which the meteor eagle has just but a moment ago stood in pride, can be pointed with the barbed steel and propelled to reach the lordly bird in his highest flight, and it can pierce him too as he floats on the summit point of the giddy elevation; depend upon it, my Lord, that when you expose yourself, a steady aim from a watchful antagonist may reach your outspread wing, and lay you prostrate on the plain. I have long considered you the most plausible, the cleverest man in the British Ministry of any shade of politics. I believe you also to be the greatest enemy that the Catholic Church has ever had during the last three centuries, and I am persuaded that unless your Sovereign dismisses you from her Councils, you will, in furthering the ends of your insatiable and unmitigable bigotry, involve our common country in irretrievable ruin. And I pray you not to make light of these remarks of mine; you must excuse me, if I tell you that I have as perfect sources of information on the subjects on which I write, as your Lordship can have; and that while you have your Parliament to cheer you at St. Stephens, I have my Parliament to cheer me wherever the English language is spoken, and have friends to publish these remarks which I here make in every capital in Europe.

I beg of your Lordship to believe, that I am not an enemy of the State; no, I am a sincere friend, as far as my humble power can go. I am grateful to the past Governments of England for every boon they have bestowed upon my unhappy country. Every one of my profession are grateful for the efficient education you have extended to our rising generation of the poor; we thank you for your generosity in educating our national Priesthood; we would fain be grateful to you for preserving the lives of our peasant population against the ruthless extermination of the needy Orange landlords of Ireland, but you will not give us the occasion. You speak of your just laws on this subject, we point to the emigrant ship; you expatiate on the rights of property, we point to the red grave; you write on the civil liberty of the English constitution, we point to "the crowbar;" you draw up long statistics of your impartial justice, your national prosperity; we point to the deserted village; you descant at public meetings called in the name of religion on the universal benevolence of your Church; we read the advertisements in the *Times* for servants, with a *nota bene* "no Irish Catholic need apply." Ah, my Lord, not all your plausible speeches and your able diplomacy can conceal from the world the palpable afflicting fact, that the Legislature of Great Britain is spoken with lips of honey, but written in rivers of blood—is published abroad in wreaths of roses, but felt within in our aching hearts, in the cold iron of persecution; like the apples in the Lake of Sodom, you offer us fine fruit in appearance, but is poison in the taste. The persecuting Protestant Church is the great Legislator of England; it is the great editor of England; it is the amusing novelist of England; it is the Prime Minister of England; and it is the parish beadle of England; it is the painter, it is the sculptor, it is the traveller, it is the teacher, the preacher, it is the general and the admiral, and, alas! in all and each of these pursuits, positions, arts, &c., it is the base maligner of Catholicity, the unscrupulous asserter of every falsehood which converts this country into a fierce battle-field, and makes Christianity resemble rather the malevolence of Satan than the charity of God.

Pray, can you tell, my Lord, what will be the next

assault of Parliament against Catholicity? Tell us, pray, my Lord, that we may be prepared for the voluminous misrepresentations of your press, your pulpit, your Exeter Hall, and your Senate House. Is there any tale of scandal in reference to a Nun on the Continent of Europe, a Convent in Asia, a Bishop in the Pacific? Can there be no story made out against a schoolmaster for whipping a child, contrary to Martin's Act? Can there be no indictment forged against Nuns, for withholding legs of mutton, bitter ale, and apple-tarts, from orphans placed in their charge? Is there no Priests to be exposed for asking questions in the confessional on the subject of *sin*, to the inexpressible horror of the spotless innocence, and of the hysterical disedification of the angelic purity of your Divine Church? Is there no book in the Catholic Church which defiles the transparent mind of Protestantism, and which, therefore, ought to be brought before Parliament, and there receive the just irrevocable condemnation of the accredited judges of Christian morality and evangelical perfection? Can no Act of Parliament be framed against the unrighteous length of our Clerical surtouts, made as they are, according to a Papal pattern, and with the clear intent of ridiculing the Russell paletot!

Ah, my Lord, you have overbalanced yourself—you have brought derision on your Government and on your Administration, and you have made the name of Whig be the by-word of broken faith and official perfidy—you are at war with the whole world and with God—your shave-beggars in Canada, in India, in Australia, at the Cape, and at home, are the theme of universal complaint in the entire journals of the country; and, in reference to my unfortunate, persecuted, plundered country, I have heard from the lips of the illustrious, the venerable, Lord Cloncurry, that in all his experience, he "had never known more than *two Viceroys who knew anything* of the government in Ireland." In the future speeches which you may deliver on the state of Catholicity on the Continent, and on the character of the Pope, and the conduct of the Priests, do, I pray you to persevere, Sir, in your ridicule and misstatements. All the world now understands you, and that it happens the contrary of your statement is the truth. Do not, therefore, Sir, malign us by your praise; do, Sir, if you please, compliment us and our Church by your distinguished misrepresentations. Do us the favor of your disapprobation, and give us the character, before all Europe, which knows you, of having earned the imperishable honor of your ministerial malignity. In these remarks, founded on historical evidence, I fancy I am the best friend of England's security, and the truest servant of the stability of the throne in thus exposing a system of policy, which has convulsed our entire national relations abroad, and has disturbed the universal peace of our fellow-subjects at home. I have the honor to be, my Lord Viscount, your humble servant, &c.

D. W. CAHILL, D.D.

N. B.—I shall send a printed copy of this letter to your Lordship, but I do not expect an answer; and I shall enclose a copy of it to all the foreign ambassadors of the Catholic Courts resident in London, that they will do justice to the injured cause of Catholicity, by publishing it in their respective capitals.

DR. CAHILL TO THE RIGHT HONORABLE THE EARL OF CARLISLE.

"I am aware that it is thought by many, that, so far from the case of the Madiai being a solitary instance, the prisons of Italy are at this moment crowded with the victims of religious persecution. * * They have continually assured us, that the old principle and codes of intolerance, once certainly (and I readily admit, not exclusively) attached to their Church, had fallen into practical disuetude, and were viewed by them with at least as much abhorrence as by ourselves. We gave them credit for the generous self-assertion. I will not waste your space by a reference to what is of so little moment, as my own career; but I feel that on the whole, it has not lagged in sympathy for their just rights. What has since happened? A man is in danger of meeting with his death under a judicial sentence, for the offence of reading the Bible. The fact, as far as yet I know, is not controverted. It is known there are some—it is believed there are many undergoing similar risks.

* * * * * * * * * * *

I must repeat, that upon the mode in which the Roman Catholic body at large treat these contemporary occurrences, their place in the estimation even of their most sincere well wishers must largely depend."

(*Extract of Lord Carlisle's Letter to the "Leeds Mercury."*)

CAMBRIDGE, *January* 27, 1853.

MY LORD EARL,—I have been very much impressed, indeed, to learn from the London journals of yesterday morning, that your Lordship has allied your most respected name, and added the prestige of your exalted character, to the insatiable calumniators of the Catholic creed; and that, in the composed moments of a deliberate letter, you have not only thought proper to make statements at variance with historical, legal, and ecclesiastical records; but, even, as may be gathered from the above extract, to introduce half assertions and covert insinuations, almost approaching to a sneer, below the dignity of Lord Morpeth, and the world-wide reputation of the Earl of Carlisle. Having followed, for many years, the influential language of your advocacy of my unhappy country, it is with great pain, that I have read your authority quoted at Exeter Hall, by the unrelenting enemies of Ireland; and although I should not have condescended to reply to the scandalous misstatements, which issue like a foul torrent against Catholicity, from the overflowing daily publications of this country, your name demands an immediate reply, and your services to Ireland, demand the most graceful answer, which personal respect and public gratitude can dictate.

You are well aware, my Lord, that the writings of Voltaire, Diderot, D'Alembert, and Frederick of Prussia, and many others, deluged the eastern and southern parts of Europe, during the latter part of the eighteenth century. These political and religious revolutions proscribed all monarchical and Christian institutions; "liberty and equality," were the two principles which their disciples published and advocated; and the united efforts of the most abandoned men that the world ever saw, were concentrated in the unchristian, sacrelegious, and treasonable combination to "uproot the altar and the throne." In order to carry out their principles of disorder, infidelity, and vengeance, they met together under the name of "a new and higher degree of Freemasonry, called Illumine-ism," and their places of meeting were so numerous, particularly in France, that Diderot was heard to say, "We have at this moment enrolled in our society upwards of six hundred thousand men, opposed to civil tyranny and Papal authority."

The German Protestants followed in the wake of these

revolutionists, and under the pretext of holding meetings for religious worship, aided, as history asserts, the progress of the infidels against Catholicity. It was under these circumstances, that both France and the Italian States took the alarm, and passed laws to protect the State and the Altar; and hence, in the year 1786, the Tuscan Government enacted a law against "private conventicles," which prohibited any one to hold a meeting in his own house, or to form a meeting in the house of a third party, under any pretext whatever—even of religion, without the sanction, and the written legal license of the civil authorities.

Two points, are therefore clear, from these premises; namely: this Law, which was never before known in Tuscany, grew out of the acknowledged and patent danger of civil revolution; and secondly, that Law had no reference whatever, either directly or indirectly, to forbidding the circulation of the Word of God, or punishing the reading of the Bible. Its object was, definitely to refuse hiding places to bands of sanguinary infidels, and to scatter the dens of perjured revolutionists.

This is the Law under which the "martyred Madiai" have been condemned—a Law, be it remembered, introduced for the first time into Tuscany, in 1786; and framed, not against the Word of God, but against perfidy; not against religion of any kind, but against blasphemy; not against liberty, either civil or religious, but to protect God and man from a scene of blood and devastation, which these monsters soon after enacted in the streets of Paris, in the autumn of 1791. The slaughter in that city on that disastrous day, the succeeding war of Europe, the blood spilled in Spain, Portugal, Germany, Russia, and Italy, and your own National Debt—all demonstrate the prudence of Tuscany in the Laws of 1786, and prove, beyond all contradiction, that your Lordship has made misstatements, in ascribing ecclesiastical tyranny in what you are pleased to call "the Roman Church," to the prudent and essential enactments of the Tuscan Government. The Catholic Church, therefore, has no necessity to retrace her steps; her office, at present, is rather to teach history to English Lords; and to entreat poets, that, before they make speeches or write letters, they will pay more attention to their loose statements, and be convinced, that the applause of Leeds, is a small compensation for the cutting and lasting iron of the Catholic historians of Europe.

I am now come, my Lord, to the precise case at issue, viz., the case against the Madiai; and I assert, that they have not been visited by a "judicial sentence," as you are pleased to write, for the reading of the Bible. I regret, for the sake of your Lordship, that you have written these words. Beyond all contradiction, you are unacquainted with the case, and, therefore, your misstatement is the result of very great culpability. Under a decided ignorance of the fact, you charge the Catholic Church with intolerance; you awaken bitter rancor in hearts not yet cooled down from a late religious burning phrenzy, which has no parallel in Europe; and you call upon all the Catholics in these countries to "earn your future esteem," by condemning laws which have never existed; and branding

Tuscany for crushing the progress of civil revolution. As I hold in my hand the indictment of the Tuscan Attorney-General, I can command your Lordship's attention, while I again beg leave to instruct you in the revival of the law of 1786, and its practical application to the case before us.

The history of Europe records in letters of fire, the scenes of revolutionary violence which have been enacted during the last six years in Switzerland, Hungary, France, Naples, and Northern Italy. You are, I am convinced, acquainted with these facts, and you have no doubt been made familiar with the names of Lord Palmerston, Lord John Russell, Lord Minto, Lord Cowley, Sir Stratford Canning, and young Sir Robert Peel. And, no doubt, you have heard of Garibaldi, Cicerouacchio, Paruzzi, the free corps of Berne, and the Red Republicans of at least five European kingdoms; and I dare say, you have seen each and every one of the revolutionists; have had the honor of corresponding with her Majesty's Ambassadors at the various Courts, being personally known to them, receiving presents from some of them; and, above all, of being patronized by those official English noblemen and gentlemen, at the very time when these incendiaries were about to involve their respective countries in civil war, banishing their lawful sovereigns, and preparing for unlimited spoliation and universal treason.

These are facts, my Lord, which may be read in the records of every city, from Constantinople to Turin, and from Berlin to Naples; in each of which cities, beyond all doubt, they, the English Embassies, were the public, palpable places of resort of the revolutionists. In this crisis, the Tuscan Government, finding herself threatened on all sides, as in the end of the last century, and from none more, than the paid spies of the English Government, revised, for the first time these last fifty years, Article 60 of the Law of the 30th Nov., 1786, and attached new binding restrictions to the ancient Law in Article 1, 4, 9, 14, on March 4th, 1849; and they gave increased power to their officials in Articles 34 and 35 of the Tuscan Police Regulations. But the revival of this Law in 1849, had no reference to the prohibiting of the Word of God; its sole object being, as was the case in 1786, to protect the State from the explosive elements of universal revolution.

The law referred to, is "The Tuscan Convention Act," which prevents men, under the appearance of religion, from meeting privately without the sanction of the civil authority. And, here again, may I beg to ask you, if this Law was not most prudent, seeing the French king hunted from his throne; the Pope concealing himself in civilian dress, as he fled from the Vatican; the Emperor of Austria threatened with imminent danger; the King of Sardinia killed by treachery; and the King of Naples all but expelled his dominions? It was in this crisis that a well-known band of fifty English evangelizers entered Florence; and, dividing themselves into five sections of ten each, proceeded to open several conventicles in this small city. They neither hed, nor sought a license. Having a place of public Protestant worship in Florence, it may be asked why have there been so many private unlicensed conventicles? Again, I have examined the statistics of the city of Rome, and I learn that fifty Protestant families are the largest number ever known to have resided there during the winter; twenty, the largest number in Florence, in the same season. Wherefore, then, the ten conventicles unlicensed? And this too, during the year when the surrounding countries were shaken to their foundations. Rosa Madiai resided in England sixteen years, and returning to Florence, became, and was a Protestant during five years previous to the trial referred to. She read the word of God to which you allude, during these five years without molestation; she could go to church without hindrance; and consequently your Lordship's statement in reference to "the offence of reading the Bible," is a shameful misstatement, wholly without foundation either in law or fact.

But I will tell your Lordship the offence of Signora Madiai and her "dear" husband. They perseveringly held closed-door conventicles against the warnings of the police, repeated ten times; they distributed at least eleven thousand copies of your Bible, containing, as I can prove, upwards of sixteen hundred variations from the original text: persuaded, inveigled, and bribed the Italian children to come to these five conventicles, to hear their instructions, and to take these anti-Catholic sources of instruction: they were associated with several *colporteurs*, as they are called, in sending these Bibles through the country: they had indecent pictures of the Blessed Virgin in fly-sheets, to be distributed by two players of barrel organs, whom they hired for the purpose: they had slips of paper, on which was written in large letters in Italian, "wafer-gods:" they had pictures of Purgatory, with representations of souls looking through the bars, and the priest in soutanne, bargaining with them for two "scuddi:" they had uttered most indecent things of the "Confessional," and ended all these readings of the word of God by an attack on the Pope, characterizing him, as the man of sin—the Antichrist.

This case, perhaps, the most atrocious that can be imagined against the feelings, the convictions, the conscience, and the peace of their quiet and unoffending neighbors—and expressed by your Lordship as "reading the Bible," was decided on the 8th of June last, by Signor Niccola Nervini, and the penalties of the violated law enforced. The "judicial sentence," therefore, has been pronounced against individuals palpably in connection with wealthy English associates; men who could import eleven thousand Bibles; pay *colporteurs*, as Clarendon did in Spain; employ barrel organ players; print caricatures of Catholicity; revile the laws of the country; insult the Pope; defy the police; ridicule our Holy Eucharist; pay printers for a constant supply of all sorts of fly-sheets, and entertain with great expense, the fifty holy men who would not read the Bible in a public church, but make the Word of God a pretext for maligning the laws, creating civil strife, and violating the public peace!

If the Duke of Tuscany, or any one else—no matter who he may be, imposed civil penalties for the religious opinions which his subjects may quietly and individually adopt, I should be the first to raise my voice against him, and cry him down as a sanguinary persecutor. But he has enforced the laws of his state against covert revolutionists, public calumniators, a band of foreign conspirators, and the unrestrained hired disturbers of the public peace. And pray, my Lord, on what authority do you state, that the prisons of Italy are "crowded with victims of persecution?" I call for your authority, and I firmly demand it. I know you are an historian and a scholar—I respect your high acquirements, but I demand the authority on which you utter this most false assertion. I challenge your Lordship to produce it; and I hereby undertake to say, that where the prisons are full, they are filled with the followers of Mazzini and Garibaldi, and with the known cut-throats of Italy.

Leaving the laws of Tuscany, my Lord, for a moment to be executed by the Italians, let me now turn to examine our laws on this identical point. And as I have formed an exalted idea of the honesty and religious feeling of the English people as a nation, I shall not allude to times gone by, when Acts of Parliament were passed, which, I am convinced, make the present generation blush in shame; when churches and lands were seized to the amount of at least fifty millions of our present currency; when laws were enacted against nonconformists and recusants, which, by fines, banishment, and death, made at least seventy thousand victims in England and Ireland; when to pray to God in public, was death; to read or write anything under a teacher was felony; and, when it was a crime even to be alive.

I shall not allude to these days, my Lord but shall confine myself to the law called, "Dissuading from Worship." This law, which was passed 35th Elizabeth, c. 1. s. 1., and afterwards confirmed by the 3rd of Charles the First, c. i v., inflicted fine and confinement on any person who would " disuade another from frequenting the Protestant worship, and who would hold a conventicle for the same." But your Lordship will assert, as is your custom, that this law has fallen into disuetude. Quite the contrary, my Lord; as the present Lord Gainsborough has been persecuted for holding a private unlicensed conventicle, and reading the Word of God in the same; and although his Lordship, like Madiai, set up a plea that he was only "reading the Bible," he was fined £20 by an English judicial sentence, and if he had not paid the money on the spot, he would have been confined, like your Italian martyrs, in an English Bridewell.

Here is a case partly in point, my Lord, which cannot be denied; and visited by English penalties although it wanted the second ingredient of the Madiai case, viz., a covert revolution against the State, and palpable combination with foreign conspirators. But, perhaps, your Lordship will again say, this odious law is now at least obsolete. Far from it. It is still unrepealed, and remains in your Statute Book, to be enforced to-morrow, against any offending British subject, as well as Lord Gainsborough. For proof of this, I beg to refer your Lordship to the Sixth Report (page 110) of the Law Commissioners appointed to revise what are called the Catholic Toleration Laws in the year 1839, two years after the accession of our present gracious Queen. Their report is as follows:

"None of the Roman Catholic Toleration Laws make any mention of

the 35th Elizabeth, or describe the offences therein contained. These offences consist in the inciting of others, by a person who obstinately refuses to repair to the church, to abstain from going there, or to frequent unlawful places of worship. Hence, there is no mode under the existing law by which a Roman Catholic who commits any of the offences can avoid the penalties."

Here is the precise case of the Madiai; divested of the revolutionary element (propagando Protestantismo,) here is the exact case, so far as it goes, of obstinately refusing to frequent the Tuscan Church, and dissuading others from the same; so that your Laws condemn for a minor offence, what is only visited with the same penalties in Tuscany when combined with covert conspiracy and political revolution.

From these premises, my Lord, it turns out, strangely enough, that your condemnation of the Duke of Tuscany, applies with far greater force, unintentionally on your part, of course, to our gracious Queen: that the speeches at Exeter Hall must be fairly shared by the Court of St. James's with the Tuscan monarch: that the deputation of Lord Roden has been a silent reproach on our own divine laws; and that the deputation from Prussia to Tuscany, at present in contemplation, would do well to come by way of London, and make a remonstrance to our beloved, upright, and decorous Lord John Campbell, before they open their sacred mission on the Italian Peninsula.

You must, I dare say, my Lord, thus concede to me, that I am well furnished with an accurate knowledge of the Tuscan laws, with a clear statement of all the circumstances of the case at issue: that similar laws, divested of revolution, remain unrepealed in your own country, and have been enforced on a man still alive; and hence, I call upon you, as a sincere friend of Ireland, and of her persecuted, maligned creed, either to substantiate your unexpected charges, or withdraw your name from the list of our calumniators. We are trodden down by a numerous host of unprincipled revilers, but Ireland has hearts and tongues, and pens, still to sustain the ancient traditions of her unblemished patriotism, and fearlessly to defend, even unto death, those points in the citadel of her creed where Augustin and Jerome once stood, clad in the invincible armor which had never been pierced by the spear of the enemy!

I have the honor to be, my Lord Earl, with the most profound and grateful respect, your Lordship's obedient servant,

D. W. CAHILL, D.D.

P. S.—I shall send a printed copy of this letter to your Lordship, and any communication which you may condescend to address to St. Paul's Square, Liverpool, cannot fail to reach me.

THE EARL OF CARLISLE TO DR. CAHILL.

Rev. Sir—Having sent my letter to a newspaper, and thus exposed it to any remark, refutation, or censure it might meet with, it is not my intention to enter into further controversy on the subject; but as you have done me the honor to call my notice to a letter you have written in reply, drawn up in a spirit of much courtesy to myself, as well as with very great ability, I think it right to acknowledge the receipt of your communication.

Upon the case in question, I content myself with observing, that in the report I had read of the sentence pronounced upon the Madiai, one of the distinct counts or heads of accusation is, that they had been engaged in reading the Bible (translated by Diodati,) in company with three persons and a young girl, who was an inmate of their house; and another is that Francesco Madiai had given a prohibited version to a young man of sixteen. I am willing to admit, that I should have expressed myself with more entire accuracy if I had said "under a judicial sentence for the offence of reading the Bible, and other acts of proselytism."

I am not prepared to name any authorities for my assertion, "that it is thought by many that the Italian prisons are filled with victims of religious persecution." The authority I give is my own. IT IS thought by many; I have found the impression current in the society in which I have mixed, and if it is a false one, it is certainly desirable that the public mind should not be disabused.

I regret that from recent change of place this brief communication will not reach you so soon as I should have wished.

I have the honor to be, Rev. Sir, your humble servant,

February 5, 1853 CARLISLE.

REV. DR. CAHILL'S REPLY.

CAMBRIDGE *February* 6, 1853.

MY LORD EARL,—I beg leave to offer to your Lordship, the unfeigned expression of my profound acknowledgments for the courteous promptitude of your generous and characteristic letter, to the humble individual who has had the honor of addressing you.

The Roman Catholics of Great Britain, who justly value your manly political career, and my unfortunate countrymen, who owe to your consistent sympathy a debt of national gratitude, will be rejoiced to learn from your communication to me, that part of your charges against the political government of a Catholic Sovereign was founded upon mere current English reports; and that the remaining portion of your public letter, arose from the circumstance of your not being minutely acquainted with the indictment and the judicial sentence of the Madiai.

I shall not dwell long on this point, except to assure the accomplished, the high-minded, and the chivalrous Earl of Carlisle, that he stands acquitted on the charge of joining the ranks of our remorseless calumniators, or of wounding our grateful national feelings.

I shall now, my Lord, take advantage of your suggestion, in reference to "disabusing the public mind of the false impressions in the Madiai case, current in English society;" and I shall direct your attention to the two leading misrepresentations circulated with such industrious malignity in this country.

The first false impression which anti-Catholic journalism has stamped on the credulous, honest English mind, arises from a passage in the reply of the Duke of Cassagliano to Lord Roden, viz:

"The Madiai, Tuscan subjects, to whom you refer, have been condemned to five years' imprisonment, by the ordinary tribunals, for the crime of propagating Protestantism."

The second false impression sought to be made, is founded on the misstatement, namely: "that the Madiais are punished for merely reading the Bible."

By the first statement, English Protestants are called on to believe that a Catholic power punishes Protestantism as a mere religious tenet; by the second misrepresentation, they are urged into the calumnious conclusion that the Tuscan Laws prohibit the Word of God, and make penal the reading of the Scriptures. I assert then, my Lord, that the first position is notoriously false, and is contradicted by the clearest records of continental history; and I say that the second is a flagrant lie, and receives a flat peremptory denial from the charge of the judge, who was president of the court, and who pronounced the judicial sentence of condemnation on the Madiai.

In proving the first point, I regret being compelled to recal past events of European history, which every generous heart would fain bury in perpetual oblivion, and which makes every honest and honorable mind shudder, at contemplating these crimsoned pages, and these antichristian deeds of our history, written in the days of "reformed gospel light, and executed in the name of God.—But these chronicled facts are necessary in the present instance, in order to show that the word Protestantism, in its commencement, its progress, and its final consummation, did not mean, nor ever has been understood to mean, in the history of Catholic Europe, the mere element of a certain religious faith. No, my Lord, decidedly not; it means, and has ever meant, in the incontrovertible records of European history, an aggregate of tenets, and a body of collateral practices clashing with Catholicity, as a conscientious creed, opposed to the sacred ties of Catholic society, originated in professed hostility against the spiritual head of the Catholic Church, and leagued by the doctrine of their first founders against Catholic monarchy, and Catholic political power. If these assertions be true as recorded, not by me, but by the Catholic historians of Europe, is it not a mean suppression of the truth to assert, that the Italian States prescribe Protestantism, as a mere conscientious creed; whereas, wherever the word occurs, it means the aggregate of the historical indictment to which I have just referred. You must understand me, my Lord; I am not in this letter making those charges; certainly not; I am explaining the language of the Laws of Tuscany and of other Catholic States, in the case before us; and in the succeeding part of this communication we shall see, if they are justified in their legislation on the aggressors of Protestantism, according to the universally received continental impression. I regret, sincerely, my Lord, the cause, and the existence of these impressions; I should efface them if I could; but I must take them as I have read them, heard them, and, in fact, felt them; I have not made the case, I merely exposed it.

Firstly, then, my Lord, Luther and associates, with one blow struck down, as the first precept of his decalogue, the spiritual authority of the Pope, as supreme head of the Church; and this point being the very main-spring of Catholicity, it is no wonder that such a levelling aggression should arouse the vigilance of every Catholic dynasty in Europe; and this step was not an impulse of the man, but a doctrine of his new creed, and violently enforced to this day.

Secondly, he and his entire evangelical staff, encouraged polygamy; and, of course, plurality of wives, by granting officially permission to the Landgrave of Hesse to marry a second wife, the first being still living. And this permission he gave not from the caprice of the mistaken friend, but from the new creed of his followers, and in order to promote the salvation of the Prince and the glory of God. In writing to the Prince on the subject, he says :—

'Your Highness, therefore, hath, in this writing, not only the approbation of us all, concerning what you desire : but having weighed it in our reflection, we beseech and beg of God to direct all for his glory and your Highness's salvation !"

And surely enough, my Lord, they all did approve of it, and all signed the document in very discreet and grave language; and in putting their names to the dispensation, so scrupulously apostolic were they, that they would not even omit the Saint's name of the day, it being executed as they wrote it, "on the Wednesday after the feast of St. Nicholas," and endorsed, Martin Luther, Philip Melancthon, Martin Bruce, Anthony Corvin, Adam Jeningue, Justus Winterte, Denis Melanther.

Here, again, my Lord, it is not surprising if Catholic States become exceedingly alarmed at the progress of the new faith, seeing that besides mere mental, and spiritual, and supernatural tenets, it introduced Mahomedanism; blasted all conjugal bliss; rent asunder the sacred ties of home, and undivided love; degraded woman into Pagan infamy; converted matrimony into a licentious scheme of perjury and adultery; and, according to the received laws of Christianity, went directly to bastardize the rising Catholic generations of the world.

Thirdly, he called on the population of the German States to rise up against their Catholic Emperor; and he openly declared, that all allegiance should be withdrawn from any king or potentate in communion with the Pope, whom he denounced as the devil and anti-christ; and the third development of his divine creed was not to be ascribed to the treasonable phrenzy of the rebel, or to the wild plans of the revolutionist. Not at all, my Lord; no such thing. It was part of the new faith—an item in the new inspiration, tending, as in the case of the Landgrave of Hesse, to the glory of God, and the salvation of the soul.

For the truth of this revealed, reformed, ethical dogma, I beg to refer your Lordship to your own historian, Sleidan, book v., page 74. Such, even, was the violence produced against monarchy, by this article of the new Protestant Faith, that the Low Countries, Switzerland, and all Germany, burst into open revolution; Zuinglius, the co-apostle of Luther, even joined the rebels in Switzerland, and was found among the dead, killed in battle.

The dominions of the celebrated Charles V. were menaced with such danger by Luther, and the princes who joined his standard, that Charles was compelled to give them battle, in which his troops were victorious, scattering the enemy, and taking the Landgrave of Hesse and the Duke of Saxony prisoners, on the Elbe, May 26th, 1547. Here again, my Lord, is it a matter of surprise, if all the Catholic Sovereigns of Europe hastened to form a defensive alliance in order to guard their conscience, their Faith, their honor, the sanctity of their families, the cause of morality, the inheritance of their thrones, and the possession and peace of their dominions from a system, which tended to change woman into a beast, man into a pagan, and which stood in naked defiance of the ordinances of God, the Gospel of Christ, and the indissoluble laws and customs of human society?

Fourthly, if these undeniable doctrines, and these authenticated historic facts, ceased with the name, character, and prestige of the first founders of these novelties, the precaution taken by Catholic countries might also fall into oblivion, and European society resume its former Christian and political peace. But, my Lord, the case is otherwise; and the history of England and Scotland, and Ireland, and France, and Germany, to which I shall not here further allude, supply the thrilling commentary—namely, that during the one hundred and fifty years which elapsed, after the death of these first apostles, a scene of practical persecution of Catholics, and a record of universal desolation, marked the track of this Faith everywhere it appeared, and made the name of Protestantism be identified with national spoliation, relentless persecution, withering penalties on conscience, together with the confiscation, banishment, and death of thousands of its defenceless and wasted victims. Let us be candid, my Lord; has not this been the universal character of Protestantism in every country where a Catholic dare raise his voice in defence of his creed or his country? Let me be plain, my Lord; is not this the cause why every Catholic country, where the standard of Protestantism has been raised in dominant triumph, has been wasted, beggared, spoliated, and ruined?

Fifthly, do you wonder, then, my Lord, that the laws of Catholic Europe have been framed with defensive, not offensive caution, against a system combining in doctrine, and in the continued practices of successive centuries, an aggregate of religious and political principles, incompatible with the security and the consistency of Catholic States and people?

My Lord, I mean no offence, either to Protestants or Englishmen, by recalling these dark scenes of your history; certainly not; I dare not offend in your presence; and I feel assured, that Englishmen and Protestants of the present day, in this country and elsewhere, blush for their ancestors in reading this sad and sullied page of their ancient story. I should not even allude to these past eventful days, under ordinary circumstances; but when I see, read, and hear, one national huge lie, spoken, cried aloud, posted, gazetted, published, printed, spouted, and preached; when I read American, Prussian, Dutch, Scotch, and German interference called, in order to mitigate the sentence of imprisonment, put publicly forward, in the grossest falsehood ever promulgated in England; and when I behold all the journals, all the Bible Societies, all the Irish Parsons, banded together in swelling the discord of an historical, public, notorious, palpable lie, against the laws, civic language, religion, creed, and defensive enactments of a foreign Catholic power, I am come fearlessly forward, sustained by the History of Europe, (to which I challenge discussion,) to defend the thesis, "that Protestantism has never meant on the Continent of Catholic Europe a code of mere religious, spiritual tenets;" but on the contrary, its acceptation has ever been an anti-christian, anti-social, anti-Catholic, anti-conjugal mixture of paganism, infidelity, spoliation, and persecution. It is false, therefore, to assert that the word "Protestantism," in the note of the Duke de Castigliano, means a mere religious tenet, detached from its social and political associations.

This assertion is unequivocally false. The Tuscan laws on heresy are written in four volumes (quarto) in Latin, to which I beg to refer your Lordship, and which, by their dates and provisions will prove to your satisfaction the position which I have taken.

And will your Lordship give me leave to ask, if the conduct of Lord John Russell and Lord Palmerston, the old decrepid family ministry, have served to awaken confidence in the case at issue? On this point, I have, for years past, already explained my views, without contradiction, but I shall add one word more—namely, that in the whole course of official recklessness, nothing, perhaps, has ever appeared in the lives and annals of English Ministers, which can bear the most remote comparison with the astounding assertion reported to have been made in the House of Commons, by Lord Palmerston, viz., "that it was the intention of the official men with whom he acted, to form into one independent kingdom all that territory which stretches from Genoa to Venice!" Hence, read, my Lord, the present history and events of Piedmont; look at the revolutionary spirit of Turin; and, (just like the deceived Hungarians, the deluded Neapolitans, the relentless Swiss, and the ungrateful Romans,) these speeches of our functionaries have encouraged the discontented of these nations to rush into rebellion, and afterwards to expiate by public degradation, banishment, or death, the evil foreign councils, when in a moment of misplaced confiding honor, they listened to heartless bigoted diplomatists, against the dictates of conscience, the voice of reason, and the call of national duty.

In fact, wherever the emissaries of the Bible Society, or the paid spies of the English Government were permitted to innoculate the public mind with the doctrines I have referred to, their victims lost all religion to God and all allegiance to the throne. Seduced by bribery to abandon the Faith of their fathers, their consciences became seared from their perjured change of creed. From perjury and apostacy, the space, my Lord, to infidelity is not far; and hence, these conventicles of Florence and elsewhere, were avowed dens of revolution and atheism. Beyond all doubt, my Lord, the Tuscan Government, or any other Government similarly situated; had, in the late circumstances of Europe, only two questions to decide—namely, "Whether their duty was to teach order and Christianity, or to preach rebellion and atheism." And they had also another principle to decide—viz: "Whether they, the Ultramontanists, should hold their tongues, and cease to protect order, morality, truth, justice, and faith, for fear of displeasing the intolerant framers of the Ecclesiastical Titles Bill; contradicting the mild, and the wise, and the grave, far-seeing Legislators of old clothes proclamation; scandalizing the sacred career of the Saints of Exeter Hall, incurring the holy anger of the modern, ancient, mortified primeval Protestant Church, the true follower of the cross, disturbing the last exemplary moments of the dying apostles, the probates of whose edifying wills amount in several cases to the truly apostolic standard of two, three, and four hundred thousand pounds! these self-denying creatures, having reserved this trifle in teaching this most sacred reforming thing called Protestantism."

When, my Lord, if I were not restrained by the presence of your Lordship, my boiling blood, and the red graves of my starved and murdered poor countrymen, plundered by this anti-Christian church, would compel me to raise my voice in loud contumely, and indignant scorn, against the universal cant, the unblushing hypocrisy, and the gigantic lies of a band of imposters and bigots; who have squeezed out the very dregs of our national existence, and who raise, whenever a pretext offers itself, at home and abroad, a cry of misrepresentation and insult, which degrades the fine, noble character of the English people as a nation—range in hostility to your name and your country the disgust and indignation of Catholic Europe; and has already laid the materials of a disastrous explosion beneath the foundation of England's power; which, if not removed in time, by truth, kindness, toleration, and national honor, may, very soon, as your Lordship has predicted, be ignited by your injured, insulted, and powerful enemies; and, in a moment of unexpected fate, like your overthrow in America, shiver to atoms the entire fabric of your national greatness.

In referring to the second point of this letter, I have already proved, that the Madiai were not condemned for "reading the Bible." The statement put forth in the public prints is utterly false. Their crime was "holding unlawful meetings with closed doors, contrary to the laws of the Tuscan Conventicle Act"—in which unlawful meetings, held without even demanding a license, a band of foreign conspirators, by bribery, by ridicule of the clergy, by caricaturing the Catholic religion, by reviling the laws, by distributing inflammatory fly-sheets, encouraged sedition, violated the public peace, and laid the foundation, as far as lay in their power, of those sudden and disastrous revolutions which convulsed all the neighbouring States, and had nearly crumbled five ancient thrones.

And while discussing this part of my subject, I shall take leave to remind your Lordship of the standing, imperishable, eternal lie which the Protestant church has stereotyped in all her books, lectures, sermons, letters, speeches, through every part of the world where her literature is cultivated, where her power is felt, and her voice heard. The enormous, unfading lie, my Lord, is "that the Catholic church will not permit the reading of the word of God." Our church declares the contrary; our bishops write it, our priests preach it, our pamphlets publish it, our writers promulgate it, our booksellers print it over their doors, in their bills, their prospectus; and the whole world knows it, except the poor wretched dupes of the swarm of bigots who stop the ears, gag the mouths, blind the eyes of their bewildered followers, to such an astounding, incredible, heartening degree of mesmeric biblicism and awful infatuation, that you hear and read statements every day made in contradiction to a fact, palpable as the earth under their feet, obvious as the Thames that runs through the city of London, and clear and unclouded as a brilliant noonday sun in a summer sky. It is a most melancholy thing to see a whole nation of people, placed in such a deplorable hopeless state of utter mental helplessness, and incapability of seeing and believing on the most notorious facts of the Old World.

The only thing which I can recollect, as approaching at all in incredibility to the biblical delusion, is the case of the man mentioned in Moore's "Gentleman in Search of a Religion." This man took it into his head "that he was made of fresh butter," and consequently could never be induced to go near the fire; and although his friends made every effort that moral ingenuity could devise to cure him, he went to his grave impervious to every human motive of persuasion, and died under ground, out of the reach of the sun, shivering with the cold. Not the least singular part, too, of this crafty hypocrisy on the part of the foreign spy biblicals, is, when they assert that the Catholics are hostile to the Word of God, because they will not receive their English perverted text. And although it is easy to see that they would not take our bibles, with our notes and comments; and they stand acquitted of all hostility to the work of God, yet they will not allow the same argument to be applied to us, when we spurn their mutilated, ill-translated text, where whole books are omitted; where inspiration is denied; where tenses are changed; particles omitted or introduced at pleasure; where philological meanings are received against the admitted practical, living, speaking interpretation; and above all, where the bible-reader, who distributes these stammering, broken records, does not write objectionable notes and comments—no, he speaks his comments; he spends hours and days, accompanying his readings with caricatures of the Host; philippics against the Confessional; ridicule of the ever blessed Virgin Mary; lies of the Pope; and, concludes all this pious reading in the Lanes and the Alleys of London; in the hovels of Clifden and Connemara; in the streets of Kells, as well as in the plains of Lombardy, where he receives perjurious bribes from the hypocrites of the Bible Societies of credulous England, and the remorseless, unmitigable Orange Parsons of Ireland.

But time may yet tell a saddening tale, my Lord, when the Legislators of England may wish to recal these crying insults to the Catholic name; when every available Irish hand may be wanted to repel the foreign foe; when every Irish heart, which now bleeds with the fresh opened wounds of centuries of persecution, may be called on to spring to the national defences, and there pour out, as poor, insulted, faithful Ireland has often done before, the last drop of her circling life-blood in defence of a nation that oppresses us; of institutions that degrade us; a Parliament that insults us; a civilization that debases us; a commerce that robs us—and a power that emaciates and kills us. Wait awhile, my Lord; but I fervently pray, that the future which your Lordship seems to dread, may never become present; and that able statesmen, and not fatal bigots; wise laws, and not insults; toleration, and not persecution; honor, and not deceit, may change the aspect of English legislation, and render England the sincere, generous parent of all her subjects, and not the tyrant and the enemy of a third of her devoted, and patient, and loyal servants.

I have the honor to be, my Lord Earl, with the most profound respect, your Lordship's obedient servant,

D. W. CAHILL, D.D.

LETTER TO THE REV. WILLIAM ANDERSON,

PASTOR OF THE UNITED PRESBYTERIAN CHURCH.

GLASGOW, *April* 12, 1853.

REV. SIR—There can be no doubt that, in reference to the Holy Scriptures, your teaching and mine are very different, indeed. I have learned the creed which I profess from the accredited voice of the Universal Church, from which your predecessors in your faith have avowedly separated. The history of all Christian antiquity bears testimony, through all nations and peoples, to the existence and the entirety of my belief at the time of your separation. There was confessed but one church, and that Church was the Roman Catholic—and as the Church of Christ was built *never to fail,* but to be always existing, living, speaking, teaching, and saving; and as the Catholic church was then *the only church in the whole world,* it follows, it must have been the only true one at the time of your separation—while not even one congregation—perhaps, not even a single individual—through all past Christian time, up to the period of what is called 'this reformation,' can be found possessing the religious opinions which you now hold. I regret that you follow these novelties, or that you teach them to others; but most certainly, I do not feel any sentiment of 'odium' towards you or your people. On the contrary, I entertain a high respect for you; and in my private intercourse, and in my public professional character, I inculcate this my own sincere impression to all those who may be guided by my words, or influenced by my example.

I respectfully beg to assure you, that you make a great mistake, in supposing that Roman Catholics have any desire whatever, either to hear the tenets of your Church discussed, or to examine over again in your Church the motives which direct them in the choice of their Faith. The disciples of the Roman Catholic Church attach very little value (in reference to divine faith,) either to accomplished declamation, or brilliant oratory; they are entirely guided by a living, speaking, infallible authority, which, in their daily reading of the Scriptures, they behold expressed in the clearest, the strongest, the most obvious, the most literal, and the most emphatic clauses of the last Will and Testament of our blessed Lord. No human being of common sense, has ever been known to bequeath in the solemn awful hour of death, metaphorical, or allegorical, or figurative property and power to his beloved children; and the Catholics believe that our Lord, at His death, has left a real, *bona fide*, substantial, living authority to guide His Church in Faith. Hence, they could no more consent to go to your Church, to subject to public discussion the tenets inculcated by this authority, than they would agree to put to the issue of a public meeting the very existence of Christ, or the value of the all-saving atonement of the cross. In fact, the very decision of consenting to such an issue, would be equivalent to the erecting you and your friends into the infallible authority which you denounce, and which you challenge me to defend in this case before us.

The second paragraph of your courteous letter to me goes to concede, in clear language, the premises—namely, that you and your friends may be wrong, since you admit the just hypothesis, that I might change your opinions. On the part of the Roman Catholics, I could not admit the *tenable* consistency of such a case, our Faith being founded on a provision which excludes the *defensible* possibility of change—namely, an infallible authority, promulgated by Christ officially, and judiciously practised by the Apostles, and still further guaranteed through all coming time by the permanent legislative presence of the Holy Ghost. No plausible sophistry, no popular discussion, no award of men's judgment, no majority of human voices can outbalance the testimony or enactment of God, which secures the immutable unity of our Faith, no more than a single ray of light can pale the meridian splendor of the sun. A Roman Catholic can never, therefore, grant the tenable possibility of the case, which you admit, and cannot therefore consent under these existing laws, to the popular issue involved in your communication.

I must say, however, that so far as you are concerned, you are strictly true to your principles, in resting your Faith on the issue of the popular will. All the varieties of all the Reformation creeds, are the results of private individual judgment, or of public Parliamentary decisions. All these creeds are acknowledged creations of human authority—all these creeds are made by man, and not by God. And they have been formed too, to fall in with the tastes, and the peculiarities, and the prejudices of the various times in which they were enacted; and the clear consequence of this accommodating principle has been the incongruous fact—namely, that, within the space of three hundred years these creeds have successively passed through upwards of seven hundred variations! The Roman Catholics smile in pity at a Faith, which admits the principle of progress; they cannot comprehend how any Christian mind can call that institution so divinely established by Christ, which is still continually altered by men; and they are astounded to hear serious men declare, that the Holy Ghost could be the propounder of seven hundred varieties of belief, from the self-same revelation. They believe, that Faith, in point of doctrine and institution, was finished by Christ and the Apostles; and they justly conclude, that men always looking for Faith have never found it; that men always changing, must necessarily *doubt*, and therefore *not believe;* that men always inquiring after truth, have never discovered it; and thus, the Roman Catholics seem to have arrived at something like a mathematical demonstration, that the interminable changes, and the constant acceptance of new doctrines contained in the Reformation principle, is the *very definition of error;* is the unmistakable mark that you have lost the one essentially true Faith, and what is worse, that you now seek to recover it in the wrong channel—namely, the decision of human reason in public controversy, and the award of human sanction in popular disputation.—Whether, therefore, you are true to wrong principles in deciding Faith in a popular assembly, is not so much, at present, the object of my unwilling animadversion, as to tell you that I am true to the ancient Catholic doctrine in not admitting such a changeable, and such an incongruous authority.

In your third paragraph, you say you select for assault "the three first canons of the Council of Trent." With respect, I presume to tell you that "the three first canons of the Council of Trent," do not treat of the Mass; they have reference to the doctrine of "justification by grace through Jesus Christ;" a belief which I fancy you do not deny. I therefore think you made a mistake in the canons referred to in your letter.

Referring to the remaining portion of your letter, I feel quite assured (judging from the tone of your communication,) that so far as could be expected, you would conduct the controversy to which you invite me with an amicable temper; but you will permit me to say, that, from my experience of public controversial discussions, a wound is always inflicted on true religion by these disputations.—Public animosities are engendered; religious rancor is inflamed; social harmony is disturbed; the charities of the Gospel are extinguished; and even the ties of long and matured friendship, are but too often rent asunder by the mutual argumentative recrimination of theological combat. Catholics, whose faith is fixed since the beginning of the New Law, can receive no benefit from these displays of argumentation. Dissenters have their old prejudices awakened, their dormant intolerance revived, and they are often driven into greater errors than their former novelties; seeking a refuge from their inconsistencies in the unbounded license of naked infidelity. These views are the result of my experience of public religious discussion; and while I place them with honest frankness before society, being convinced they will meet the approval of every reasonable Christian man in the community, who witness the religious contentions, and reads the accounts of the fanatical bigotry with which this country is convulsed and degraded; I should therefore suggest to you, Reverend Sir, that our doctrine can be better learned from the cool, clear pen of learned Divines, than from the incautious extemporaneous expression of heated debate; and I shall add, that the mind, and a heart seeking really a knowledge of the truth (as I feel confident you are,) are more aptly fitted to receive the impressions of grace in silent prayer, and in deliberate, dispassionate study, than in a crowded meeting of contending parties, where the passions are inflamed, and the judgment warped by the excitements of public rivalship, and the hostile prejudices of party triumph. My long professional studies; the various chairs of science which I have filled, are, I presume to say, a sufficient guarantee, that the foregoing observations are the sole considerations which influence me, in the course which I am about to adopt in the case at issue; and for these reasons, therefore, you will be pleased, Sir, to excuse me, if I decline the challenge to which you invite me.

In the course of religious lectures, which I am called on to deliver in this country and elsewhere, I have invited Protestants to attend. If they honor me by their presence, I take care never knowing to wound their conscientious feelings, either directly or indirectly; and I never address my instructions to any hearers but to Roman Catholics. You, therefore, have no right to call upon me, to account for the doctrine which I have a right to teach to my people. You have thought proper to send me the challenge referred to in this letter, and I have considered it my duty (from the tone of that communication) to reply to it; but as you can have no claim on me for the continuance of your respected, yet gratuitous correspondence, you give me leave to say, that my numerous engagements will not permit me to answer any future letters which you may think proper to address to me on this subject.

I have the honor to be, Reverend Sir, with high and courteous regard, your obedient servant,

D. W. CAHILL, D.D.

P. S.—As your challenge has been already made public, through newspapers and placards, I shall send this communication to the *Glasgow Free Press* for reluctant publication.

FIVE PROTESTANT CLERGYMEN, WITH THE PROTESTANT ARCHDEACON OF RAPHOE, TO DR. CAHILL.

LETTERKENNY *May* 30, 1853.

"REV. SIR—We, the undersigned, having heard you deliver a controversial lecture this evening in the Chapel of Letterkenny, feel it our solemn duty, as ministers of God and ambassadors of Christ, to protest against the doctrines set forth by you, as unscriptural and contrary to the teaching of the Catholic church. We would therefore take the liberty of inviting you to a public discussion, to be carried on in a kind and Christian spirit, in which we call upon you to prove, that the doctrines contained in the twelve supplementary articles of the creed of Pope Pius the IV were ever propounded and set forth in the Christian church as a creed, before the year 1564.

"Secondly—We invite you to bring on the platform your rule of faith, and give us your church's authorised interpretation of the 6th, 9th, and 10th chapters St. Paul to the Hebrews—or, if you prefer it, your church's *authorised* exposition of the simplest portions of the Holy Writ—the Lord's prayer.

"Thirdly—We invite you and any number of your brother priests to meet an equal number of clergy of the church of England, to prove the assertions you used in endeavoring to establish the unscriptural doctrine of the sacrifice of the Mass. Trusting you will receive the invitation in the same spirit in which it is dictated, we remain yours faithfully in Christ.

F. GOOLD, Archdeacon of Raphoe.
J. IRWIN, Rector of Aughaninshin.
R. SMITH, Curate of Cornwall.
J. W. IRWIN, Curate of Raymohy.
J. LINSKEA, Glenalla.

REV. DR. CAHILL'S REPLY.

REVEREND SIRS—I have the honor to acknowledge the receipt of your polite note, dictated in a spirit of great courtesy, and having stamped on it the clear impress of the distinguished character of the gentlemen whose names it bears. I shall then at once proceed to give a hasty reply to these passages in your respected communication, which demand commentary from me.

Firstly, then, I solemnly deny, and conscientiously protest against your unauthorised assumption, of calling yourselves " the ministers of God and ambassadors of Christ;" and I complain loudly of your most unjustifiable intrusion, in designating your modern local conventicle by the name of the "Catholic Church." Gentlemen, I assure you I do not mean, even remotely, to utter one offensive sentiment to you personally by telling you that you are libelling God, and calumniating the Apostles in using this language. You are, on the contrary, the ecclesiastical ministers of the British Parliament, you are the clerical ambassadors of the Queen of England, and you are the rebel children of the most terrific apostacy the world ever saw. The Thirty-Nine articles of your creed (which learned Protestants call contradictory and incongrous,) are the *accidental result* of a majority of voices in the British Senate-house of that day. This act of Parliament forms the preface of your Book of Common Prayer, and the decisions of that Parliamentary Session, are unavowedly the very basis and the theological title of the Anglican creed, as expressed in these Articles. In point of fact, and according to the language of the English Parliament, that creed should be appropriately called a "bill," like any other parliamentary bill passed by a majority in that House. Beyond all doubt, its proper name should be "the Protestant Religion Bill" or some other such designation, proceeding, as it does, professedly, and originating officially from the decision of the Senate-house, and from the authority of the Crown. The authority does not even pretend to be derived from Christ, as it acknowledges itself to be fallible, and of course, progressive and human.

And the Prime Minister of England can lay aside any of your present opinions when he thinks fit, as was recently proved in the case of the Rev. Mr. Gorham; and the Queen can annul the united doctrinal decision of your national convocation at her pleasure. Argue this case as you will, and call this authority by whatever name you please, there it is, the supreme arbiter of your Church, the essential sanction and source of your Faith. Thus, in point of fact, you pray to God as the Premier likes; and you believe in God, as the Queen pleases; and you multiply or diminish the articles of your "Religion Bill," as the Parliament decides. You are, therefore, judicially and officially, the very creatures of the State; and you wear your surplices, and preach by precisely the same authority with which a midshipman wears his sword, or a Queen's Counsel appears in a silk gown; you derive your jurisdiction from an authority, at which the very Mahomedans stand in stupid amazement—viz.: an authority, which places a child in a cradle, a young girl in her teens, or a toothless old hag in the place of the twelve Apostles; standing in the footsteps of Christ, the seat of wisdom, the oracle of divine truth, and the expounder of revelation. Except that we know this statement to be a fact, from undeniable evidence, no man living could ever think, that any man in his senses would submit to such an outrage on the human understanding. Sir Thomas More, the Chancellor of England, with thousands of others, preferred to die at the block, sooner than submit to this mockery of God. This is the ludicrous jurisdiction under which you teach and preach; but to call yourselves "the Ministers of God and the Ambassadors of Christ," is an act of such reckless forgetfulness of your position (in reference to jurisdiction,) as to set all the delicacies of truth and fact at defiance, in a matter of the most public and palpable notoriety; in truth, it is unbecoming effrontery.

Again, all Christians of all denominations, admit that the repeated pledges and promises of Christ guarantee the indestructible existence of a true Church for ever on the earth. The Word of God, the Father, fixing our sun in our skies for ever, is not more clear and emphatic than the Word of God, the Son, in placing the true Church in a permanent unclouded existence on the earth for ever. At the time of your separation there was only this one universal Church on earth; there being but *one* in existence, it must have been this true one so guaranteed. You have avowedly separated from this Church; and at that time, in order to mark the doctrinal character of your conduct, you called yourselves by the appropriate name of Protestants. You, therefore, at that time, resigned your title to the Catholic Church, which you abandoned. You rebelled against her authority, and from that hour to this you stand expelled from her spiritual territory, and excommunicated by her judicial penalties. On that occasion you severed yourself from the source of all her spiritual power, and broke the link that bound you to the long chain of apostolic jurisdiction. Will you kindly inform the world when and where did you become reunited to that Church? You now call yourselves "Catholic!" Or, are you now beginning to be ashamed of the word "Protestant?" You see that this word argues the want of legitimate title to the Christian inheritance, and you are trying to insert a word by fraud into your forged deed.

Why do you not use the other three marks of the true Church, and call yourselves, "One, Holy, Catholic, and Apostolic?" Ah, reckless as you are in your assumption, you are afraid of the jibes of the historian to assume the other three marks. As long as your interminable (750) changes in Faith are recorded, it would be injudicious to invest your Church with the attribute of unity; as long as the public reads the plunder of the abbeys, and hears the universal spoliation of the poor; while the red gibbet of Elizabeth surmounts your communion table, and while your modern towers publish your recent origin, it would be drawing rather too largely on the public credulity to stifle this glaring evidence of your sins and character, and to call yourselves, "One, Holy, Catholic and Apostolic." No, no; you are too clever and discerning to attempt this palpable imposture; and hence, you are content to assume slyly the single term of "Catholic;" and thus you endeavor to regain the place you have forfeited, and repair the connection you have broken. But, Gentlemen, this dodge will not do; you may impose on your own flocks, who don't know you as well as we do; but as long as I am placed as a sentinel at the ivy doors of the old Church you shall not enter under false colors. Come in your own clothes as Protestant ministers, Parliamentary ambassadors, modern biblemen, from a petty district, but you shall not assume the mark of the universality of time and place while I am present. Like sparrows hatched in an eagle's nest, I shall teach you, that, although you have been born near us, you have neither the shape, color, or genealogy of the royal breed of the Apostles, under whose wings your Church has been fraudulently introduced and nurtured into an illegitimate existence.

Whenever, therefore, you may in future honor me with any communication, may I beg you will announce yourselves in your Protestant profession; appear in your own modern dress—assume your own Parliamentary titles—and do not add to your former prevarications to the living, by coming now in the end of time laden with the spoils of the dead. Dress yourselves like Luther and Calvin, and Knox and Cranmer; come with a sword in your hand like Zuinglius, and with an axe like your first apostles; don't assume the holy cross; do not put on the robes of Jerome or Chrysostom; do not, for shame, rob the dead of their hoary honors; do not appear in the unsullied robes of the Apostles, whom your ancestors have betrayed; do not wear the crowns of More and Fisher, won on the block, which your Gospel had erected. This passage brings me in presence of the second part of your note.

In consequence of the existence of an infallible authority framing our laws, and promulgating our faith, it would be clearly an act of the most palpable inconsistency to subject to your decision, or to the award of a public meeting of fallible men the doctrines already fixed by an unerring tribunal. You are true to your principles in seeking and yielding to this decision, since private judgment is your first principle; but I cannot subject my faith to such a standard, believing, as I do, that a living authority has been permanently appointed in the Church of Christ, invested with a command from Heaven to teach all men, and sustained by the official presence of the Holy Ghost, as a legislative guarantee for the immutable truth of its decisions. There are no passages in the Scriptures on any subject of divine faith, put forward in stronger or more emphatic language, than these parts of Revelation which enforce the permanent unchangeable existence and practicable agency of this tribunal. The existence of Christ, or the facts of the cross, the Resurrection and Ascension, are not expressed in a clearer official enactment than the record of this living court of infallible decision. I can no more doubt the existence of the Saviour than disbelieve this official prerogative of the Church of Christ. I believe the one with the same precise amount of evidence I believe the other; and if you bring a doubt on the authority of this court, you necessarily call in question all the other parts, of the record of salvation. So perfectly logical is the inference, that history sustains my assertions on this vital point: and it is quite true to say, that since the fatal period of your separation, and since you preached the overthrow of this first principle, you have opened the floodgates of latitudinarianism, and filled every Protestant country in Europe with wild rationalism and naked infidelity.

In a thousand years hence, when Protestantism will be only recollected in name, like Arianism or any of the other varieties of human wickedness or folly—the future ecclesiastical historian will write the thrilling record—namely, that of all the phases of irreligion which have appeared on the earth, the Anglican heresy has inflicted the deepest wound on revelation, from its encouragement to human pride, and its official flattery of human passion. Human reason in its practical workings has never been the same in the same country, the same age, or even the same man. If we except the truths of mathematical science, human reason is ever changing, and I think it ought to be readily admitted, that a God of rigid justice and truth, could never build the unerring enactments of revelation and salvation, on a shifting basis of such a variable construction.

Within the last twenty-five years, I have seldom read the proceedings of any Protestant assembly on matters of religion, in which the principal topics have not been, viz: The *usurped* infallibility of the Church of Rome, and the *new* articles of faith of the Roman church." The ancient Protestant clergy of Ireland did not utter these falsehoods—they lived contented with their titles, and enjoyed their glebes, and drunk their claret without this eternal calumny of the plundered Catholics. But, within the last quarter of a century, a swarm of young clerical aspirants invade all the public places, stand in all the thoroughfares, and are heard on the four winds roaring and bawling, wherever you turn, against the church of Rome. They are to be seen at all the Protestant printshops, bookstands, railroad stations, bazaars, excursion trips, botanical reunions; and I dare say, you will admit the powerfull fact, that they have no conversation, no entertainment for all who have the misfortune to come within the range of their clerical contact, save one ceaseless, indecent abuse, misrepresentation, and calumny of the principles of the Catholic creed. And I am quite willing to admit, that these gentlemen are persons of finished education, and of delicate truth, and of elegant courtesy in their social character on most other points; but in reference to Catholicity, they are not ashamed to utter statements too foolish to be noticed, or too gross to be told. Having apparently no parochial duties to discharge, their sole occupation seems to be calumniating their Catholic neighbors, and forging misstatements of the Catholic clergy, who never speak a word of offence to them, either in our public or private intercourse. We cannot in these days instruct our people without public insult, nor can we defend our doctrines from misrepresentation without sickening challenges from schoolboy declaimers, raw, *jejune* clerical graduates seeking notoriety in the service of God (?) by falsehood, malignity, and sedition. This is a painful state of society; the conduct of your brethren on this subject has long since formed the topic of public condemnation, even throughout Europe, and has by its excess and extravagance, nauseated the public taste, and, beyond all doubt, has raised the spirit of inquiry in the detection of this indecent imposture, and now universal exposure.

I am led into these observations, by your remarks on the creed of Pius IV., in which you assert that novelties have been introduced into our faith.

Gentlemen, in all the public speeches and writings of your brethren, they all (I hope not through calumnious design,) make one common mistake, viz:—You call "a new decision of a council," by the name of a new act of faith—an addition to the old creed. It is not so. The new decision of a council is rather a proof of an old doctrine, than the evidence of a new one; it is the collected expression of the old belief of the church embodied in a new decree; so that, so far from being an evidence of a new thing, it is, on the contrary, an inevitable demonstration of an old thing. It is the official application of an old truth and principle, to some new heretic, or some new error; so that while the heretic is new to whom it is addressed, and the case is new to which it is applied, the principle and the truth so applied, is *ipso facto* already known as the statute law of the church; and ten thousand new cases may be settled by one old principle, just as the Chancellor settles the unnumbered new cases of his court, without adding one tittle to the old Statute Law of England. When Moses brought down from Mount Sinai the ten commandments, embodied in a written decree from God, will any man assert that this was the first time for twenty-five centuries, that men received the commandments of God? Certainly it was the first written decision of God that men ever saw; but will any man say, that this was a new faith or morality received under the Theoarchy, and that this was the first time when God forbid the crimes of murder, adultery, robbery, perjury and idolatry, &c.! If, then, our doctrine of an infallible tribunal be true, as it is; it follows that a general council, directed by the Holy Ghost, stands in similar circumstances (as far as Revelation goes,) with this Theoarchy, and hence that these new decisions, so far from being acts of faith, are on the contrary, the best evidence of the already universally received opinions on the point decided. All the new decisions of the church against Arianism and Pelaglanism; and the decisions on the consubstantiality of the Son with the Father; and all the decrees on the natures and person of Christ, are all nearly expressed in one sentence of the creed:—"I believe in Jesus Christ, his only Son, who was conceived by the Holy Ghost, and born of the Virgin Mary, was crucified dead and buried, and rose again on the third day from the dead, and ascended into Heaven. I believe in the Holy Catholic Church &c. &c." This short sentence with some few additional texts, form, if I may so speak, the statute laws on the varied decisions, alluded to. In fact, all the new decisions, such as your brethren allude to, and such as you have referred to in the point at issue, are merely so many legitimate deducibles from the record of Revelation subjected to this competent authority, and settled and published by a decree founded on the ancient truths of Christ's Gospel as taught by the Apostles.

The Catholic rule of Faith, therefore, is the Word of God interpreted and taught by this living Authority, as it was from the beginning; and this rule is so clear, so obvious, so comprehensive, and so easily attainable, that, with a penny catechism in your hand, and in the society of a Priest, the accredited officer, you can learn, to your perfect satisfaction, our entire faith, in construction, plan, and indefectible legislative guarantees, within the short space of one hour; and the authorized version of any portion of Holy Writ is to be learned not so much from its philosophical or philological construction, as from its inferential adjustment, and its substantial agreement with the known truths, already believed and taught in connection with the passages under the examination referred to. We do not receive our Faith from disputing, contentious schoolmasters, but from ordained priests; we are occupied with the substance, not the names of things; we take our Faith from the guaranteed inspiration of the Holy Ghost, not from the inflections and the rules of grammar; and as the incarnation and the death of our Lord are beyond our reason, we have no idea of consulting that same reason in laws beyond its reach, no more than the mysteries which it cannot comprehend.

In conclusion, I beg to assure you, that I have felt much complimented by your attendance at my lectures on the Holy Sacrifice of the Mass, and I have felt rather honored by the united note of the five Protestant clergymen, transmitted to me through the courtesy of the Protestant Archdeacon of Raphoe, and the brother-in-law of our late Viceroy. I have not, I hope, in any words which escaped me at that lecture, uttered any sentiment which could offend; and I here disclaim again, intending to say one word in this note (beyond my professional duty,) to give the smallest uneasiness to gentlemen, towards whom I feel much personal respect, and to whom I beg unfeignedly to offer the expression of high and distinguished consideration.

I have the honor to be, Reverend Sirs, your obedient servant,

D. W. CAHILL, D.D.

P. S.—As you nave gratuitously originated this correspondence, you can have no claim on me for its continuance; and, therefore, I respectfully decline taking any further notice of any letters which you may do me the honor to send to me in future.

IMPORTANT LETTER OF DR. D. W. CAHILL

TO TWENTY-ONE PROTESTANT CLERGYMEN

FROM BIRKENHEAD.

On the 19th October, 1853, the Rev. H. P. Linton, calling himself Secretary to the Local Comittee for special mission to the Roman Catholics of Birkenhead, wrote to Dr. Cahill "notifying him the intention of the Clergy of that place and its neighborhood, of calling on him publicly for proofs of his assertions in reference to the recent numerous conversions from the Roman Catholic Church in Ireland." He adds, that "popular controversialists on your side have even seemed more anxious to sustain their reputation by *ad captandum* arguments, than by a strict adherence to facts." Lastly, he enclosed a copy of a letter directed to Dr. Cahill, saying: I sincerely hope, that as you have, unprovoked by us, brought charges against our Church and missions, necessarily calling for controversy, you will not now shrink from that public test of their truth, which you must consider as the inevitable result of your own acts of aggression."

The inclosed letter was signed by several clergymen, and made the following proposals to Dr Cahill:—"1st. If you furnish us wiih definite charges against the Irish Church Missions, giving names, dates, and other circumstances connected with your charges, we undertake to bring forward credible witnesses to disprove those charges, and to give you a public opportunity of proving your assertions in the presence of those witnesses.

"2nd.—We are ready, on our part, to appoint a clergyman to meet you, before the same assembly to discuss the points of controversy between our respective Churches.

"Having come amongst us with charges seriously affecting the character of the "united Churches of England and Ireland" and also assailing doctrines, which we hold sacred, we feel assured that the proposition which we hereby make will be accepted as reasonable by all thinking men, and we also hope that they will meet with your concurrence."

On the 20th of the same month, Dr. Cahill addressed a private note in answer. He said:

"I assure you I feel rather happy in the distinguished position in which the united communication of so many eminent persons has placed so humble an individual as I am; and I trust I shall not, in my reply, depart from the example which is set before me in the politeness of their language.

"I may here state that their letter has been conceived under some most unaccountable mistake, as I am not conscious at this moment of having said or written anything to justify the position they have taken. Will you kindly grant me the favor of not requiring the manuscript of my letter, but be content with receiving the *printed* answer in the *Mercury* of next Tuesday."

REV. DR. CAHILL'S REPLY.

St. Werburg's Birkenhead, *Saturday, Oct*, 22, 1853.

Rev. Sirs—I have acknowledged through your Reverend Secretary, your public letter to me, of last Wednesday's date; and I feel bound to say, that the courteous tone of your communication, combined with the numerous distinguished names attached to that document, demand from me the sincerest expression of grave respect. I shall at once enter on the subject of that le ter, by assuring you of my entire surprise at what I must call, your most unwarrantable assumptions. Firstly, then, I did not come to this town to deliver lectures "on the character of the Irish Church missions;" and secondly, I have never either in this town, or in any other town or city in these countries, lectured "on the points of controversy between the Churches of England and Rome." It is my invariable practise to explain and defend my own doctrine against Protestant calumnies, but never to discuss or ridicule the creed of others. Such a mode of lecturing is at once opposed to *my own feeling*, and *strictly prohibited* by my superiors: and I have never in my numerous subjects departed from this rule, except occasionally on one doctrine—namely, whenever I maintain "the infallibility" of the Catholic Church, as distinguished from "the Bible" as a rule of faith. You, Gentleman, have fallen into the common mistake of editors of anti-catholic newspapers, and of some Protestan clergymen who are continually calumniating me, and who are really putting forth statements, before the public, which in general and in detail, are one unbroken tissue of gross (and I am compelled to say) malignant falsehood. I shall now place before the public, the *placards* which invited Catholics (not Protestants) to my Lectures ; and the people of Liverpool and Birkenhead will thus no doubt form a correct judgement whether you have been justified (without reasonable data and without waiting for a reply from me) in fixing on all the walls of your city and neighborhood, the letter which appears at the head of this reply. There were two placards, as follows:—

"On Sunday, the 16th inst., the Very Rev. Dr. Cahill will preach two sermons (morning and evening) in St. Werburgh's church, in aid of the funds of the poor schools of this parish."

My subjects were—1. "The parable of Dives and Lazarus."—2. "The casting out the dumb devil and the return of seven other devils, worse than the first."

The second placard was as follows:—"And the Reverend Doctor will lecture in the same church, three evenings of the next week—viz. Tuesday, the 18th; Wednesday, the 19th; and, Friday, the 21st.—on the following subjects:—

1. On Mortal Sin. 2. On the Triumphs of the Catholic Church over the world. 3. On Protestant Conversions, or the late attempt at Reformation in Ireland."

It must be borne in mind, that your letter was delivered to me on Wednesday evening, the 19th inst., that is, two whole days before I discussed my last subject. And now, will you give me leave, Gentlemen, to ask how can you account, before the impartial decision of honorable, peaceful public opinion, for the clear, palpable misstatements of your letter? Where have I, as you say, "unprovoked," committed an "aggression" on your doctrines? Where have I "attacked the character of the Irish Church Mission?" and, above all, how could you accuse me on *Wednesday evening* of charges which were to be made on the *following Friday?* How could you know on Wednesday, what I should say on the next Friday? And how could gentlemen of education, character, station, eminence, and, I shall add, punctillious delicate honor, (which I willingly admit,) be guilty of deliberately writing and publishing statements, which *you ought to know* (by referring to the placards,) were an entire falsehood. With your hands, therefore, you have written in large capitals your own blushing condemnation; and if you had printed your names in red ink, it would be a more suitable color to express the ridicule and scorn with which every one of you stands at this moment branded, before the clear public decision. You would involve me in difficulties if you could, (a position in which I would not certainly place you, or any one of you,) and in your intemperate precipitancy, you have overstepped common discretion, and you charged me with saying, what I have never even intended to utter.

But, on the other hand, as you have the peculiar logical talent of drawing conclusions without premises, who knows, but you took it into your heads to think, that I was describing the genius of the Protestant Church, while I denounced the rich glutton; perhaps you indiscreetly fancied, as I shuddered at the eternal furnace, where he was buried, that I was depicting the future condition of your archiepiscopate; and that while I unfolded the rich drapery of purple and fine linen, worn by Dives, or while I described the sumptuous feast of the monster, as he gazed the while on poor starving Lazarus, ten to one, but you have uncharitably understood me as painting your fat angel of Canterbury, or, what is more ungenerous, perhaps our own apostolic Tom of Dublin. And as you have the singular power of reasoning, without any imaginable data, I dare say, you believed my description of the unfortunate man repossessed by the seven devils. as entirely applied to the members of the Protestant Alliance of England; and it is not improbable, that in your jealous zeal, you conceived my graphic description of the evils of mortal sin, as a mere allegorical subterfuge, in order to cover a pointed delineation of the doctrines and practices of the Reformation Church. Gentlemen, you have originated this correspondence, without any provocation on my part, either directly or indirectly; and I think it will be admitted by the thousands, who have seen the placards of my lectures, and heard me during the past week, that you made two unbecoming mistakes—first, in making charges, in a clear ignorance of your case; and secondly, in printing these charges without waiting for my reply.

I have been particularly struck with the first sentence in Rev. Mr. Linton's letter to me, where he styles himself "Secretary to the Local Committee for special mission to the *Roman Catholics* of Birkenhead." This announcement has led me to inquire, if the Catholics of this place had any connection with this society; and, after a minute and an accurate investigation, amongst those whose office and duties enable them to form an unerring judgment, I am instructed to say, that Mr. Linton's secretaryship is an office without a duty, a position without a place; and that "the mission to the Roman Catholics," is something like the echo of an imaginary sound. I have never read anything like this pompous announcement, except the inscriptions on the signboard of a London tradesman, who, within the last few years, placed over his door in large capitals, that he was "barber and hair-dresser to her present Majesty." Now this announcement could only gull the mere simple ignorant, as it is *evident that this man never will or never can shave the Queen!* and, therefore, the Birkenhead puff, is the only parallel that can be drawn to the show-board of the absurd barber, since every man, woman, and child in this parish knows with a smile, that no Catholic here ever receives one particle of these frothy missionary ministrations.

But under other circumstances, it is notorious, that Catholicity supplies an abundant theme for the pulpit harangues of these missionaries. The platform where you speak, the columns of the English press where you write, the festivals where you declaim, might be supposed to give a field wide enough for the display of your zeal and talent, against the tenets and discipline of the Catholic Church; but it is only in your pulpits that your oratory acquires the full bulk and growth of Protestant perfection, and where it is poured forth on all occasions in a devastating flood against the profession and the name of what you are pleased to call "Popery." The sober, religious of your congregations, as I am credibly informed, look in vain on the peaceful Sabbath, for some words of charity from your reverend lips. They are deceived; there is only one subject at Birkenhead and Liverpool, viz.: the errors of Popery; your race, being still true to the original instinct of your progenitry, still, still *protesting* against the existing form of our worship, without adopting permanently any fixed symbol of your own. These inflammatory speeches from your pulpits, have produced the natural and expected result. Grace can never arise from calumny, nor faith from falsehood; and hence, your churches are empty, your ranks are thinned, and your professional character is weakened. Your statements are doubted, your assertions disbelieved, and while I am prepared to concede to your honor, (as a matter of course,) the highest and the most spotless truth, on all social, commercial and national subjects; I am reluctantly compelled to say, that from your known and unceasing deviations from strict statement, in matters *connected with the Catholic doctrine and practices,* it is now universally whispered, and (without wishing to give the slightest offence,) it is the familiar adage at home and abroad, *throughout Europe, and the civilized world,* to brand the statements of your Church, *in reference to Catholicity,* as "unscrupulous, unprincipled Protestant lies." And while you have forfeited the public confidence abroad, you have, beyond dispute, infidelized your own country at home. From undeniable statistics, it is demonstrated that one half the Protestants of Liverpool, never attend Church; it is the same in Manchester, and in all the manufacturing towns; the poor are never seen in the churches. The *Times* has lately stated, that fifty persons are the largest number known to attend worship in any church within the city of London on Sunday. Rev. Mr. Jones, in his examination before a Committee of the House of Commons, has proved the existence of forty-nine known conventicles of avowed infidelity in England; and he has demonstrated that Protestant laborers and tradesmen, &c., to the number of at least 300,000 in London and the suburbs, live and die without any practical religion or any form of worship. In fact, the entire Protestant ecclesiastical records of this country prove at once, the total failure of your Church Establishment, and publish the awful existence of a growing and wide-spread infidelity; and the impartial ecclesiastical historian will yet tell the sad truth, that this most deplorable national condition is beyond all doubt to be ascribed to the teaching of the Protestant Church; which, by breaking down all authority, removing the evidences of all antiquity, and taking away all checks from the heart, has flung the public mind on a troubled ocean of doubt, has unbridled human passion, and precipitated the national character into an inevitable demoralization and a wild infidelity.

And not content with unchristianizing your own followers, your Church has, of late years, by a system of the most unparalleled vituperation and misstatement, attempted to undermine the Faith of the Catholics of these countries, and thus involve our creed in one common ruin with your own. The very title under which your society has been organized, contains in the first line a palpable and notorious falsehood. It exists on the assumption that the Catholic Church withholds the Scriptures from her faithful, and it is set in motion under the pretext of distributing amongst our people the Word of God. This assumption and this pretext, are, without any exception at all, the most flagrant instance of unblushing imposition which has ever been practised on the public credulity, at any period of Christian history. It is the widest calumny which the Protestant malignity has ever forged; it is beyond all comparison the most unprincipled lie which English apostacy has ever promulgated. Now, mark me, Gentlemen, I disclaim uttering one syllable disrespectful to you personally. I have no reason to entertain towards you, individually and collectively, any other sentiments than those of exalted estimation; but I again repeat my utter abhorrence of the flagitious system which lives on falsehood, grows fat on calumny, and claims the venerable spotless honors of sanctity, from perjury to man, and blasphemy to God.

Beyond all doubt, there never was invented, so gross a fabrication as the nauseating cant—that the Catholic Church has never encouraged the reading of the Bible. In the early ages she could not, of course, circulate the Scriptures with such efficiency as we can do at present, because the art of printing was then unknown; but she alone collected them; she alone decided their integrity and their authenticity; the Protestant Alliance not being well known in those days! She alone stamped them with her authority, without which they could no more vouch for themselves, than a dead man could tell his name and parentage; she alone, like a witness before a jury, proved their inspiration before mankind; she alone, by her infallible reputation, chained the universal belief in them; and she alone, preserved them amidst the wreck of the Roman Empire, the convulsion of ages, and the changes of dynasties and races, creeds and tongues. The sickening cant of the beardless strippling clerics of the modern Reformation conventicles, asserting their claim to the Scriptures, is the same kind of humbug and imposition on the undiscerning mind of your dupes, as if a green set of young English architects, declared it was the Protestant Sir Christopher Wrenn, who built and preserved the Pantheon at Rome; or that it was the present London School of Design, which planned and kept in repair the Pyramids of Egypt! Of all the instances of audacious, bare-faced, cool, imperturbable insolence of Protestantism, their claiming the Scriptures as preserved by them, and promulgated by them, is the highest point of wicked, exaggerated, extravagant misrepresentation to which the ingenuity of man could build up a lie.

So unceasingly laborious, on the contrary, was the Catholic Church in making copies of the Bible, that she kept the Monks, and the religious of all countries continually writing them; and whoever will attentively consider for a moment the extraordinary labor of even making one copy of the Old and New Testament—whoever will visit any ecclesiastical library, and count over the folio volumes of Saint Augustine, Saint Jerome, Saint Chrysostom, and all the Greek and Latin Fathers, and calculate then the difficulty of making unnumbered copies of these Greek ponderous volumes—whoever will, like a candid man, reflect, that all the profane and Church histories of these days—all the sermons—all the works on piety were copied, re-copied, and one thousand times copied by the Monks of the Catholic Church, the surprise of the generous man, and the scholar amounts to a feeling of impossible expression, how the Church could have been able to furnish copies of these vast accumulated biblical, and classical, and historical works to every part of the world, such as we know them to have existed before the Christian libraries were destroyed, and before the art of printing was discovered. And further, to prove this statement, the moment printing was discovered, and made the vehicle after many improvements, of communication between men, the Catholic Church, so early as the year 1412, (almost immediately after the discovery of printing and paper,) published the Latin Vulgate, at once to circulate the word of God, and that too in a language then *most known* to the whole Christian world. When the Scotch Sir Walter Scott lampooned the Catholic Church for her want of library facilities, in the middle ages, he might as well accuse King Alfred of ignorance, for not using the electric telegraph, or charge Hannibal with a blundering strategy, for not meeting the Romans with artillery. The truth is, that the present issue of the *Times* newspaper, at the rate of sixty copies in every minute by steam, is not a whit more wonderful in its way, than the manuscript copying of the Fathers, and of the Scriptures in the middle ages by the Monks, who supplied the whole world with as many copies, as the skill of thousands of expert penmen could have executed.

In order to arrive at the palpable refutation in this Reformation lie, I shall make a few quotations for you, Gentlemen, which I do not intend for you (who already know them so well,) as for the numerous readers who will see this letter of mine, in every part of the known world :—

Aware of the manifest dangers to faith and morals that are found in *corrupt versions* of the Bible.....insidiously issued amongst the people .... we have not ceased to deplore this great evil, and to labor for its correction. It occurred to us that the publication of genuine versions of *the Vulgate* would be found amongst the most efficient means to neutralise the poison of these counterfeit productions. Accordingly we aprove of this edition of the Douay Testament, Published by Thomas **Brennan, of this city, and** *recommend* it to the faithful.

† JOHN, ARCHBISHOP OF TUAM.

St. Jarlath's Tuam, 1846.

BELFAST, *July* 24, 1839.

This new and portable edition of the Douay Bible, has been diligently and carefully collated with the most approved versions in the English language, previously to its publication. I sanction *its circulation* among the faithful. † CORNELIUS DENVIR. D.D.
Bishop of Down and Connor.

The new edition of the English version of the Bible, printed with our permission by James Duffy, carefully collated by our direction, with the Clementine Vulgate of 1606, and with the Rhenish version of the New Testament of 1582, and with *other approved English versions*, we, by our authority, approve; and we declare the same may be read *by the faithful* with great spiritual profit.
Given at Dublin, Nov. 4, 1846. † D. MURRAY.

Extract of a letter of Pope Pius the Sixth to Anthony Martini, Archbishop of Florence, in the year 1778:—

Calends of April, 1778.

At a time when a vast multitude of bad books, which grossly attack the Catholic religion, are circulated even amongst the unlearned, you judge exceedingly well that the faithful should be excited to the reading the Holy Scriptures; for these are the most abundant sources, *which ought to be left open to every one*. This you have seasonably effected by publishing the Sacred Writings in *the language of your country*, suitable to every one's capacity. We, therefore, applaud your eminent learning, and we return you our due acknowledgements.
PHILIP BUONAMCI, Sec.

For proof of the above extracts, I beg to refer you to Mr. Rockliffee, the eminent bookseller of Liverpool, who will place these editions in your hands, with at least ten other editions of the Bible in England. I refer you again to Mr. James Duffy, the eminent publisher and bookseller of Dublin, who, I dare say, will show you at least twelve editions of the Bible in Ireland. I again wish to inform you, that there are forty-seven different editions of the Bible, published in Italian on the Italian peninsula; and I beg in addition, to tell you that, in France there are 126 different editions of the Bible published in French, within the last 300 years, since the art of printing has been found out. And, now, "Gentlemen of the Home

Mission for Distributing the Bible amongst the Catholics of Birkenhead," will you satisfy the public on the morality of organizing a society founded on a lie known to every Catholic in England, Ireland, and Scotland—on a lie perfectly understood in every Catholic country in Europe—a lie denounced by the very first principles of the Catholic Church, and contradicted by the extracts I have made, by Popes, Bishops, and the public historical facts of your own country. No man of honor and conscience, except yourselves, can understand how, in the teeth of the most notorious facts, you can ascend your pulpits, and there promulgate, before your unfortunate congregations, what all the Catholic world knows to be the grossest misstatement ever yet uttered on any one subject, between man and man, in any age or in any country.

This is the conduct which has earned your Church the character all over the world, of unblushingly and unscrupulously asserting anything, however unfounded, provided it raises a momentary hostility against the Catholic Church; and it is the practice, too, which has led the impartial historian of your day, to say, "that of all the Christian inhabitants of the civilized world, there is no one nation on the earth kept in such a fatal ignorance of God's real Gospel as the Protestants of England." Your bishops write pastorals, by which the clergy can believe what they please: Prime Ministers issue ecclesiastical appointments, which sustain men in adding or curtailing any doctrines they like; and the preachers publish such lectures as induce the laity to follow any imaginary creed they may fancy to adopt. The most fashionable, and the most modern phase which your chameleon church has assumed, is what is termed "believing on the Saviour."— And in fact, these words are uttered in such a strange vague signification, that your Protestant saints seem to think, that belief in the mere existence of Christ is an inspired act of heroic Protestantism; and it is impossible to avoid feeling, that they imagine the *historical belief in His existence and person,* ranks far higher in their Christian estimation than the *precepts of His law,* the *definitive conditions* of His revelation, or the *expressed reward and penalties* of His judgments.

Depend upon it, Protestantism can no longer deceive even your own dupes; it is detected, exposed, and scouted wherever mankind are free from national acerbity and professional bigotry. Austria, Bavaria, Northern Italy, Naples, France, Spain, Portugal, all know the spirit of Exeter Hall, and feel fully the revolutionary antichristian genius of your creed; and never since Luther first lifted the standard of apostacy, has Catholic Europe entered into such a united defensive compact, as she has adopted since the famed year 1847, against the intrigues, the machinations, and the conspiracies of your insatiable and exterminating novelties. If our opponents were men of honesty in controversy, they would state the fact—namely, that the Catholic Church encourages the circulation of her own version of the Scriptures, but that she strictly prohibits the Protestant versions, because they contain 1,600 errors in grammatical accuracy, in sense, and in doctrine. And besides these errors, the Catholic Church has an objection that your missionaries should call on our people, even to distribute our own version, as experience has proved, that wherever they go amongst Catholics, they are unceasingly ridiculing our worship, misstating our principles and practices, and ever and always calumniating our clergy and our conventual societies.

It is not true, then, that our people are not taught the Scriptures, or are not allowed the use of the Scriptures; our people are taught their doctrine by the teachers, with (not without,) the Scriptures in their hands. Your people are taught their creed by their own judgment on these Scriptures. The difference between us lies in the teachers; and we believe that the entire sacred volume, furnishes no other position stronger than the one on which we rest this doctrine of ours. There was no legal document drawn with such consummate comprehensive provisions, as the warrant from Christ, by which we believe in our official essential character as teachers. We believe no one can infallibly learn Christ's law without our teaching; and we believe that the very provisions of the divine revelation itself, are not more forcibly expressed and urged, than our legal and essential appointment. We do not believe that the teacher ranks as high as the thing taught; but we believe, that according to the clear legislation of Christ on the subject, the thing to be learned canot be securely taught without the agency of the accredited minister; or, can never be duly acquired by individual unofficial judgment. The document of appointment on this subject, is, the finest piece of legislative jurisprudence published in the sacred volume:—

1. The appointment, and the Source of the power—"As the Father sent me, *I send you.*"

2. The knowledge requisite to discharge the duties—"All things whatsoever I heard from the Father I have made *known* to you."

3. The office to be discharged—"Go ye into the whole world and *preach the gospel*"

4. The subjects of their jurisdiction—"Go ye and preach the gospel to *every creature.*"

5. The extent of territory subject to their duties.—"Go ye into all nations."

6. The authenticity of their appointment, and the obedience to be paid to them—"He who hears you, hears me."

7. The crime of not hearing and obeying them—"He who despises you, despises me."

8. The rewards and penalties attached to their authority—"Go ye and preach * * * * and he that believeth shall be saved, and he that believeth not shall be damned."

9. The security which is attached to the discharge of their office—"Lo! I am with you."

10. The term and tenure of their office—"All days even to the consummation of the world."

11. The legislative bond of Christ, like a legal security to all men as a guarantee, that these officers so appointed, can never violate their trusts to the public—"And the gates of hell shall never prevail against it."

12. The presence of the Holy Ghost, as a further security to the performance of their duties "I will send the Holy Ghost, the Spirit of Truth, who will bring to your recollection all things whatsoever I told you, and who will abide with you forever."

In the foregoing section of this letter, I have merely glanced at what may be called the legislative enactment, under which the Catholic Church holds her office of God-like, universal, boundless, permanent, and infallible teacher of men in the Law of the Saviour. I assure you, Gentlemen, I have often read over this commission in astonishment, as a mere product of legislation; and I have arrived at the conclusion in my own heart, my own mind, and my own soul, that there are no passages in the entire Last Will and Testament of our Lord, put forth with even so much emphatic legal earnestness and literal energy, as the comprehensive provisions which place in the hands of duly appointed men the whole power of teaching and deciding Christ's law. There is decidedly no evidence in favor of the very existence of Christ, or in support of the very atonement on the cross, which ranks higher in testimony than the clauses in reference to the subject before us; and hence I place this authority precisely on a level, in point of essence and necessity, with any other provision of God's Gospel. And beyond all doubt, if I would be made to believe that all the provisions, and legal statements, and high constitutional enactments which I have quoted, had all failed, fallen into disuse, and ceased to be necessary or essential; I tell you frankly, gentlemen, that the character of the rest of the volume, the reputation of the remaining provisions, the credence of all other clauses of the will, would be so much lessened, damaged, and, indeed, forfeited, that I could have decidedly no reasonable motive for relying on one word of the rest of the Testament. If you take away credit from the sincere, serious, didactic legal passages which I have adduced, I publicly avow that I could not be a Christian: and hence I presume to say with St. Augustine, "that I am held to the doctrines of Christianity, only by the authority of the Catholic Church."

Gentlemen, will you kindly excuse this long letter to you? I beg to express again my unfeigned respect for you, although I do think you have not used me well, in the indiscreet, precipitate, unfounded public letter you have written to me. I pity you all much in the unchristian mission in which you are engaged. You can no more teach the truth, than I can teach falsehood. You are doomed to a permanent error, by the very same evidence by which I am appointed to essential truth. You must be forever wrong, by the very self-same laws by which I am forever right. I act under a commissioned authority, you speak from a self-appointed intrusion ; and by the same bond by which Christ is bound, always to set right the Catholic Church, precisel yon the same cause, it follows that your local modern conventicles, must be through all coming ages and unborn time, permanently wrong.

I have the honor to be, Reverend Sirs, your obedient servant,

D. W. CAHILL, D.D

P.S.—As I shall leave Birkenhead to-morrow for t. North of England, and as you have gratuitously commenced this correspondence, I beg to say, with the highest respect that I cannot attend to any valued communication with which you may condescend to favor me in future.

www.ingramcontent.com/pod-product-compliance
Lightning Source LLC
LaVergne TN
LVHW020112110826
845151LV00001B/134

* 9 7 8 1 4 2 5 5 4 3 3 2 7 *